The Illustrator in America

1900-1960's

"Two Strikes and the Bases Full." Drawing by Charles Dana Gibson for *Collier's Weekly*, 1904.

The Illustrator in America

1900-1960's

Compiled and edited by

Walt Reed

Reinhold Publishing Corporation / New York

Vignette by Tom Lovell for *True* magazine, 1963.

Acknowledgments

The idea for this book has generated an enthusiastic response from nearly everyone approached for information or assistance during the long period of its preparation. I should like particularly to thank the eminent illustrators whose commentaries have furnished personal insight and added stature to this record. Among the many who lent source material or pictures were Lyman Anderson, Rudy Belarski, Arthur William Brown, Helen Card, Richard Case, Howell Dodd, Robert Fawcett, Lucius O. Gauger, Peter Helck, Fritz Henning, the late Donald Kennicott, Robert Lambdin, William MacLean, Henry C. Pitz, Paul Rabut, Norman Rockwell, Milburn Rosser, Amos Sewell, Harold Von Schmidt, and William H. White.

Others who helped were Hal Rogers, Gerald Clarkson, and Myron Hall III, art direction; Zoltan Henczel, photography; Mary Lyon, Gordon Carroll, Sterling McIlhany, and Edward Boyd, writing and editing; The Society of Illustrators library and particularly the records maintained there by the late Norman Price; the many publishers of copyrighted material; and finally my wife, Mary, for her faithful work as typist and secretary.

Walt Reed

Printed in the United States of America
Library of Congress Catalog Card Number: 66-24545

Designed by Walt Reed

Edited by Mary Lyon

Typeset by Lettick Typografic Inc.

Printed and bound by The Guinn Company Inc.

Color printed by The Guinn Company Inc.

Published by Reinhold Publishing Corporation
430 Park Avenue, New York, N.Y.

Contents

Is Illustration Art?

by Albert Dorne

In recent years, it has been fashionable for art critics to couple the word "mere" with "illustration" in dismissing pictures that tell any kind of story. And, since illustration is usually commissioned, it has also been viewed as impure, commercial art when contrasted with the nobler motivation of the fine arts in which the artist is free to express his innermost feelings.

This distinction, if applied consistently, would reject a Fra Angelico, a Giotto or a Michelangelo, who made paintings of Biblical subjects on commission from wealthy patrons or the Church. To come closer to the present, many American painters such as Winslow Homer, William Glackens or Frederic Remington, whose works now command honored places in our museums, contributed much of their life's output to illustration. Certainly for them it was a valid form of art, and they gave their best to it.

More appropriate, to me, would be a distinction between good artists and bad artists. Throughout history there have been thousands of mediocre artists, many good ones, and a few who were great. In many cases we have no record of the original reasons the artists had for painting their pictures, and whether or not the pictures were painted to specification. This no longer seems very important. The real question is, what did the artist contribute of his own particular individuality to make his picture a masterpiece?

The form in which an artist chooses to create is secondary. He may work with stone, metal, canvas or water-color paper; he may paint murals, portraits, illustrations or landscapes; his viewpoint may range from highly detailed academic realism to abstract expressionism. Each artist, however, works within the restrictions of his medium, his purpose, and his ability.

The illustrator, in his turn, is subject to the limitations of his assignments and a responsibility to his client. His success is measured by whether or not the function of the picture is realized — to tell a story or to present an idea effectively. He must, therefore, be able to communicate his intention clearly.

DRAWING BY ROBERT FAWCETT

In translating the requirements of an advertising director or a magazine art editor into a picture, there is no reason why the same standards of art cannot as appropriately be applied here as for gallery walls. Many illustrators do, in fact, paint as many pictures for exhibition as they do for reproduction, without compromising their integrity in either area.

This is not to imply that *all* illustration is art. We have seen far too many pictures of stereotyped clinches or models with toothpaste grins promoting a product to be sold. In these instances, the vision of the advertiser or art editor, as well as the artist, is shallow and deserves but little respect.

Furthermore, some artists, and often the public, mistakenly confuse technique or facility with art. An artist must have much more than virtuosity. A painting may approach technical perfection and yet be completely vacuous. And even a crudely made drawing or painting can be important if the artist has a really worth-while statement to make.

This does not mean that the illustrator must always say something profound. He may use humor or exaggeration, present a glimpse of beauty, a fresh insight into a familiar scene, or even use a line in such a sensitive and expressive way as to stimulate the imagination. The artist may also be a reporter, adding his special dimension to that of the camera, the recording, or the printed word.

In other words, opportunities for the illustrator are limited only by the imagination of the individual. It is up to each one of us to realize his fullest potential both as individual and as artist.

This volume covers a period during which illustration became a vital art form in the United States. Since it is, perhaps, too early for a definitive judgment, each reader should draw his own conclusions from the varied contents of this book. He should do so because the final worth of the pictures will be based on these conclusions, plus the opinion that will ultimately be filed by posterity.

Albert Dorne

A. Howard Pyle illustration, “Marooned,” engraved on wood by Henry Wolf, 1887. Actual size.

B. An enlarged detail of the above shows the merged skills of illustrator and engraver.

DRAWING BY ROGER VERNAM

The Earlier Days
by Walt Reed

The selection of the year 1900 as a beginning for this record of American illustration may appear to be an arbitrary one. In fact, the work of several illustrators included here reaches back into the 1880's.

However, it was the invention of photoengraving, as a mechanical process for reproducing drawings or paintings, that was responsible for the spectacular development and expansion of the whole field of illustration at that time.

Earlier, the illustrations in books, newspapers or magazines were largely reproduced by wood engravings. Although the technical skill of the engravers was extraordinary, the method of reproduction had changed very little since the days of Albrecht Dürer. The artist was required to make his drawing directly on a block of wood (in reverse) as a guide for the engraver. It was then the job of the engraver to cut away the wood *between* the lines, thus creating the white areas in the final printed form. Later, it became possible to transfer the artist's drawing photographically to the wood block, freeing the artist considerably; but the final printed result still tended to reflect the personality of the engraver as much as that of the artist. In fact, the artist and the engraver both signed the work and shared the credit.

The transition from the use of wood engravings to line or halftone photoengraving was a gradual one, dating from the early 1880's to as late as 1910. The early halftones (which also made full color printing practical) tended to be gray and muddy, requiring a great deal of additional handwork by the engraver. However, by 1900, leading monthly periodicals such as *Harper's, Century,* and *McClure's,* were able to obtain halftone reproductions of good quality and hence began to make lavish use of illustrations. Many of the finest artists of the time were attracted to illustrating for the magazines and their names became widely known to the general public.

This period thus marked the real beginning of illustration as a popular art; and it is the interval from then to the present that determines the scope of this book. During this short time, an immense amount of exciting and creative work has been produced. Because of the impermanent nature of periodicals, however, the record of much of this art has vanished; the originals are scattered or lost. In such cases where the originals were not obtainable, it was necessary to reproduce from proofs in order to include particular pictures which best represented the artists.

This book has been compiled, therefore, to pay tribute to the talents of these illustrators, to preserve their record as Americana, an invaluable part of our heritage.

The Decades: 1900-1960's with Introductory Commentaries

1900-1910

ILLUSTRATORS 1900-1910

Edwin Austin Abbey
Stanley M. Arthurs
Reginald Bathurst Birch
Robert Frederick Blum
Clifford Carleton
Walter Appleton Clark
Benjamin West Clinedinst
Joseph Clement Coll
Will Crawford
Thomas Fogarty
Arthur Burdett Frost
William Gilbert Gaul
Charles Dana Gibson
William J. Glackens
Phillip R. Goodwin
Elizabeth Shippen Green
Thomas King Hanna
Charlotte Harding
Lucius Wolcott Hitchcock
Henry Hutt
Edward Windsor Kemble
Edwin Penfield
Joseph Pennell
Howard Pyle
Frederic Remington
Henry Reuterdahl
Charles Nicolas Sarka
Everett Shinn
William Thomas Smedley
Dan Smith
Jessie Wilcox Smith
Frederick Dorr Steele
Albert E. Sterner
Alice Barber Stevens
Sarah S. Stilwell-Weber
Thomas S. Sullivant
Will Ladd Taylor
Thure De Thulstrup
Albert B. Wenzell
George Hand Wright
Rufus Fairchild Zogbaum

DRAWING BY JAMES MONTGOMERY FLAGG

The Decade: 1900-1910

by Harold Von Schmidt

Although this was a period of American illustration in which I did not directly participate, throughout my career as an illustrator I have felt a direct kinship with it, both in the Old West, as exemplified in the paintings of Frederic Remington and Charles Russell, and with the mainstream of American illustration as a pupil of Harvey Dunn who, in turn, taught the philosophy of Howard Pyle, "father of American illustration."

A magazine was thought of in those days as a purveyor of the finest in literature and art. Advertising was limited to the front and the back; any tailing-in of advertising material with editorial matter would have been unthinkable. This lofty standard was reflected in the work of some of America's greatest illustrators: Edwin Austin Abbey, Walter Appleton Clark, A. B. Frost, E. W. Kemble, Edward Penfield, Charles Dana Gibson; and men who later became famous as American painters: Winslow Homer, William Glackens, John Sloan, Ernest Blumenschein, Everett Shinn, and others. From 1900 on, I clipped and filed reproductions of their work.

This was an illustrious company. Among them, Howard Pyle was preëminent and probably the greatest illustrator America has ever produced. His career had begun 24 years earlier, in 1876, when he first did illustrations for the old *Harper's* magazine. His work continued through the next 35 years until his death in 1911. During this time he both wrote and illustrated a prodigious amount of work.

As an artist, Pyle's greatest love and interest was in Americana. He eagerly sought all information available about early Colonial times and actually interviewed a survivor of the Revolutionary War. His illustrations, as a result, carry an authentic stamp not only because of the accuracy of detail, such as in buttons or ruffles, but also because of his ability to portray the spirit of a rough-hewn but forthright American pioneering period.

Pyle's influence, had it rested on his pictures alone, would have been great; as a teacher his talents were equally important and created an even more lasting influence. For some time Pyle taught at the Drexel Institute in Philadelphia, but his dissatisfaction with the limitations of conventional classroom teaching and his passionate desire to help deserving and talented young students led him to form his own school at Chadd's Ford, Pennsylvania. No tuition was charged, and Pyle gave generously of his valuable time to the development of his pupils. As N. C. Wyeth, one of his pupils at the time, wrote later: "Howard Pyle's extraordinary ability as a teacher lay primarily in his penetration. He could read beneath the crude lines on paper, detect therein our real inclinations and impulses; in short, unlock our personalities. This power was in no wise a superficial method handed out to those who might receive. We received in proportion to that which was fundamentally within us."
(Quoted from "*Howard Pyle, A Chronicle,*" by Charles D. Abbott, published by Harper & Bros. 1925)

As part of his teaching, Pyle made his students fully aware of the practical use to which their pictures would be put. Through his contacts with publishers and art directors, he arranged that the students work on actual commissions or that finished pictures be shown to art directors for possible use. As he taught, "When you are making pictures to be reproduced in print, you are then given no favor and your pictures must be good as pictures or else they are of no possible use . . ." As he described it, ". . . my final aim in teaching will not be essentially the production of illustrators of books but rather the production of painters of pictures, for I believe that the painters of true American art are yet to be produced."

Pyle's high purposes were more than justified. His pupils have gone on to achieve eminent names in their own right and, in turn, have continued to pass Pyle's spirit on to a third and fourth generation of illustrators. The total influence of his personality on the whole field can never be measured; but it is a privilege for me to pay this small tribute to him.

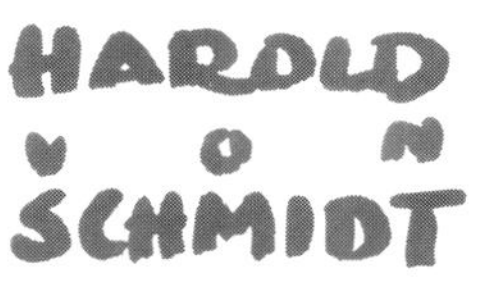

A

E. A. Abbey

EDWIN AUSTIN ABBEY, N.A., R.A. (1852-1911) was both illustrator and artist in the fullest sense. His work, beginning with small black-and-white illustrations for the old *Harper's* magazine, and culminating in the huge mural decorations for the Boston Public Library and the State Capitol in Harrisburg, Pennsylvania, was done with extraordinary artistic dedication.

Abbey's drive for authenticity was legendary among his fellow-illustrators and eventually led him to live in England where the original props and costuming required for his historical illustrations were still to be found.

Many of his later illlustrations were rendered in water color or in oils for reproduction in full color, but he continued to use pen and ink as a serious art medium. The brilliant draughtsmanship of his pen-and-ink drawings for the plays of Shakespeare has never been surpassed.

A full record of his life and work is contained in the two-volume *Edwin Austin Abbey* by E. V. Lucas, published in 1921 by Charles Scribner's Sons in New York, and Methuen and Company Limited in London.

A permanent collection of his drawings, paintings, and pastels is retained in the Edwin Austin Abbey collection at Yale University in New Haven, Connecticut.

A. Illustration for Shakespeare's *King Henry VI*, Part III, Act III, Scene III, from Harper and Brothers, 1905.
B. Drawing for *King Henry V*, Act IV, Scene III, from Harper and Brothers, 1909.
C. "The camp of the American Army at Valley Forge, February, 1778," mural painting for Pennsylvania State Capitol, 12′6″ by 6′, 1909-10.
D. "And every pang that folly pays to pride," illustration for *The Deserted Village*, by Goldsmith, Harper and Brothers, 1902.

B

C

D

S. M. Arthurs

STANLEY M. ARTHURS (1877-1950) was a student of Howard Pyle and one who was very close to him personally. Arthurs devoted his career to depicting American historical subjects, painting a series of episodes from earliest Colonial times through the Civil War era.

After Pyle's death, Arthurs occupied his studio and set for himself the same high standards Pyle had taught. Every detail of his pictures was painstakingly researched, and he immersed himself as thoroughly as possible in the mood and character of his picture subjects.

Arthurs' use of color was rich and varied; he produced a valuable contribution to the American historical record. Many of his pictures are reproduced in James Truslow Adams' *History of the United States,* in the 15-volume *Pageant of America* edited by Ralph H. Gabriel, and in *The American Historical Scene* published by the University of Pennsylvania Press in 1935.

Arthurs also painted a number of murals including the "Landing of DeVries" at Delaware College and "The Crusaders" at the State Capitol, Dover, Delaware.

"The First Voyage of the Clermont — 1807," published by *Scribner's* magazine.

REGINALD BATHURST BIRCH (1856-1943) was known as "the children's Gibson" because of the great number of pen-and-ink illustrations for children's stories and fairy tales he did for *St. Nicholas* magazine.

His drawings give the appearance of great spontaneity and directness resulting from his practice of using models only for his preliminary sketches and rendering the finished drawings freely from them.

Although Birch also illustrated for the *Century* magazine, *Harper's, McClure's, Scribner's, Collier's,* the old *Life, Youth's Companion,* and nearly 200 books, his best known illustrations were done for *Little Lord Fauntleroy,* by Frances Hodgson Burnett in 1886. These were responsible for a whole generation of Victorian boys' being forced to wear black velvet suits, lace collars and curls, patterned after Birch's prototype.

Birch was born in England, grew up in San Francisco, and studied at the Art Academy in Munich, Germany.

Reproduced from *St. Nicholas* magazine, January, 1889.

C. Carleton

CLIFFORD CARLETON (1867-1946) was born in Brooklyn, New York, and studied at the Art Students League under H. Siddons Mowbray. Carleton was at his best with rural subjects, such as the water-color painting reproduced here. He produced a great amount of work and illustrated for most of the leading magazines of his day, including the old *Life*, *Harper's Weekly*, *Harper's Bazaar*, and *Scribner's*. Books he illustrated include: *Pembroke*, by Mary Wilkins, *People We Pass*, by Julian Ralph, and *Their Wedding Journey*, by William Dean Howells.

"The Barn Dance," published by E. R. Herrick & Company, 1898.

In this beautiful pen-and-ink rendering by ROBERT FREDERICK BLUM, N.A. (1857-1903) there is evidence of the influence of Fortuny, the Spanish master, but the soundness of draughtsmanship and form were his own.

Blum was born in Cincinnati, Ohio, and was apprenticed to a lithographer's shop in 1871. He studied nights at the McMicken Art School of Design in Cincinnati, later attended the Pennsylvania Academy of the Fine Arts in Philadelphia. Blum made many trips abroad, and the majority of his pictures are of foreign subjects. He lived for some time in Japan where he produced some of his finest drawings and paintings — one of which, "The Ameya, or Itinerant Candy Vendor," is owned by The Metropolitan Museum of Art.

"Mr. Joseph Jefferson as Bob Acres," for Sheridan's comedy, *The Rivals*, *Scribner's* magazine, 1880.

B. West Clinedinst.

BENJAMIN WEST CLINEDINST, N.A. (1859-1931) was one of the original ten founders of the Society of Illustrators in 1901. He was born in Woodstock, Virginia, and studied at the Ecole des Beaux Arts in Paris where he was a pupil of Cabanel and Bonnat. In addition to his illustrations for many magazines and books, he painted portraits of several national figures including President Theodore Roosevelt and Admiral Peary.

From 1903-'05 he was art editor of *Leslie's Weekly*. He exhibited widely and was elected to membership in the National Academy in 1898. The last years of his life were devoted to painting and teaching of illustration at Cooper Union in New York.

"A Levee at the President's House in 1813," from *The Century* magazine, 1901.

JOSEPH CLEMENT COLL (1881-1921) was perhaps America's greatest virtuoso in the use of pen and ink. He commanded an awesome technical dexterity. He employed his pen point as freely as a paint brush, showed it capable of the finest subtlety as well as the boldest slashes of black. As an illustrator, he also made masterful use of the white areas of his pictures, incorporating them to create a full spectrum of values.

His skill had been acquired through careful study of his predecessors, particularly Vierge, and the demanding pressure of deadlines in his earlier employment as a newspaper sketch-artist.

This technical skill was coupled with a vivid and unusual imagination which he displayed best in illustrations with exotic settings or for mystery stories by such authors as A. Conan Doyle and Sax Rohmer.

Coll illustrated several books and his work appeared in many periodicals, including *Associated Sunday Magazines, Collier's* and *Everybody's,* up to the time of his sudden death at the age of forty while his talents were still developing.

Illustration for "King of the Khyber Rifles," by Talbot Mundy for *Everybody's* magazine.

WILL CRAWFORD (1869-1944), a staff artist for the *New York World*, had a special flair for humor. With thorough mastery of his pen, he loved to contrive very elaborate situations based on actual historical incidents, poking fun at or exposing what *really* happened. He did a number of these illustrations, called "Historic Bits," for the old *Life* magazine at the turn of the century. The example reproduced here, published in 1900, was from this series entitled, "Our First Railroad Accident."

Crawford, who was born in Washington, D. C., began drawing for the old *Newark* (N.J.) *Call* while still in his teens and later also illustrated for *Puck, Munsey's,* and *St. Nicholas.*

"The belt rails used would occasionally loosen, and 'snakehead'."

Walter Appleton Clark

The life of WALTER APPLETON CLARK (1876-1906) was tragically short, but even in that time he established himself as a mature and versatile artist.

While Clark was still a student at the Art Students League, one of his drawings on the classroom wall was seen by the art editor of *Scribner's* magazine. This led to his first commission as an illustrator. He thus fortunately began his career very early and worked industriously for the remaining ten years of his life.

He took on a wide variety of subjects and had a faculty for executing each assignment in an original and arresting way. The treatment of this illustration done for *Scribner's* magazine in 1898, for instance, is as fresh and charming as if it had been done for publication today.

"Impromptu Theatricals in College Parlors," for "Undergraduate Life at Smith College."

A

A. B. Frost.

ARTHUR BURDETT FROST (1851-1928) was our best illustrator of rural America. He usually treated his characters with humor, and in his drawings there was a directness and honesty which showed his sympathetic understanding of his subjects. His sound draughtsmanship was combined with an intimate knowledge of nature. The details in his picture are always very specific, as though drawn on the spot, and so artfully chosen and placed as to carry out the picture's idea in a natural and entirely convincing manner.

He may be best remembered now, however, for his charming illustrations for the *Uncle Remus* tales by Joel Chandler Harris. In the preface and dedication by Harris for the 1896 edition, he wrote of Frost ". . . you have conveyed into their quaint antics the illumination of your own inimitable humor, which is as true to our sun and soil as it is to the spirit and essence of the matter. . . . The book was mine, but now you have made it yours, both sap and pith . . ."

C

B

A. "The Game between the Squire and the Postmaster," from *A Book of Drawings by A. B. Frost*, published by P. F. Collier & Son, 1904.
B. "A Sporting Print," one of the many variations of hunting and fishing scenes which, with golf, were favorite picture subjects for Frost.
C. From *Told by Uncle Remus*, by Joel Chandler Harris, published by McClure, Phillips & Company, 1905.
D. "Br'er Fox and Br'er Rabbit," from *The Tar Baby*, published by D. Appleton & Co., 1904.
E. "Mr. Rabbit Meets his Match Again," from *Uncle Remus — His Songs and Sayings*, D. Appleton & Co., 1885.

E

D

Thomas Fogarty.

THOMAS FOGARTY (1873-1938) has imbued this pen-and-ink illustration with his own nostalgia for an earlier era when the local blacksmith was a hero, and his shop the most attractive place in town to awed youngsters.

Fogarty did much illustration in many media but was at his best with simple homespun subjects in pen and ink or wash and crayon, as exemplified by his interpretive pictures for the David Grayson books.

For many years he was a famous teacher at the Art Students League; among his pupils were Walter Biggs, McClelland Barclay, and Norman Rockwell.

Illustration from *Cosmopolitan* magazine for an article by Calvin Coolidge entitled, "The Scenes of my Childhood," published in 1929.

Gilbert Gaul-

WILLIAM GILBERT GAUL, N.A. (1855-1919) specialized in military subjects to which he gave a feeling of great authenticity. His characters were not paintings of polished, costumed models, but of real people revealed by carefully observed gestures. The uniforms looked lived-in, powder-stained, torn or patched. Like Matthew Brady's photos, the effect is one of raw honesty to which he added the drama of lifelike action.

He won a Gold Medal from the American Art Association in 1881 for his painting, "Hold the Line at All Hazards." "Charging the Battery," won a medal at the Paris Exposition in 1889.

"The Captain," from *The Quarterly Illustrator,* October-December, 1893.

WILLIAM J. GLACKENS, N.A. (1870-1938) began his career as a newspaper artist in Philadelphia. John Sloan, Frederic R. Gruger, and Everett Shinn were his co-workers and together they covered fires, riots, parades, and public ceremonies. Glackens' rapid facility made him the expert in sketching crowds.

McClure's magazine sent him to Cuba as an artist-correspondent during the War with Spain, but even before the success of these drawings he had entered the field of magazine illustration.

Hard work preceded the apparent ease of his drawings. He would sketch an action or pose of a figure over and over until he knew it thoroughly. Then discarding the sketches, he would be able to put down the essence of the pose with a deceptive economy of means.

Glackens had been early attracted to the work of Manet and Renoir and had adopted the Impressionist approach in his own work. Gradually, his interest shifted entirely to painting. He became one of The Eight, that famous and controversial group of painters who exhibited independently of the National Academy in 1908, and who gave a new impetus and direction to American art.

"The Generous Mr. Dean" by Abby Meguire Roach. This illustration for *McClure's* magazine in July, 1906, clearly shows the influence of Glackens and F. R. Gruger on each other. They had joined the art staff of the old *Philadelphia Press* at the same time and worked together there, and for *The Ledger,* for several years.

Philip R. Goodwin

PHILIP R. GOODWIN (1882-1935) of Norwich, Connecticut, was a student at the Rhode Island School of Design and the Art Students League in New York. He also studied with Howard Pyle. His work exhibits much of Pyle's earnestness and discipline but is restricted almost entirely to subjects of hunting and fishing. In this limited area, however, he produced many notable pictures, the subject matter always convincing, dramatic in color.

"October Hunting" from *Scribner's* magazine of October, 1911.

CHARLES DANA GIBSON, N.A. (1867-1944) could draw a pretty face. His drawings of women were so beautiful, so gracious, that it was the highest compliment to a young woman to say that she looked like a Gibson Girl. She was depicted on the stage; her likenesses were printed on pillow covers, painted on chinaware, molded on silver spoons. The Gibson Girl, although aloof and refined, was everyone's "ideal" sweetheart.

However, the popularity of Gibson's art was based on much more than a pretty girl. First, he was a master-draughtsman with pen and ink. He used a penpoint almost as a brush, "painting" in his values with sure capability.

Not that his sureness of technique was an overnight acquisition. Years later, John Ames Mitchell, art editor of the old *Life* magazine, who bought Gibson's first drawing, related that he "detected beneath the outer badness of these drawings peculiarities rarely discovered in the efforts of a beginner . . . his faults were good, able-bodied faults that held their heads up and looked you in the eye. No dodging of the difficult points, no tricks, no uncertainty, no slurring of outlines . . . there was always courage and honesty in whatever he undertook." Gibson's later virtuosity was developed through many years of solid application and gradual refinement.

Most important, he was a commentator on the social life and mores of his day, with a satiric but gentle point of view. His people, like "Mr. Pipp," were those with whom everyone, rich or poor, could identify. This happy combination of abilities made Gibson the highest paid illustrator of his time. In 1904 Gibson accepted a contract from *Collier's Weekly* for $100,000 for one hundred illustrations over a period of four years, a contract, incidentally, that repaid *Collier's* many times over in increased circulation.

During World War I, Gibson, as President of the Society of Illustrators, formed and became the head of the Division of Pictorial Publicity under the Federal Committee of Public Information. The top illustrators of the day were recruited to design posters, billboards, and other publicity for the war effort.

After the war, Gibson became owner and editor of the old *Life*, a step which greatly curtailed his own drawing output. By the early 'thirties, he had retired to paint exclusively. In his long career, however, Gibson had compiled a warm and eloquent pictorial record of his era.

A. "A Love Song." Irene Langhorne, later Mrs. Gibson, was the model for this picture, Life Publishing Co., 1896.
B. "Reading the Will," Life Publishing Co., 1895.
C. "The Champion," published by *Collier's Weekly*, 1904.

B

C

ELIZABETH SHIPPEN GREEN

ELIZABETH SHIPPEN GREEN (1871-1954), later Mrs. Huger Elliott, was born in Philadelphia and studied at the Pennsylvania Academy of the Fine Arts with Robert Vonnoh and Thomas Eakins. She also studied with Howard Pyle at the Drexel Institute where she met Jessie Willcox Smith and Violet Oakley. The three women became close friends and shared a studio for many years.

Although Elizabeth did some early illustration for the *Ladies' Home Journal* and *The Saturday Evening Post*, as well as a number of books, she was for many years under an exclusive contract with *Harper's* magazines. Her work is essentially decorative, especially in her brilliant use of color, and is similar in treatment to that of stained-glass windows. It is interesting here to see how effectively she has used the major shapes of the picture as directional pointers to the face of the heroine in "The Chair of Judgment."

From "Felice," published by *Harper's Monthly*, December, 1904.

C. Harding. 00.

CHARLOTTE HARDING (1873-1951), later Mrs. James A. Brown, was a student at the Philadelphia School of Design for Women, Pennsylvania Academy of the Fine Arts, and of Howard Pyle at Drexel Institute.

Pyle's influence in her compositions is clearly apparent, but she had her own strong decorative sense as shown in her use of linear shapes and flattened tonal areas. Her work evinces her special sympathy and understanding of children who were her favorite subjects.

Charlotte Harding was awarded a Silver Medal at the St. Louis Exposition in 1904 and at the Panama-Pacific Exposition at San Francisco in 1915.

Illustration for "The Play's the Thing," from *Harper's Monthly*, September, 1904.

-T-K-HANNA-

The illustrations of THOMAS KING HANNA (1872-1951) are strong and straightforward, yet very skillful. Observe how effectively he placed the heads of the three principal characters in "Darius and Alexander," silhouetting light against dark and dark against light. He was at home with both contemporary scenes and historical costume subjects such as the one reproduced here.

Born in Kansas City, Missouri, Hanna studied at Yale University and at the Art Students League in New York under Kenyon Cox and C. S. Reinhart.

After a long career in illustration for magazines such as *Harper's*, *Scribner's*, *Life*, *American*, *Liberty*, *The Saturday Evening Post*, and *Woman's Home Companion*, he turned to painting and exhibited widely. One of his paintings is in the collection of the National Art Gallery in Sydney, Australia.

From "Darius and Alexander," *Scribner's* magazine, 1914.

- HENRY - HUTT -

In a day when the illustrators set the fashion, no artist was more influential in depicting the stylish, up-to-date female than HENRY HUTT (1875-1950). In spite of the differences of silhouette and time, the subtle detail and good taste of Hutt's illustrations are still apparent.

Hutt was born in Chicago, Illinois, and studied at the Chicago Art Institute. He sold his first picture to the old *Life* magazine at the age of 16 and thereafter illustrated for most of the magazines of his day.

The *Henry Hutt Picture Book*, a volume containing more than eighty of his illustrations, published by the Century Company, was a popular gift book in 1908.

From *Life* magazine, April 26, 1900.

LUCIUS WOLCOTT HITCHCOCK

LUCIUS WOLCOTT HITCHCOCK (1868-1942) painted in the academic tradition of the Laurens and Colarossi School of Paris where he studied with Lefebvre and Constant. His pictures were extremely well painted, and he was especially effective in presenting the social élite.

He was one of the early members of the Society of Illustrators, also joined the Salmagundi Club and the New Rochelle Art Association. His awards were many, including a Silver Medal for illustration in Paris in 1900, Silver Medal for Illustration, and a Bronze for Painting at the St. Louis Exposition in 1904.

Illustration for "The Master Strategist," by Katherine Holland Brown in *Scribner's* magazine, 1913.

Kemble

EDWARD WINDSOR KEMBLE (1861-1933) was a self-taught artist whose work reveals a strong sense of humor and an acute observation of character. His outlook was similar to that of A. B. Frost and, like Frost, he illustrated many of the *Uncle Remus* stories by Joel Chandler Harris.

Kemble illustrated several other famous books, including Mark Twain's *Huckleberry Finn*, and *Puddin' Head Wilson*, Harriet Beecher Stowe's *Uncle Tom's Cabin*, and Washington Irving's *Knickerbocker History of New York*.

He had a special empathy for Negro characters and drew them with an understanding and geniality uncommon in his day.

"The Plantation Bell," from "Sugar Making in Louisiana," *The Century* magazine, November, 1887.

JOSEPH PENNELL (1860-1926) was a pictorial reporter interested chiefly in architectural subjects. He ranged the world on assignments for *Century*, *McClure's*, and *Harper's* magazines, sending back exquisite etchings, pen-and-ink drawings or lithographs of cathedrals, plazas, street scenes, and palaces. He also skillfully depicted the panoramic aspects of major construction or engineering projects – the Locks at Niagara Falls, the construction of the Panama Canal and the war production efforts in Britain, France and America during World War I.

He was a friend and great admirer of James McNeill Whistler, whose biography he wrote. He also wrote a number of books on various art and travel subjects, many in collaboration with his wife, Elizabeth Robins Pennell.

"Chartres Cathedral – the North Porch," dated 1892, published by *The Century* magazine, January, 1907.

EDWARD PENFIELD (1866-1925) produced some of America's finest posters. His clean style and large silhouetted shapes resulted from much careful preliminary refinement and elimination of detail. Horses and coaches were a favorite subject with him, as typified by this cover for *Collier's*. A notable series of his illustrations were contained in his book, *Holland Sketches*, published by *Scribner's* in 1907. Another was a series of calendar illustrations, re-drawn in 1918 from the 1843 "Old Farmer's Almanack" for The Beck Engraving Company.

Penfield had a profound influence on American illustration through his own work, in his post as art director for *Harper's* magazine, and through his teaching at the Art Students League. He was president of the Society of Illustrators in 1921 and 1922.

Collier's cover, December 22, 1906.

A

B

H. Pyle.

The illustrations of HOWARD PYLE, N.A. (1853-1911) are as exciting now as they were over 60 years ago, while pictures by many of his contemporaries today look dated and mannered.

Several special qualities combined to make Pyle America's foremost illustrator. Pyle was interested in pictures, first of all, as drama. As a young man his initial visit to a theatrical performance had made a great impression on him and influenced his point of view from then on. In his illustrations, Pyle sought to dramatize themes with universal appeal. The pictures portrayed basic human emotions: the ruthlessness of pirate greed, raw grief in the break-up of Lee's army after Appomatox, smug pride, humble petition.

Pyle's concept of a picture was never trite. He deliberately looked for new ways to tell a story and involved himself in his subject so thoroughly that his picture makes the reader an eye-witness to a vivid experience.

Having evolved his basic pictorial idea, Pyle developed his compositions; his pictures are fascinating to analyze. No area of a picture is wasted; each makes its contribution, through placement, line, tone, or color, to the whole story. Through the details, the viewer's eye is purposefully led toward the focal center.

Pyle wrote, as well as illustrated, many books himself. He did original research on the obscure subject of the buccaneers in the New World. It is from his famous *Book of Pirates* that our present-day concept of pirates has come. School children still read his *Men of Iron, The Story of King Arthur and his Knights, The Merry Adventures of Robin Hood,* and many other tales.

As a teacher, Pyle attracted a large number of students, inspiring them as much by his idealism as by the high standards he set for picture-making. Over the years he taught at the Drexel Institute in Philadelphia, lectured at the Art Students League in New York, and eventually conducted special classes for gifted students both at Wilmington, Delaware and, during the summer, at Chadd's Ford, Pennsylvania. He made no charge for his teaching and, in fact, built a set of studios for the students to work in. N. C. Wyeth, Harvey Dunn, Stanley Arthurs, and Frank Schoonover were among the beneficiaries of this instruction, and passed along to others Pyle's unique approach as they, in turn, became illustrators and teachers.

At a time when it was customary and fashionable to study in Europe, Pyle had a strong conviction that students should seek their training and inspiration in America. Many of Pyle's greatest pictures came from his intense and loyal interest in Americana. His renditions of the Revolutionary War period and of Civil War subjects have since become standard pictures in our history books, among them Woodrow Wilson's *History of the American People*, and James Truslow Adams' *History of the United States.*

After Pyle's death, his students collected many of his original paintings as a nucleus for the present comprehensive collection of his work in the Wilmington Society of the Fine Arts. An excellent biography entitled, *Howard Pyle, a Chronicle*, was written by Charles D. Abbott and published in New York and London by Harper & Brothers in 1925.

A. Illustration from the King Arthur series. These books, written and illustrated by Pyle, are still kept in print by Charles Scribner's Sons after nearly 60 years of continued popularity.

B. La Salle petitions the King for permission to explore the Mississippi, *Harper's Monthly,* February, 1905.

D. "Lincoln's Last Day," illustration for *Harper's Monthly*, September, 1907.

C. Illustration for "Washington and the French Craze of '93," *Harper's Monthly*, April, 1897.

E. "The Cock Lane Ghost," written and illustrated by Howard Pyle. *Harper's Monthly*, August, 1893.

A Courtesy Amon Carter Museum, Fort Worth.

A. "The Smoke Signal," one of Remington's finest pictures, from the Amon Carter Museum of Western Art, Fort Worth, Texas. This painting was made the subject of a Frederic Remington Centennial commemorative postage stamp issued in 1961.
B. "Setting a Mink Trap," a pen-and-ink drawing from *Harper's Monthly*, 1892.

FREDERIC REMINGTON

FREDERIC SACKRIDER REMINGTON, A. N. A. (1861-1909) was a huge, hearty man who loved adventure and hard work equally. After a brief period of training in art at Yale University, he departed with the romantic idea of striking it rich in the West of the 1880's.

Remington arrived on the scene during the final period of the old lawless West. Today, we are the richer for the record of those picturesque days in the prodigious outpouring of drawings, paintings and bronzes his vigorous talent has left with us.

If his earliest work was somewhat crude, and had to be re-drawn for publication by a staff artist for *Harper's* magazine, the vigor and authenticity of his subject matter won him immediate recognition; and as his technical ability improved, he was given assignments as a reporter-artist, not only in the West, but also in other parts of the world.

In 1898 he accompanied the Fifth Corps to Cuba as a war-correspondent during the war with Spain when he made many notable paintings and drawings of the action. His painting, "Charge of the Rough Riders at San Juan Hill," helped enhance Theodore Roosevelt's reputation as a soldier. They had become personal friends, and he later illustrated several of T. R.'s books and magazine articles.

Remington loved horses. He made a lifelong study of horses and knew at first hand, the several strains of the western broncos, their peculiarities and strengths. His article, "Horses of the Plain," was published by *Century* magazine in 1889. He has well earned his own suggested epitaph: "He Knew the Horse."

After his death, a Remington Memorial Museum was established in his home town of Ogdensburg, New York. Here are to be found some of the finest of his paintings and bronzes. His Indian Collection, together with his studio effects, are preserved in the Whitney Gallery of Western Art in Cody, Wyoming.

B

C. "An Old Time Plains Fight," reproduced courtesy of the Remington Art Memorial, Ogdensburg, New York.

D. "Cavalry Charge on the Southern Plains," 1907.

The Metropolitan Museum of Art, Gift of several gentlemen, 1911.

Reuterdahl.

HENRY REUTERDAHL (1871-1925) was a master-painter of ships and the sea. His early pictures were literal and factually accurate, but in his later pictures his knowledgeability allowed him a more impressionistic approach in the manipulation of sea and ships, with a brilliance of color in keeping with his ageless subject.

During the Spanish-American War, he served as an artist-correspondent. He also accompanied the American Fleet on several voyages including one through the Straits of Magellan in 1907, and another to the Mediterranean in 1913. As a Lieutenant Commander during World War I, he was artistic adviser to the United States Navy Recruiting Bureau in New York and made paintings for many of the Navy's most effective and dramatic posters.

He is represented in the collections of the National Museum in Washington, D. C., the Naval Academy at Annapolis, Maryland, the Naval War College in Newport, and in the Toledo Museum.

"Camouflaged Ships," published by *Everybody's* magazine.

Sarka

CHARLES NICOLAS SARKA (1879-1960) had a chronic wanderlust which, if it interfered with the volume of work he might have done, nevertheless gave him a first-hand knowledge of the exotic subjects of his pictures.

He traveled to many remote areas, from Tahiti and the South Seas to North Africa and the hill tribes of Morocco, paying his expenses on the way with his brush. Thomas "Pop" Hart was one of his traveling companions. His credo was: "This was my art school: to travel and paint: to paint and travel."

Sarka first did illustration for newspapers in Chicago, San Francisco and New York. By 1904, he was illustrating for *Judge* and *Cosmopolitan*, and later added to these most of the other major magazines.

He was a fluent water colorist and a life member of the American Water Color Society. But his early work was in line, and the mastery of his pen-and-ink drawings is brilliant, full of tonal subtleties, rich in texture.

Reproduced from *American* magazine in 1907 for "Arethusa, a Princess in Slavery," by F. Marion Crawford.

"The Rich and the Poor," *Harper's Weekly*, 1891.

W. T. Smedley

WILLIAM THOMAS SMEDLEY, N.A. (1858-1920) was born in West Chester, Pennsylvania, received his art education at the Pennsylvania Academy of the Fine Arts in Philadelphia and later studied with Jean Paul Laurens in Paris.

He began his career in the early 1880's as pen-and-ink artist for Harper and Brothers; later, as halftone engraving was introduced, he changed to working in opaque water color.

An active painter, Smedley was a member of the American Water Color Society, National Association of Portrait Painters, and National Institute of Arts and Letters. He won many awards, including the Evans Prize, A.W.C.S. 1890; Proctor Prize, National Academy of Design, 1906; and the Carnegie Prize, National Academy of Design, 1916. His work is also represented in the National Gallery of Art, Washington, D. C.

Everett Shinn

As one of The Eight EVERETT SHINN, N.A. (1876-1953) greatly influenced American art both in the gallery and on the printed page.

His milieu was New York, Broadway, the theatre, and colorful public gatherings. His immense technical facility is evident here, developed in his early career as a newspaper illustrator which demanded rapid, on-the-spot drawings for immediate deadlines. An individual of great enthusiasms and many interests, Shinn was also an accomplished inventor, playwright, and actor.

A mural, done for the residence of his friend, Clyde Fitch, led to a large number of other such projects, including those of the Belasco Theatre and a large 22-by 44-foot mural for the Trenton, New Jersey, City Hall.

Shinn is represented in many collections and museums, including the Metropolitan Museum of Art, Whitney Museum of American Art, and the Phillips Memorial Gallery in Washington, D. C.

"Street Scene at a Fire," one of a series of four midwinter scenes in pastels for the *Century* magazine, February, 1901.

Albert Sterner

ALBERT E. STERNER, N.A. (1863-1946) was a versatile performer in many media including pen and ink, water color, oils, lithography, pastels, etching, monotypes, crayon, red chalk and charcoal.

Born in London, Sterner studied on a scholarship at the Birmingham Art Institute. He came to America at 17 to start his career working as a scene painter, then went on to lithography and drawing for engravers on wood blocks.

By 1885 Sterner had moved to New York and begun illustrating for the old *Life, St. Nicholas,* and *Harper's* magazines. He later taught at the Art Students League, the school of the National Academy of Design, and the New York School of Applied Design for Women. During his long career he also received commissions to paint portraits of members of socially prominent families including the Vanderbilts, Lamonts, and Whitneys.

Sterner was president of the Society of Illustrators in 1907 and 1908 and was elected a full member of the National Academy of Design in 1934.

From the story, "Etelka Talmeyr," *Harper's Monthly*, 1893.

T. S. Sullivant

THOMAS S. SULLIVANT (1854-1926) was not an illustrator of serious subjects, yet his humorous drawings were so skillfully done that no collection of American illustration would be complete without them. He was born in Columbus, Ohio, and studied at the Pennsylvania Academy of the Fine Arts. His work reveals him as a master-draughtsman even though he chose to distort the facts rather than to record them as they were.

Here, for instance, Sullivant shows a thorough knowledge of the anatomy of the horse, the construction of the buggy and the special character of the figures. His drawings of animals of all kinds are a delightful combination of this anatomical knowledge and a calculated exaggeration.

From *Judge* magazine, 1903.

ALICE BARBER STEPHENS

Sincerity and good taste, as well as her technical excellence, make the illustrations of ALICE BARBER STEPHENS (1858-1932) a pleasure to look at. The early discipline of her work as a wood engraver for *Scribner's* was in some measure responsible for her fine draughtsmanship. She was most successful in quiet settings, with humble subjects — among her best is a series of pictures of old men and women, inmates of the Philadelphia almshouse.

She was trained at the Pennsylvania Academy of the Fine Arts and at the Philadelphia School of Design for Women, where she later taught portrait and life classes.

Among her many awards were the Mary Smith prize, Pennsylvania Academy of the Fine Arts, 1890; Bronze Medal, Atlanta Exposition, 1895; and a Gold Medal in London, 1902.

Illustration for *John Halifax, Gentleman,* published by Thomas Y. Crowell & Co.

SARAH S. STILWELL-WEBER (1878-1939) was fortunate as a student to attend the Drexel Institute in Philadelphia at the time Howard Pyle conducted his illustration class there, (1894-1900). She also attended his summer classes at Chadd's Ford, Pennsylvania.

Although Pyle's influence is evident in her work, her point of view was often highly imaginative; she did story illustrations about or for children particularly well. This illustration of Blue Beard's wife painted in full color in oil is a typical example of her art.

Reproduced from *Thirty Favorite Paintings by Leading American Artists.*

Published by P. F. Collier and Son, 1908.

Courtesy of the Procter & Gamble Company.

JESSIE WILLCOX SMITH

JESSIE WILCOX SMITH (1863-1935) never married but throughout her long career specialized in drawing and painting mothers, babies, and children. Her training was acquired at the School of Design for Women, the Pennsylvania Academy of the Fine Arts with Thomas Eakins, and at the Drexel Institute under Howard Pyle.

She had first planned to be a kindergarten teacher but turned to an art career with the stimulus and assistance of Howard Pyle. Some of her best-known illustrations were for books: *Little Women, Heidi, A Book of Old Stories,* and Robert Louis Stevenson's *A Child's Garden of Verses.* She also painted a great many illustrations for magazines such as *McClure's* and did nearly 200 covers for *Good Housekeeping.*

She painted and exhibited widely, receiving many awards, including a Silver Medal at the Panama-Pacific Exposition at San Francisco in 1915.

This appealing advertising illustration was done for Ivory Soap in 1902.

DAN·SMITH

DAN SMITH (1865-1934) was born of Danish parentage in Ivigtut, Greenland. He came to America as a child; later went to Copenhagen where he studied at the Public Arts Institute. Eventually, he returned to the United States and studied further at the Pennsylvania Academy of the Fine Arts.

Smith's first work was done as a member of the art staff of *Leslie's Weekly*; and at the time of the Spanish-American War, he joined the Hearst organization.

Through drawing for newspapers, Smith developed a remarkable dry-brush technique that made him the star attraction for many years in the Sunday supplement of the old *New York World*. His drawings were syndicated and distributed throughout the country. During this time he also illustrated for the national magazines and exhibited his etchings and oils.

Illustration for *Everybody's* magazine demonstrating Dan Smith's masterful control of dry brush.

FREDERIC DORR STEELE (1873-1944) was a prolific illustrator for *Century, McClure's, Scribner's,* and other publications, but he is best remembered for his portrayal of Arthur Conan Doyle's Sherlock Holmes, as depicted on this cover design for *Collier's* magazine. Steele's drawings were almost always made in line, with either a pencil on a textured paper or in dry brush. Benday screens were sometimes used for tonal effects in these illustrations.

Steele illustrated the works of many other famous authors, including Mark Twain, Richard Harding Davis, F. R. Stockton, Rudyard Kipling, Booth Tarkington, O. Henry, Joseph Conrad, and Arnold Bennett.

Born in a lumber camp near Marquette, Michigan, Steele studied at the National Academy of Design, and at the Art Students League in New York where he also later taught illustration.

He became a member of the Society of Illustrators in 1902, and was awarded a Bronze Medal at the St. Louis Exposition in 1904.

Cover illustration, *Collier's* magazine, 1904.

W. L. TAYLOR -

WILLIAM LADD TAYLOR (1854-1926) had a thorough art education in art schools in Boston, New York, and with Boulanger and Lefebvre in Paris.

Taylor returned to settle in Boston and to record a long series of subjects usually of a historical or regional nature. His interest in antiques and in recreating the era of their use was reflected in an excellent series of paintings of the nineteenth century in New England. Other series included "Old Southern Days," "Home Scenes," and "Frontier Scenes," the latter painted during the course of an illness and a year's stay in Colorado.

For many years these pictures were a regular feature as full-color, full-page reproductions in the *Ladies' Home Journal*; reprints of the pictures for framing were very popular. A large number of the pictures were also published in a book, *Our Home and Country*, published by Moffat, Yard and Company in 1908.

"Homekeeping Hearts are Happiest," the most popular picture ever printed in the *Ladies' Home Journal*, published in 1904.

THULSTRUP.

THURE DE THULSTRUP (1848-1930) was a Swedish subject born in Stockholm. He fought with the French Army during the Franco-Prussian War of 1870-71. Shortly after immigrating to the United States in 1873, he attended the newly organized Art Students League in New York. His first illustrations were made for the old *Daily Graphic* of New York; later he became a staff artist for Frank Leslie's periodicals. By 1881 he was a regular contributor to *Harper's* magazine, then to *Century, Scribner's, Cosmopolitan,* and other leading magazines.

His work is forthright and without frills, whether rendered in pen and ink, black-and-white wash, or in full color. His careful observance of fact and a strong compositional sense gave him the versatility to depict any subject convincingly, but he was especially competent with horses and military subjects.

Two illustrations from *Harper's Monthly* for "The Refugees," by A. Conan Doyle, 1893.

ALBERT B. WENZELL (1864-1917) was born in Detroit, Michigan, and was sent to study art first in Munich and then in Paris where he stayed for seven years. Upon his return to America, he became the acknowledged master of fashionable society and drawing-room subjects. His paintings were done with much "technique," in oils, often in full color, although usually reproduced in black and white. If his preoccupation with the rendering of the sheen of a silk dress or a starched shirt sometimes lessens the message of his pictures, he did, nevertheless, leave us an historic record of the settings and costumes of fashionable society at the turn of the century.

He was awarded a Silver Medal at both the Pan-American Exposition at Buffalo in 1901, and the St. Louis Exposition in 1904.

"A Passing Cloud," from *Drawings by A. B. Wenzell,* published by P. F. Collier and Son, 1903.

G. Wright

The son of a blacksmith, GEORGE HAND WRIGHT, N.A. (1873-1951) always retained a sympathy for rustic subjects and working people in his illustrations for *Century, Scribner's, Harper's, The Saturday Evening Post,* and other publications. He researched his pictorial material as a reporter, filling innumerable sketchbooks and making his finished illustrations from these on-the-spot drawings. In fact, many of his sketches were reproduced directly in the magazines as reportorial coverage for accompanying articles. He made no distinction in approach between these commissioned illustrations and the fine arts prints, etchings or pastels to which he restricted himself in his later years.

Wright studied at the Spring Garden Institute and the Academy of the Fine Arts in Philadelphia. He was a member and past president of the Society of Illustrators, the Westport Artists, and the Salmagundi Club, also a member of the Dutch Treat Club and the Society of American Etchers.

Illustration for "On Horseback to Kingdom Come," a story by John Fox, Jr., published by *Scribner's* magazine, 1910.

R. F. Zogbaum

RUFUS FAIRCHILD ZOGBAUM (1849-1925) was a lifelong student of and expert in the depiction of battle scenes. (He wrote a scholarly article on "War and the Artist," for *Scribner's* magazine in the January 1915 issue.) He himself specialized in American war illustrations, of the Civil War, the skirmishes with the Indians, and the Spanish-American War. In his pictures, as in this episode at the close of the Civil War, there is an originality of approach and authenticity of detail that mark him as a master. Unfortunately, the great bulk of his work predated halftone engraving and was reproduced by the cruder method of wood engraving.

He painted the "First Minnesota Regiment at the Battle of Gettysburg," as a mural at the State Capitol in St. Paul, and the "Battle of Lake Erie," for the Federal Building in Cleveland.

"The Message of Peace," from "The Closing Scene at the Appomattox Court House," by General George A. Forsyth, U.S.A., published by *Harper's Monthly* in 1898.

1910-1920

ILLUSTRATORS 1910-1920

Samuel Nelson Abbott
John Wolcott Adams
Edmund M. Ashe
Clifford Warren Ashley
William James Aylward
Ernest Leonard Blumenschein
Franklin Booth
John Paul Bransom
George Brehm
Worth Brehm
Arthur William Brown
Charles Livingston Bull
Charles Shepard Chapman
Howard Chandler Christy
Walter Jack Duncan
Harvey Dunn
William Herbert Dunton
Charles Buckles Falls
Harrison Fisher
James Montgomery Flagg
Frederic Rodrigo Gruger
George Harding
Arthur Ignatius Keller
Frank X. Leyendecker
Joseph Christian Leyendecker
Walt Louderback
Angus Peter MacDonall
Charles Davis Mitchell
Wallace Morgan
Harold James Mowat
Thornton Oakley
Rose Cecil O'Neill-Wilson
Maxfield Parrish
Clara Elsene Peck
Coles Phillips
Norman Mills Price
Henry Patrick Raleigh
Charles Marion Russell
Frank Earle Schoonover
John Sloan
Frank Walter Taylor
Harry Everett Townsend
John Scott Williams
Edward Arthur Wilson
Newell Convers Wyeth
Frederick Coffay Yohn

DRAWING BY AL PARKER

The Decade: 1910-1920

by Arthur William Brown

Honorary President, Society of Illustrators

The year 1910 continued what we now think of as the Golden Era with Pyle, Abbey, Penfield, Parrish, Remington, Wenzell, Glackens and many other notables carrying on the fine tradition of illustration.

If you were lucky enough to work for the Big Four: *Century, Harper's, McClure's* and *Scribner's,* you had arrived. Other fine magazines were: *American, Everybody's,* the women's *Ladies' Home Journal, Woman's Home Companion, Good Housekeeping, Delineator* and *Pictorial Review.* There were others, too — *Collier's* and *The Saturday Evening Post, Youth's Companion, St. Nicholas, Smith's, Success, Circle,* and many smaller ones. Finally there were the humorous weeklies: *Life, Puck,* and *Judge.* The market for art was large. Most of the magazines were a great help financially to the illustrator. When your drawings were accepted you went to the cashier and got your money at once in cash or by check.

Compared to today, reproductions of drawings were small. One magazine required that the head of a character be no more than one-and-one-quarter inches in height. Most work was in black and white; color was seldom used and then only sparingly.

Art editors were men of education, taste, and culture but few of them had been artists; however they knew the artist's ability and showed their confidence by giving him a free hand. They rarely asked for sketches or layouts; you were simply told how many illustrations to make for most illustrators had their own style and stuck to it consistently.

As a rule, illustrators drew from live models; anyone using photographs was frowned on; he was prostituting his art — a far cry from the present where camera is king. No mechanical gadgets like balopticons. Models' fees were low, whereas today, top models earn as much as many illustrators did then. This is a fact. Many models we used then, later became stars of stage and screen — Frederic March, Norma Shearer, Neil Hamilton, Joan Blondell, to name a few.

Artists who illustrated stories by popular authors became well known to readers who often were attracted by their pictures. With no radio and TV, illustrations created styles according to fan mail received. As an example, girls would write to say they liked a hat or dress in a drawing and would have it copied by a local milliner or seamstress. There was also what we called the Mistake-Finders' Society. They loved to write to the editor when catching the artist in a mistake; he hadn't followed the story and they pointed out details that were wrong. These letters were sent to us to answer; it was a command.

There were no artists' representatives then, and illustrators' contact with editors, art editors, and authors was on a warm personal basis. We enjoyed a certain prestige and dignity seldom found today. Illustrator and author often teamed up to talk over picture situations and continued to collaborate, sometimes for years. A case in point was the Ephraim Tutt series by Arthur Train, started in 1919 in *The Saturday Evening Post* and continuing regularly until 1944 when the author died.

Most young illustrators followed the work of the top men. Frederic R. Gruger was one who began a new trend. Starting as a newspaper artist on a Philadelphia paper, his work appeared in the first issue of *The Saturday Evening Post.* His compositions were monumental even in miniature. His characters were part of the story and believable. To Henry Raleigh, H. J. Mowat, and me — all close friends — Gruger was our hero.

When the United States entered World War I in 1917, many illustrators were in the Armed Forces, but those at home did everything possible to help the war effort and sell Liberty Bonds. A division of Pictorial Publicity of the Committee on Public Information was formed with Charles Dana Gibson as chairman. We met weekly at Keen's Chop House on West 36th Street in New York City where we received assignments for art work; anything from a newspaper spot to posters and billboards. James Montgomery Flagg created his famous poster of Uncle Sam pointing "I WANT YOU" and he posed for it himself. To help sell Liberty Bonds, Flagg and I did billboards in front of the New York Public Library. He did the figures, and I smeared in the background. We used live models and, with a girl wrapped in the Stars and Stripes, we did one on a scaffold high up in Times Square. The wind was strong; the street below looked safe and inviting. When traveling to Washington and other cities painting these billboards, we always attracted large crowds.

In January 1918 a number of illustrators were commissioned as official war artists and were sent overseas as Captains in the Engineers' Reserve Corps. These men often lived at the Front with the troops; in some cases, went over the top with them. Notable artwork resulted. These vivid drawings and paintings by Wallace Morgan, Jack Duncan, Harry Townsend, Harvey Dunn and others are part of the permanent collection in the Smithsonian Institution in Washington, D.C.

As this era ended, many of us went on to the next. Even with the War it was a great and glorious ten years for American Illustration.

S.N. ABBOTT

The fact that the life and work of SAMUEL NELSON ABBOTT (1874-1953) are not better remembered today is largely due to the artist's own extreme modesty and sense of loyalty. Born in Illinois, he had saved up enough to study in Paris under Laurens and Constant. Upon his return to the United States, he was given his first assignment to do the cover design and fashion illustrations of a catalog for Hart, Schaffner and Marx, clothing manufacturers. This began a collaboration that lasted for the next twenty-five years. These booklets, in full color, were greatly admired and collected by other illustrators, designers and agencies. Abbott always turned down offers for any other commercial illustration assignments out of intense loyalty to his first employer, although he did some editorial illustration and cover paintings for the *Ladies' Home Journal, The Saturday Evening Post* and *Collier's.* His fine sense of design, color and his draughtsmanship deserve recognition here.

Cover illustration for the *Ladies' Home Journal,* August, 1922.

THE LADIES' HOME JOURNAL

John Wolcott Adams

JOHN WOLCOTT ADAMS (1874-1925) was born in Worcester, Massachusetts, a descendant of two illustrious United States' Presidents. He studied at the Art Museum in Boston, the Art Students League in New York, and with Howard Pyle.

His illustrations appeared in *Scribner's, Harper's, Century,* the *Delineator,* and other magazines, usually as pen-and-ink drawings to accompany old songs, poetry, and historical incidents.

Adams, who was also interested in the theatre, designed the stage settings for one of Walter Hampden's productions. He was a member of The Players and the Society of Illustrators.

This fine drawing is one of a series illustrating "The Hard Cider Campaign of 1840."

From the *Century* magazine, September, 1912.

E. M. ASHE

One of the earliest members of the Society of Illustrators (he joined in the first month), was EDMUND M. ASHE (1867-1941), a founder of the Silvermine Guild in Norwalk, Connecticut.

During Theodore Roosevelt's administration, Ashe was an artist-correspondent at the White House and was able to secure several scoops through his personal friendship with the President.

In addition to his illustrations for most of the magazines, he taught for many years. In the early 1900's he instructed at the Art Students League, later at Carnegie Institute of Technology from 1920 to 1939.

In this small vignette, Ashe reveals his complete mastery of the pen-and-ink medium.

C W Ashley

CLIFFORD WARREN ASHLEY (1881-1947) who was a student of Howard Pyle, came by his interest in the sea naturally. He was born in New Bedford, Massachusetts, the center of the early whaling industry, and specialized in illustrations of fishing and whaling subjects.

Ashley was also the author and illustrator of several books relating to seafaring, including the *Yankee Whaler,* and *The Ashley Book of Knots*, an 11-year project, with some 7,000 drawings and diagrams, and the definitive work on the subject.

Ashley is represented by paintings in the Brooklyn Museum, The Whaling Museum in New Bedford, the Canajoharie (New York) Museum, Massachusetts Institute of Technology, the Society of Fine Arts in Wilmington, Delaware, and the Mariner's Museum, Newport News, Virginia.

"Spearing a Swordfish," from the *Century* magazine, September, 1907.

W. J. Aylward

WILLIAM JAMES AYLWARD (1875-1956) was born in Milwaukee, Wisconsin, but like Ashley, his greatest interest was in the sea and related nautical subjects. He, too, was a student of Howard Pyle.

Aylward's interest embraced more of the history of seafaring, however, and he both illustrated and wrote articles describing the earlier days of sailing. He also illustrated Jack London's *Sea Wolf*, Jules Verne's *Twenty Thousand Leagues under the Sea,* and other books on naval or marine subjects.

Aylward belonged to many art societies and exhibited widely, winning the Shaw purchase prize at the Salmagundi Club in 1911; the Beck prize, Philadelphia Water Color Club in 1912; the Salmagundi prize for Illustration in 1914. He was also an official artist with the A.E.F. during World War I.

"The Breeches Buoy," from *Thirty Favorite Paintings*, published by P. F. Collier & Son, 1908.

Franklin Booth

As a farm boy near Carmel, Indiana, FRANKLIN BOOTH (1874-1948) wanted to be an artist and so studied pictures in all of the books and magazines available. Most of the reproductions at that time were printed from steel or wood engravings. Mistakenly believing the drawings were made with pen and ink, he painstakingly copied their character line by line. This was eventually to become the basis for his unique line technique.

Booth described his working methods in the *Professional Art Quarterly* in 1934, ". . . In doing a drawing it has been my custom first, of course, to lay in my entire conception with the pencil. This penciled sketch is not a completed thing, but a generalization. Parts of this I then draw in more fully and follow immediately with the pen. My drawings are usually somewhat involved and a completed pencil drawing to begin with would, in places, become smudged and lost in the process of inking in other parts. So I proceed and complete a part or section at a time and follow through, in this way, to the outer edges of my drawing. At times in the making of my drawings, in one section or more, a completed picture will be seen in the midst of white paper and penciled suggestions.

"By this method, also, the general relationship of values of the whole drawing, at the start, can be established in one small part. This becomes the guide. The point, therefore, of the beginning of a picture will usually be a place where a section of the darkest dark, the grays and the highest whites appear together."

If this method of rendering was a laborious one, it does not appear to have restricted Booth's picture concepts. All of his compositions are characterized by a feeling of space and lofty grandeur. Many of his pictures were used to accompany poetry or to decorate editorial articles. This same sense of beauty and taste was carried over into his advertising assignments. In an introduction to a book of 60 drawings by Franklin Booth, published by Robert Frank in 1925, Earnest Elmo Calkins wrote:

"Mr. Booth has done more than almost any one man to break down the barrier between the pure art of decoration as applied to the book or magazine page and the same art applied to the advertising page. Anything undertaken by him is approached in the same creative spirit and executed with the same sure touch . . . His two great qualities are his dexterity with his pen and his imagination. His work appeals to the spirit. It has an uplifting effect. It suggests something just beyond, an ideal almost realized. His fine craftsmanship never becomes mere dexterity. It remains always as it should be, the instrument for expressing a fine creative imagination."

Advertising illustration for the Estey Organ Co.

A. One of the most popular and enduring series of short stories in *The Saturday Evening Post* was about the famous lawyer, "Mr. Tutt," written by Arthur Train and depicted here by Brown.
B. Illustration for *Harper's Bazaar*, 1917.

ARTHUR WILLIAM BROWN (1881-1966) has had one of the longest and most prolific careers of any American illustrator. Born in Canada, he landed his first job as a chalk-plate artist, on the local Hamilton, Ontario, *Spectator* at the age of 15. These drawings were made directly through chalk-coating on a steel plate in a crude process preceding halftone engraving. After four years of this, he saved enough money to go to New York where he studied at the Art Students League under Walter Appleton Clark.

Brown's first chance at magazine illustration came when a friend of his was assigned to write a circus article for *The Saturday Evening Post*. "Brownie" took a chance that he could make acceptable accompanying drawings and spent six weeks traveling with the circus. The *Post* was pleased with the result and the published illustrations became the first of a long and busy association which lasted over 40 years.

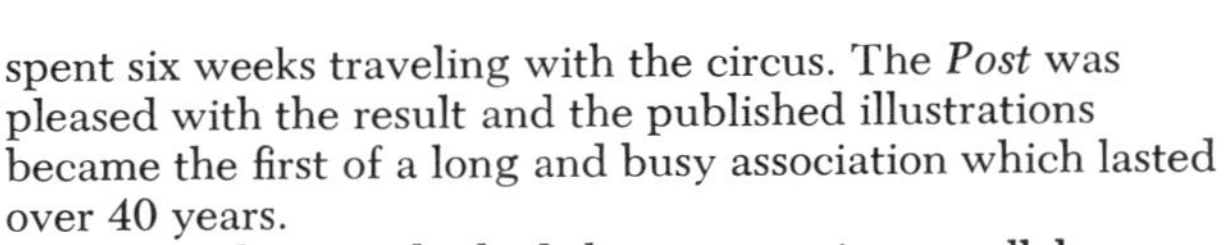

During this time he had the opportunity to collaborate with many famous authors, including O. Henry, F. Scott Fitzgerald, Booth Tarkington, Irvin Cobb, Edna Ferber, and Sinclair Lewis. In the early stages of their careers, Frederic March, John Barrymore, Neil Hamilton, Joan Blondell, and Dean Jagger all posed for him.

Brown has always been an active member of the Society of Illustrators. He was its president from 1944 to 1947 and has been president emeritus ever since. In 1964 he was unanimously voted to the Illustrators' Hall of Fame.

ERNEST LEONARD BLUMENSCHEIN, N.A. (1874-1960) was among the group of artists who settled early in or near Taos, New Mexico, attracted by the Indian life and pictorial color. Blumenschein painted many award-winning pictures there and is represented in several museum collections by his fine interpretive pictures of Indian subjects.

This Taos period came comparatively late in his life, however; earlier he had had an active career as an illustrator in the East. Born in Pittsburgh, Pennsylvania, he had attended the Cincinnati Art Academy and the Art Students League in New York. Later he studied with Joseph Benjamin Constant, Laurens and Collin in Paris. He was a very versatile and competent painter with a fresh, unusual viewpoint. Although he worked realistically, there was always strong design underlying his pictures.

For many years Blumenschein divided his time between New York and New Mexico, eventually settling permanently in Taos.

"The Peacemaker," typifies Blumenschein's interest in Indian life and in decorative pictorial concepts.

-G-BREHM-

Both GEORGE BREHM (1878-1966) and his younger brother, Worth, had the ability to illustrate stories about children, particularly boys, sympathetically and convincingly. Perhaps this insight developed from their small town, Hoosier upbringing.

George studied at the Art Students League in New York with Twachtman, DuMond, and Bridgman, but did his first illustration for the *Reader's* magazine, published by Bobbs-Merrill Company near his home in Indianapolis. On the strength of this work, he obtained an assignment from *Delineator* in New York, and his career was launched. Over the years he illustrated for most of the magazines; his most memorable pictures were done for *The Saturday Evening Post* for story series by Booth Tarkington, Octavius Roy Cohen, and M. G. Chute.

Illustration for *The Saturday Evening Post*.

WORTH BREHM

WORTH BREHM (1883-1928) became interested in art through his brother. He prepared a series of sample drawings in Indiana, brought them to New York, and *Outing* magazine bought them all. Publication of these pictures led *Harper's* to commission him to illustrate *The Adventures of Tom Sawyer* and *Huckleberry Finn*.

He later did general illustrations for many magazines; the best known were for the *Penrod* stories by Booth Tarkington, in *Cosmopolitan*; the M. G. Chute boyhood stories in *Good Housekeeping* magazine, and the Irvin S. Cobb stories of the Mississippi in *Cosmopolitan*. His work was always in demand from both magazines and advertisers up to the time of his death at the age of 44.

"Marbles," illustration for *Outing* magazine, 1908.

Paul Bransom

PAUL BRANSOM (1885-) began drawing animals from early childhood. He was born in Washington, D. C., and, after leaving school at 13, became an apprentice-draftsman assisting with mechanical drawings for patents. This rigorous discipline in drawing, combined with his free-time sketching at the National Zoo, developed in him the habit of making a careful analysis and recording of the individual characteristics of each of the animals he drew. His work later led him to New York — and the chance to take over a vacancy at the *New York Evening Journal* doing a comic strip, "The Latest News from Bugville." He credits Walt Kuhn and T. S. Sullivant (both of whom did animal cartoon subjects then) with having most influenced his career, and . . . "of course, the greatest of all animal illustrators, Charles Livingston Bull."

During this time he haunted the Bronx Zoo to such a degree that he was permitted to set up a studio at the Lion House. His goal was to draw and paint animals for the magazines. The work in his portfolio so impressed the editor of *The Saturday Evening Post* that he bought, on the spot, four pictures for covers and several smaller drawings.

Since then, Paul Bransom has had a long and distinguished career. He has illustrated nearly 50 books on wildlife subjects, including Jack London's *Call of the Wild*, and hundreds of stories and articles for almost all of the major magazines.

Paul Bransom is currently painting for exhibitions and teaching in the summer at the Teton Artists Associated, an outdoor art school at Jackson Hole, Wyoming.

"Black Bear at Bay," illustration in charcoal for the *Country Gentleman*.

Charles Livingston Bull

CHARLES LIVINGSTON BULL (1874-1932) learned about animals almost literally from the inside out. His first job, at 16, at Ward's Museum in Rochester, New York, consisted of scraping out the inner linings of animal pelts preparatory to their being mounted. Later, he became an accomplished taxidermist and worked for the National Museum in Washington, D. C., as an expert on the anatomy of birds and animals.

He studied at the Philadelphia Art School and drew and painted his subjects in the course of his work, soon becoming one of our foremost animal illustrators. Both his taxidermy and paintings were greatly admired by President Theodore Roosevelt for whom he mounted many specimens now in the National Museum.

Bull lived directly opposite the Bronx Zoo in New York for many years in order to be able to sketch from living models. A lover of the outdoors, he also made numerous field trips into Mexico and Central and South America where he studied wildlife in its natural habitat. His book, *Under the Roof of the Jungle*, is a collection of illustrations and short stories of animal life in the Guiana wilds based on his explorations there.

Bull was active in bird-banding for the United States Biological Survey and particularly interested in the plight of the American eagle. To arouse public interest in their preservation, he made many drawings and posters for pictorial publicity, as reproduced here.

Charles S. Chapman N.A.

CHARLES SHEPARD CHAPMAN, N.A. (1879-) is an illustrator and painter whose compositions convey a feeling of spaciousness and dignity. Part of the effect is achieved through his use of scale, but his subject matter also contributes. He is interested in the beauty of nature, especially in forest subjects, painted with much imagination and experimentation in textural effects.

Chapman was born in Morristown, New York, attended the New York School of Art, studying under William Merritt Chase and Walter Appleton Clark.

He and Harvey Dunn conducted a school of illustration in Leonia, New Jersey, for several years. He also taught at the Art Students League, exhibited regularly, and won many awards. His painting, "In the Deep Wood," was purchased by The Metropolitan Museum of Art in New York.

"The Loon Call," illustrates Chapman's fine sense of composition and decorative use of texture.

Howard Chandler Christy.

HOWARD CHANDLER CHRISTY (1873-1952) had a long, colorful, and varied career. He had made his early reputation in accompanying the United States troops to Cuba during the Spanish-American War when articles illustrated by his drawings and paintings were published by *Scribner's* and *Leslie's Weekly*. The famous Christy Girl resulted from his picture, the "Soldier's Dream," in *Scribner's*. From then on he did beautiful girl pictures, for *McClure's* and other magazines, almost entirely.

Christy's painting technique was sumptuous, and he was in great demand as a portraitist. Among the notables he painted were Mrs. Calvin Coolidge, Secretary of State Charles Evans Hughes, Amelia Earhart, Lawrence Tibbett, and Mrs. William Randolph Hearst.

He was also a popular teacher and at various times instructed at Cooper Union, the Chase School, New York School of Art, and the Art Students League.

In later years, Christy painted several murals, including his well-known decorations for the Café des Artistes in New York. His most famous mural, however, is a 20 by 30-foot canvas, "The Signing of the Constitution," which hangs in the rotunda of the Capitol in Washington, D. C.

For three years, Christy researched conscientiously the material for this painting; he got hold of Washington's watch fob, the original quill used in the signing, and even Benjamin Franklin's books, as models. The faces of two signers are hidden since no authenticated likeness existed.

W J Duncan

WALTER JACK DUNCAN (1881-1941) came from Indianapolis to study at the Art Students League in New York. His first work was for *Century* magazine in 1903. *Scribner's* sent him on assignment to England in 1905, and he subsequently worked for *McClure's*, *Harper's*, and the other major publishers. In 1917, he was one of the artists, commissioned as officers in the Engineer Corps, who went overseas with the A.E.F.

Duncan specialized in pen and ink which he employed with great directness and skill. The directness resulted from his very careful and thoroughly worked out preliminary studies. He had been attracted to line because of its harmony with the text of the printed page and his interest in both books and writing. Most of his best friends were writers, among them Christopher Morley, for whom he illustrated several books, including *Tales from a Roll-top Desk*, *Pipefuls*, and *Plum Pudding*. Duncan himself wrote and illustrated a scholarly book entitled, *First Aid to Pictorial Composition*, published in 1939 by Harper's.

Some of his finest work was done for the late Henry B. Quinan, art director of the *Woman's Home Companion*. This example was published in 1928.

W. Herbert Dunton

WILLIAM HERBERT DUNTON (1878-1936) who was born in Augusta, Maine, studied at the Cowles Art School in Boston and the Art Students League of New York under Andreas M. Anderson, Joseph De Camp, Frank Vincent DuMond, William Ladd Taylor, E. L. Blumenschein, and Leon Gaspard. This thorough training is evident in his accomplished and well-composed illustrations for *Harper's*, *Scribner's*, *Everybody's*, and other magazines. His subject matter was spirited, usually of the West or other outdoor scenes, his use of color effectively keyed to the mood.

Dunton settled permanently in Taos, New Mexico, in 1921. In addition to his illustrations, he also painted and exhibited widely, received a Gold Medal in Nashville, Tennessee, in 1927, and won many other awards. He is represented in the collections of the Peoria Society of Applied Arts (Illinois), the Witte Memorial Museum, San Antonio, Texas, the Museum of New Mexico in Santa Fe, and by murals in the Missouri State Capitol, Jefferson City, and in the White House, Washington, D.C.

"The 'Breed' Trapper, 1830." Reproduced from *Scribner's* magazine, July, 1914.

A

A. "The Prairie is my Garden," is one of Dunn's best known pictures.
B. "Something for Supper." These two pictures are part of the Harvey Dunn Collection at South Dakota State College, Brookings, South Dakota.

B

C. Illustration for a *Saturday Evening Post* story.

HARVEY DUNN

HARVEY DUNN, N.A. (1884-1952) was a large, powerful man who paid for his art schooling by "sod-busting," plowing under the thick, virgin, prairie grass for his homesteading neighbors of the Red Stone Valley of South Dakota.

From the Art Institute of Chicago, he was invited by Howard Pyle to study at Chadd's Ford. Of all Pyle's students, Dunn was perhaps most deeply imbued with his philosophy, and as a teacher passed it along together with his own straightforward honesty and intolerance of pretense. Among his students were Dean Cornwell, Harold Von Schmidt, Amos Sewell, Lee Gustavson, Mario Cooper, Mead Schaeffer, and many others.

Dunn's pictures, like the man, were forceful, yet combined great sensitivity with brilliant use of color. During World War I, Dunn was commissioned a Captain as an official war artist with the A.E.F. He lived in the trenches, shared their dangers, and went over the top with the men. These experiences produced many striking documentary drawings and paintings, now part of the archives of the Smithsonian Institution in Washington, D.C.

From notes taken during one of his classroom criticisms, the following* fittingly describes his credo:

"Art is a universal language, and it is so because it is the expression of the feelings of man. Any man can look at a true work of art and feel kin to it and with him who made it — for he has the same number of heartbeats a minute, comes into the world to face the same joys, sorrows, and anticipations, the same hopes and fears. A vastly different vision may arise in the consciousness at the mention of a word, but our feelings are the same. By this you may know that the Brotherhood of Man *is*."

* quoted from "An Evening in the Classroom," notes taken by Miss Taylor in one of Dunn's painting classes and printed at the suggestion of Mario Cooper in 1934.

Falls

CHARLES BUCKLES FALLS (1874-1960) approached illustration primarily as a designer. Realism in his pictures was always tempered by a strong sense of decoration. This quality was first exemplified in the fine posters he made for many of the old vaudeville theatres in New York, now collectors' items.

In 1918 he designed a famous "Books Wanted" poster for the Armed Forces which provoked an enthusiastic flow of books to the training camps and gained an international reputation for Charlie Falls.

His pictures were ideally suited for books. As a personal project, he did an ABC book for his daughter, then three years old, comprised of colored woodcuts. This book has become a classic of its kind, and has been in continuous publication since the first edition in 1923.

The long career of C. B. Falls included much illustration for advertising, magazine covers and editorial art for fiction and articles. In addition, he taught at the Art Students League in New York and produced his own woodcuts and paintings. He executed numerous mural commissions, among them a series of historical portraits for the ceiling of the New York State office building at Albany.

Illustration for article on the Arts by H. G. Wells in the *New York Herald Tribune*, 1926.

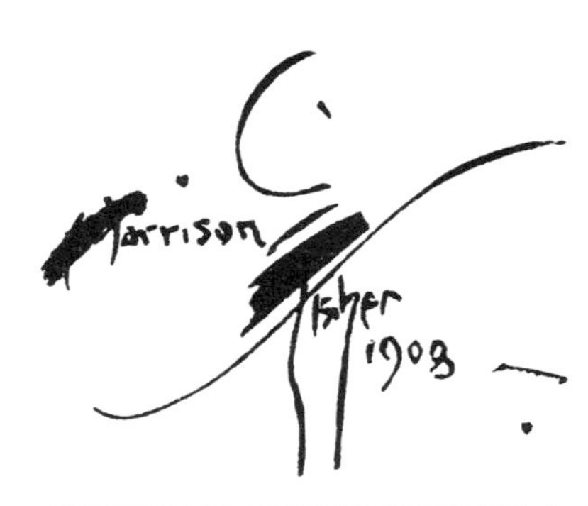

HARRISON FISHER (1875-1934) showed an early interest in drawing and from the age of six was instructed by his father, Hugh Antoine Fisher, a landscape painter. When his family moved from Brooklyn to San Francisco, Harrison studied there at the Mark Hopkins Institute of Art. At 16, Fisher had begun to make drawings for the *San Francisco Call* and later for the *Examiner*.

Soon after returning to New York, Fisher sold two sketches to *Puck* magazine which also hired him as a staff artist. He became noted for his ability to draw beautiful women, and his Fisher Girl became a rival to those of Gibson and Christy. The American Girl was a favorite theme for the magazines then, and Fisher did cover illustrations for most of them. For many years he was under an exclusive contract to do covers for *Cosmopolitan*; but eventually he restricted himself to painting portraits.

Pastel rendering for *Cosmopolitan* magazine, October, 1924.

JAMES MONTGOMERY FLAGG

JAMES MONTGOMERY FLAGG (1877-1960) lived with gusto. He epitomized the public concept of the handsome bohemian artist, surrounded by beautiful models, dashing off pictures with sheer exuberance of talent. In Flagg's case, this was nearly true. He worked rapidly and easily in all media and with any subject matter. Humor and satire were his special forte; early in his career he did a cartoon feature entitled, "Nervy Nat." His rapid portrait studies and incisive caricatures were prized by many prominent sitters.

For over 30 years he turned out an immense amount of work, including many posters during World War I. Probably his best known illustration was the famous "I Want You" Uncle Sam recruiting poster (shown below). Over four million copies of this were printed and distributed throughout the country.

Flagg was a painter of serious portraits, too. He exhibited in the Paris salon of 1900, at the National Academy of Design, and the New York Water Color Club. His well-known mural painting of the Dempsey-Willard fight may be seen in Jack Dempsey's restaurant in New York City.

A. World War I illustration for the American Red Cross.
B. Flagg gives us a vignette of a brief stage in the development of the automobile, and of traffic control in 1913, in this illustration for an advertisement of the Willys-Overland.

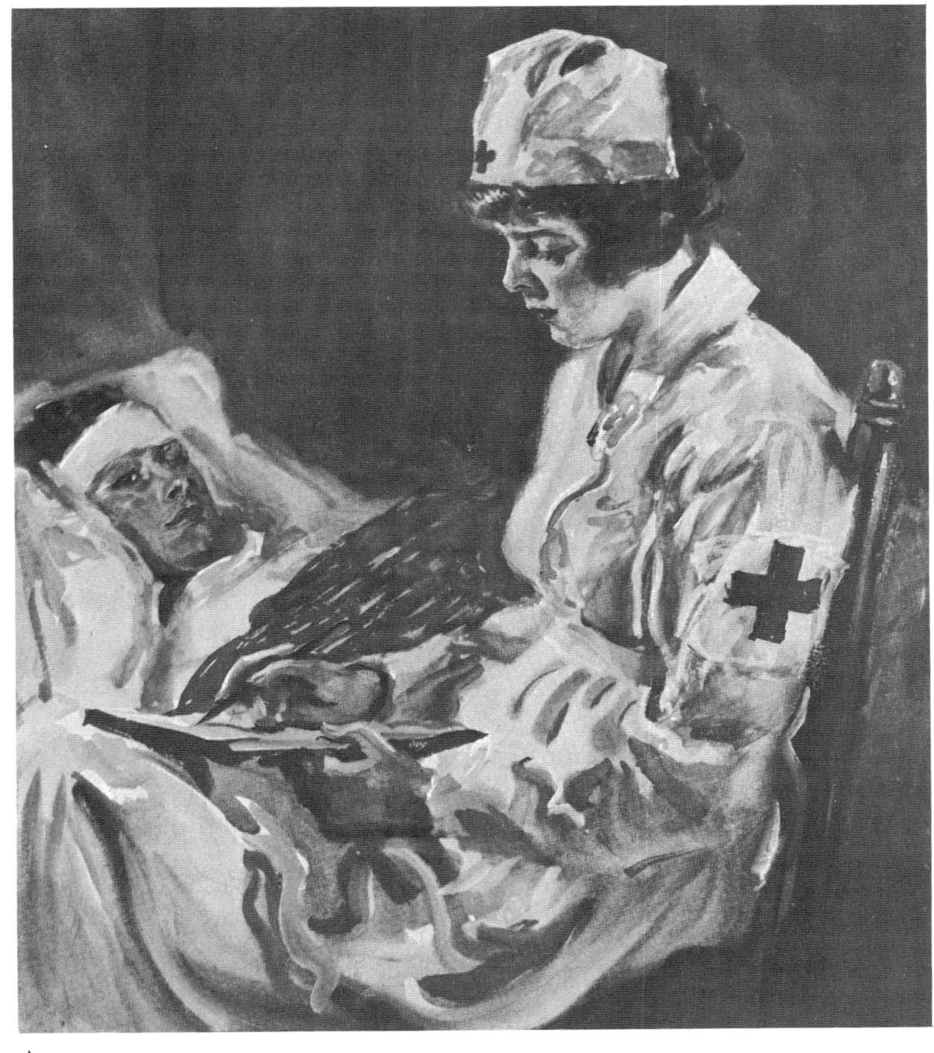

A

I WANT YOU

for the U.S. ARMY

B

A

F. R. GRUGER

FREDERIC RODERIGO GRUGER (1871-1953) wrote on the subject of Illustration for the Encyclopedia Britannica, describing the illustrator's role as follows:

"... Illustration may become a great art, but to become a great art, it must be creative. It cannot hope to compete with the camera in the reporting of facts. It has no business with the outer shell of things at all. It deals with the spirit. Dealing with the psychological aspects is a great opportunity and a serious handicap. Presupposing a pictorial presentation of the relations of people, the telling of a story is inevitable. A great and simple story, akin to truth, or a poor and trivial one, akin to meagre facts, may be told by the same incident — depending upon the insight, the vision of the artist. The nature of the story portrayed is the measure of the artist who portrays it ..."

Gruger demonstrated this insight and vision in his work. His pictures were always concerned with the larger themes, and although the original drawings were actually quite small, they appear monumental in scale.

He worked in a medium developed out of his earlier work for the *Philadelphia Ledger*. The drawing was made with Wolff pencil, rubbed with a stump or eraser, oftentimes over an underlying wash, which produced a full range of values, particularly a rich, velvety black. The board itself was an inexpensive cardboard used by newspapers for mounting silver prints. It had a receptive, soft surface and has since become known as "Gruger board."

Gruger got his start with the old *Century* magazine and worked subsequently for many other publishers and advertisers, but was most closely identified through his long career with *The Saturday Evening Post*.

A. Illustration for *The Saturday Evening Post*.
B. *Cosmopolitan* magazine, August, 1925, for "True Thomas."
C. Illustration for Edna Ferber's "Show Boat," *Woman's Home Companion*, 1926.

B

C

A. I. Keller

A

Perhaps the first reaction to the work of ARTHUR IGNATIUS KELLER (1866-1925) is one of admiration for the brilliant facility of his technique. His preliminary studies, especially, show a mastery of drawing itself, the result of his long training both at the National Academy of Design and with Loefftz in Munich. The studies are not a stolid assimilation of facts, however, but rather a poetic exploration of the forms, freely and directly made from the model, for his own use in the finished illustrations.

This feeling of interpretation and poetry is carried further in his compositions, often crowded with figures, but controlled through passages of light or accents of carefully placed tones rendered with an impression of great spontaneity.

A. Painting in water color of Ichabod Crane's courtship of Katrina Van Tassel for a gift book edition of *The Legend of Sleepy Hollow*, published in 1906 by The Bobbs-Merrill Company.
B. Illustration for *Her Letter* by Bret Harte, published by Houghton Mifflin & Company, 1905.
C. One of Keller's preliminary drawings for an illustration.

C

B

GEORGE HARDING

GEORGE HARDING (1882-1959) was the younger brother of Charlotte Harding and through her work became interested in illustration. With her influence, he was admitted to Howard Pyle's illustration classes in Wilmington. He later spent several months studying and sketching the life of Newfoundland fishing families. With this background, he returned home to find a market for his work with *The Saturday Evening Post* and other major magazines.

He was one of eight official artists sent overseas, with the A.E.F. during World War I, with roving assignments to document the war in drawings and paintings. In his drawings he was concerned more with the effect of war on the men themselves than with portraying panoramic scenes of battlefields or ruins. These are now part of the permanent collection of the Smithsonian Institution in Washington, D.C.

Harding subsequently taught illustration at the Pennsylvania Academy of the Fine Arts; he exhibited widely and painted many murals.

"Mont Saint-Père, July 23, 1918," Smithsonian Institution.

Walt Louderback

The work of WALT LOUDERBACK (1887-1941) is broad and direct, with few subtleties. Yet for all his sledge-hammer technique, romanticism permeates his pictures. His characters and their emotions seem heroic, larger than life. As in the picture reproduced here, the mood of the desolation of burial is compellingly dramatized; emphasized by the cold, the wind, and the sombre grayness of the massed figures.

Louderback was born in Valparaiso, Indiana, and studied at the Art Institute of Chicago. He lived in Europe for some time in the 'twenties, delivering his pictures by ship. A painter, as well as an illustrator, he was awarded the Daughters of Indiana Purchase prize and a special honorable mention at the Hoosier Salon in 1933.

Illustration for "Pig Iron," from *Cosmopolitan* magazine, October, 1925.

FRANK X. LEYENDECKER (1877-1924), born in Germany, was always overshadowed by his older brother. His work was more sensitive but though very competent, never matched the assurance and dramatic poster quality of Joseph's. He, too, did illustrations and cover designs for leading publications and, later, also designed stained-glass windows.

The two brothers, neither ever married, worked together in a large studio estate in New Rochelle. The fascinating story of their personal lives is related in Norman Rockwell's *My Adventures as an Illustrator*.

Cover design for *Collier's* magazine, July 15, 1905.

JOSEPH CHRISTIAN LEYENDECKER (1874-1951) was born in Montabaur, Germany, and came to America at the age of eight. Showing an early interest in painting, he got his first job at 16 in a Chicago engraving house on the strength of some large pictures he had painted on kitchen oilcloth. In the evenings after work he studied under Vanderpool at the Chicago Art Institute, and saved for five years to be able to go to France to attend the Académie Julian in Paris.

Upon his return, as a thoroughly trained artist with immense technical facility, Leyendecker had no difficulty in obtaining top commissions for advertising illustrations and cover designs for the leading publications. His first *Post* cover was done in 1899, and he did well over 300 more during the next 40 years. Among the most famous of these was the annual New Year baby series.

His advertising illustrations made his clients famous. The Arrow Collar man was a byword for the debonair, handsome male, and women wrote thousands of love letters to him care of Cluett Peabody & Company. His illustrations for Hart, Schaffner & Marx were equally successful in promoting an image of suited elegance.

A., B., C., Typical *Saturday Evening Post* covers.

D. Painting for the 1931 *Post* cover showing J. C. Leyendecker's brilliant technique and decorative use of color.

E. One of the long line of Arrow Collar men depicted over a period of 24 years, beginning in 1907. Illustration courtesy of the Arrow Company.

A

B

C

D

E

W.MORGAN —

WALLACE MORGAN, N.A. (1873-1948), at the turn of the century, went through the tough school of the newspaper artist as did his friends and fellow-artists, Glackens, Shinn and Sloan. Forced to draw a constant variety of subjects under pressure, on the spot or from memory, he emerged with such facility that he never needed models in his later work. His finished renderings were attempted directly, without preliminary sketches. If difficulties arose, he'd abandon the drawing for a new try. This was the secret of that inimitable spontaneity.

Wallace Morgan viewed the human comedy with warmth, wisdom and humor, laced with irony. He traveled across the country with Julian Street, sketching, while Street wrote *Abroad at Home*. This ran serially in *Collier's*, was published in 1914 by the Century Company — a witty chapter in Americana.

Morgan was of the official artists assigned to the A.E.F. during World War I. His quick sketching was especially useful for documentary recording of life in the trenches, as it was for his swift, salty portraits of top brass.

This special flavor made his style a natural for illustrating the P. G. Wodehouse stories which ran in *The Saturday Evening Post*; equally so for evoking the spirited action of the polo at Westbury for Men's Shop advertisements at Saks Fifth Avenue.

Morgan taught at the Art Students League, at intervals, from 1905 to 1929. He was made an honorary member of the League, a rare honor reserved for such greats as Bellows, Pyle, Henri, DuMond and others. He was elected a full member of the National Academy in 1947; received an award from the National Institute of Arts & Letters.

Morgan's clubs included The Players, Century, Dutch Treat; he was president of the Society of Illustrators from 1929 to 1936. In January, 1949, a memorial exhibition of Wallace's drawings was given at the Society of Illustrators, of which he was honorary president at the time of his death in May, 1948.

The Union League and F.D.R. ". . . the need of an experienced hand at the helm. And so let us fervently hope that the great pilot who has steered us so surely through the perilous currents of the past 8 years may be prevailed upon . . ."

MOWAT.

HAROLD JAMES MOWAT (1879-1949) always preferred to work in black and white, obscuring many of the details, highlighting others out of an overall tonality. In this method he shared the approach of a number of fellow artists: Henry Raleigh, Arthur William Brown, and especially Frederic R. Gruger.

Mowat was born in Montreal, Canada, and received his art education at the New York School of Art. His first illustrations were made for the *American* magazine. He lavished so much time and expense in models' fees on his work that he barely broke even. This kind of conscientiousness made him a relatively slow worker throughout his career, and he never became as popular with the public as did many of his more facile co-workers. However, other illustrators paid him the compliment of great respect and acknowledged his preëminence. He illustrated for most of the top publications, including *The Saturday Evening Post, Ladies' Home Journal, McCall's, Woman's Home Companion*, and *Redbook*.

Describing his work, Mowat said, "My medium is a piece of white paper and a black pencil. Sometimes a bit of dirt from the floor. When at work, I'm at it from early morning until far into the night. I haven't known the meaning of true peace of mind for years, but I infinitely prefer the uncertainties and struggles of the illustrator to any other game on earth."

Illustration for the *Ladies' Home Journal*.

CHARLES D. MITCHELL

CHARLES DAVIS MITCHELL (1887-1940) had great drawing facility, and most of his illustrations were done in a technique somewhat similar to that of Arthur William Brown.

Mitchell drew very attractive young females, successfully adapting their changes in style and taste over three decades. His work appeared regularly in *McCall's*, *Redbook*, *Good Housekeeping*, *Cosmopolitan*, *Pictorial Review*, *Delineator*, *The Saturday Evening Post*, *Ladies' Home Journal*, and other magazines.

Originally from Wilmington, Delaware, Mitchell had his studio in Philadelphia and was a member of the Artists' Guild, New York, and the Art Club in Philadelphia.

Illustration for "Scandal Street," *Cosmopolitan* magazine, 1923.

ANGUS MAC DONALL

ANGUS PETER MacDONALL (1876-1927), who came from St. Louis, was one of the early group of artists who settled in Westport, Connecticut, to make it a famous art colony. MacDonall was especially popular with fellow-illustrators because of his three beautiful daughters who were in great demand as models.

MacDonall illustrated for most of the magazines including *Scribner's*, *Harper's*, *American*, and *Ladies' Home Journal*. For several years he did a regular double-spread illustration of human interest or social commentary for the old *Life* magazine.

Illustration for *The Modern Priscilla* magazine, 1919.

T Oakley -

This illustration by THORNTON OAKLEY (1881-1955) is typical of the artist's strong, carefully composed pictures. Note the thorough planning in the placement of the lampman's head, the perspective lines all converging on it. In addition, the head is treated as a virtual silhouette against the light steam behind, creating a strong contrast. The result, as planned by the artist, is that the viewer's eye is irresistibly led to the worker's face.

Oakley studied architecture at the University of Pennsylvania; he also studied illustration with Howard Pyle. Throughout his career, he both illustrated and painted for exhibition. His work is represented in many major museums in the United States and abroad. During World War II, he painted a series of 48 paintings of "American Industries Geared for War," and related subjects, for the *National Geographic* magazine published in 1942, 1943 and 1945.

"In the Railway Yard," a series of four illustrations published by *Century* magazine in January, 1907.

A

M . P

MAXFIELD PARRISH, N.A. (1870-1966) throughout his long lifetime created and painted a world of his own. As a child he made careful drawings of figures, cutting around their outlines and mounting the silhouetted shapes. This flat, almost two-dimensional treatment was later carried over into his mural decorations, in which the figures were superimposed against highly detailed backgrounds.

Parrish's subject matter, too, seemed to have originated with his childhood interests, in fairy tales, giants, castles, and other make-believe. His most successful illustrations were made for such books as Eugene Field's *Poems of Childhood*, and Kenneth Grahame's *Golden Age* and *Dream Days*. He used the same kind of material for his mural subjects. His 30-foot wall decoration depicting "Old King Cole" was painted for the old Knickerbocker Hotel, later reinstalled in the St. Regis Hotel in New York. Other subjects included "The Pied Piper," for the Sheraton-Palace Hotel in San Francisco and "Sing a Song of Sixpence," in the Hotel Sherman in Chicago.

He was a sumptuous, rich colorist, noted especially for his luminous "Maxfield Parrish blue." Reproductions of his cover designs or illustrations were saved and framed by tens of thousands of families. One of the most popular of all his pictures was "The Dinkey Bird," originally for Field's *Poems of Childhood*. This mass appeal also made Parrish a favorite calendar illustrator for several subsequent decades.

A. Illustration in color for "Jason and the Talking Oak," from *A Wonder Book and Tanglewood Tales for Boys and Girls*, published by Duffield, New York, 1910.
B. "The Wond'rous Wise Man," from *Mother Goose in Prose*, published by George M. Hill Company, 1901.

B

The familiar and pleasing legacy of ROSE CECIL O'NEILL-WILSON (1875-1944) is the Kewpie doll. The dolls were patterned after her drawings of Kewpies — fanciful, elf-like babies who solved all sorts of problems in a bumbling, good-natured way. Her drawings and stories were immensely popular for over two decades, appearing as a special feature in *Good Housekeeping* magazine and the *Ladies' Home Journal*. The dolls were sold all over the world.

A self-trained artist, Rose O'Neill became nationally known as an illustrator at 19. Her pictures appeared in *Puck*, *Truth*, the old *Life*, *McClure's*, and *Harper's*. She was also a novelist and poet, a member of the Société des Beaux Arts in Paris and the Society of Illustrators in New York.

From the *Ladies' Home Journal*.

COLES PHILLIPS

The Fadeaway Girl was the particular hallmark of COLES PHILLIPS (1880-1927). Phillips pictured fashionably beautiful young women, using the device of tying the figure into the background by either color, value or pattern. This approach produced an intriguing poster-like effect of great simplicity; yet actually it was based on the most careful preliminary planning of shapes to carry out the illusion of the full figure.

Phillips was born in Springfield, Ohio, and had his first pictures reproduced as a student contributor to the *Kenyon College Monthly* magazine. Upon graduation he tackled a New York career, first as a solicitor for an advertising agency. Later he formed his own studio of artists. After further study at the Chase Art School, he decided to launch his art career. His first effort was sold to the old *Life* magazine as a double-page spread. When *Life* began to use color on its covers, the Fadeaway Girl made her initial appearance and was an instant success. For many years thereafter she appeared in a variety of guises, but was always the patrician beauty.

Phillips prided himself on being a good businessman-artist. His pictures, both for covers and for advertising campaigns, such as Holeproof Hosiery and Community Plate Silverware, were the product of a meticulous, cerebral craftsman.

Good Housekeeping cover, February, 1915.

Clara Elsene Peck

CLARA ELSENE PECK, (1883-   ), as an illustrator, specialized in drawing women and children. Her pictures are decorative in composition, sensitive in rendering. They were particularly appropriate to articles she illustrated in the women's magazines on such subjects as education, child psychology, and the expectant mother. She also illustrated fiction in magazines and books, did advertising campaigns for Procter & Gamble, Aeolian Company, Metropolitan Life, and others.

Miss Peck was born in Allegan, Michigan, acquired her art education at the Minneapolis School of Fine Arts, the Philadelphia Academy of the Fine Arts, and with William M. Chase, the painter. She is a member of the American Water Color Society, has exhibited extensively and won many awards.

Illustration for *In the Border Country*, by Josephine Daskam Bacon, published by Doubleday, Page and Company, 1909.

B

NORMAN MILLS PRICE (1877-1951) never fully received the popular recognition that his work deserved. Because he was so intently interested in historical subjects, he restricted his work to these almost exclusively.

However, the dedication and artistry he brought to his work was especially appreciated and respected by a select group — his fellow-illustrators. His painstaking research into every detail made each picture an authentic documentary, but the detail was never allowed to detract from the dramatic concept of the illustration itself. Although Price made effective use of tone and color, his pen-and-ink drawings were especially effective, exhibiting a full range of values and textural effects.

Price was born in Canada, studied art there and in London and Paris. By 1912 he had established himself in New York and had begun to work for American publications. Some of his most successful illustrations were done for a series of historical novels by Robert W. Chambers. He was a charter member of the Guild of Free-Lance Artists, and honorary president of the Society of Illustrators at the time of his death.

A. "Slave Auction," reproduced from the bulletin of the Society of Illustrators for the 37th Annual exhibition in 1939.

B. Illustration for Metropolitan Life Insurance Company, 1942.

RALEIGH

HENRY PATRICK RALEIGH (1880-1944) was one of the most prolific of all our illustrators. In spite of this, he maintained a consistent high quality and good taste in all his work. His renderings in line, line and wash, colored inks or other combinations were ideally suited to the printed page.

In his illustrations he was able to translate the mood and setting of the story with easy versatility. His pictures look as though they flowed from pen or brush. He was probably at his best with society subjects and for many years depicted the ultimate in fashionable society for the Maxwell House Coffee advertisements.

Raleigh was born in Portland, Oregon; later moved to San Francisco. He left school at 12 to help support his mother and sisters. Befriended by the head of the coffee firm for which he worked as a clerk, Raleigh was sent to Hopkins Academy, a San Francisco art school, for two years.

At 17 he got a job in the art department of the *San Francisco Bulletin* where he learned to make drawings for the chalk-plate process. As a reporter-artist, he was later sent on assignments to sketch newsworthy subjects, such as fires, floods, or corpses at the city morgue.

By the age of 19 he was working for the *San Francisco Examiner* as one of its highest paid artists. His work attracted the attention of William Randolph Hearst, who sent him to New York to work for the *Journal*. He next went to the *New York World*, doing special features three days a week. This experience served as a base for his entry into the magazine field.

Raleigh was also a serious etcher and produced many fine plates, but these were seldom exhibited. Among his many awards were the Shaw Prize for Illustration at the Salmagundi Club in 1916 and the Gold Medal for Advertising Art in America in 1926.

Illustration in brown ink for *Harper's Bazaar*, 1922.

From the Sanford Low Memorial Collection of American Illustration, New Britain, Connecticut, Museum of American Art.

A

"In the Wake of the Buffalo Runners," reprinted by permission of and copyrighted by Brown & Bigelow, St. Paul, Minnesota.

The life and career of CHARLES MARION RUSSELL (1864-1926) has a number of singular parallels with that of Frederic Remington. They were both largely self-taught; both spent their early years living the rugged frontier life of the West; they both recorded in drawings, paintings, and sculpture, the panorama of a vanishing era. Yet they pursued their goals separately. Remington had early success but died young. Russell had several years of struggle before gaining a national reputation and had a relatively long career.

B

Russell was the more compassionate observer of the Indians' side of the "civilizing" of the West. His open-hearted, direct manner led the Indians to trust him instinctively. He lived with the Blackfeet in Alberta for several months, learning the language and making many drawings and paintings. For a while he even seriously considered becoming a squaw man himself.

Most of Russell's early pictures were made for himself or to give away to friends, until the economic necessities of marriage forced his wife to find a market for them. Within a few years, Russell's paintings and bronzes commanded high prices, and today his original works are eagerly sought by collectors and museums. Among the museums with good collections of his pictures are the Historical Society of Montana in Helena and the Trigg-Russell Gallery at Great Falls. One of his finest paintings is a mural, 24′9″ by 11′7½″, entitled "Lewis and Clark meeting the Flathead Indians at Ross's Hole," in the Montana State Capitol.

A. "In the Wake of the Buffalo Runners."
B. Illustration for "Finger-that-Kills Wins his Squaw," a story written and illustrated by Russell for *Outing* magazine, April, 1908.

A

Frank E. Schoonover

FRANK EARLE SCHOONOVER (1877-) owes much to Howard Pyle's belief that an illustrator should thoroughly immerse himself in his subjects, painting those things he knows best. After studying with Pyle, both at the Drexel Institute and at Chadd's Ford, Pennsylvania, Schoonover began to receive assignments to do Indian and frontier subjects. In order to qualify himself properly, he made two trips to the Hudson Bay country in 1903, by snowshoe and dog team, and in 1911 by canoe, observing there the life and customs of the Indians. Over the years he did a great number of excellent, authentic illustrations based on these expeditions.

Similarly, he made field trips to other locations, such as the Mississippi Bayou country for a book which he both wrote and illustrated, *Lafitte, the Pirate of the Gulf*.

Over his long and productive life he has illustrated for many magazines and books, designed stained-glass windows, taught at the John Herron Art Institute and at his own studio, and continues to paint landscapes of the neighboring Brandywine and Delaware River valleys.

A. Illustration for *Outing* magazine, 1905, now in the permanent collection of The Wilmington Society of the Fine Arts, Delaware.
B. Illustration for "White Fang," by Jack London, *Outing* magazine, 1906.

B

JOHN SLOAN, N.A. (1871-1951) worked for the *Philadelphia Press* as a young newspaper artist, together with William Glackens, George Luks and Everett Shinn, all of whom studied at the Pennsylvania Academy of the Fine Arts. They subsequently became members of The Eight, but for some years continued to paint for exhibitions and, at the same time, to do illustration for the magazines.

Sloan came to New York in 1905 and became interested in recording city life and the social upheaval as he saw it around him. He became famous for his illustrations on this subject for that short-lived magazine, *The Masses*. He also contributed to *McClure's*.

He later devoted himself exclusively to painting, etching, and lithography and is represented in many major collections and museums including the Museum of Fine Arts, Boston, and The Metropolitan Museum of Art in New York City.

For several years Sloan taught at the Art Students League in New York. He summarized much of his painting philosophy in his book, *Gist of Art*, published by American Artists Group in 1939.

Cover drawing for *The Masses* in 1913.

FRANK WALTER TAYLOR (1874-1921) worked almost exclusively with charcoal in which he employed a full tonal range from white to rich blacks.

Taylor was born in Philadelphia and studied at the Pennsylvania Academy of the Fine Arts. There he was awarded a traveling scholarship which enabled him to study in Paris. Upon his return to America he worked, as an illustrator, for numerous magazines and also contributed a number of his own short stories. He was awarded a Medal of Honor for illustration at the Panama-Pacific International Exposition in 1915.

One of a series of illustrations done for the best-selling novel of 1911-1912, "The Iron Woman," by Margaret Deland, published serially in *Harper's* monthly, 1910.

Townsend

Although HARRY EVERETT TOWNSEND (1879-1941) painted and exhibited in full-color oils, some of his best work was done in black and white, including his drawings in line for the old *Adventure* magazine.

Townsend was born in Camp Grove, Illinois, and attended school at the Art Institute of Chicago. In 1900 he was invited to study with Howard Pyle in Wilmington, Delaware, staying there until 1904. Moving to New York, he was soon illustrating for the leading magazines.

In 1917, Townsend, with seven other artists, was commissioned as a Captain with the A.E.F., and assigned to record the war. These drawings and paintings are now in the War College and in the Smithsonian Institution in Washington, D.C.

Active in art circles, Townsend was a member of the Society of Illustrators, Allied Artists' Association, Salmagundi Club, Architectural League of New York, Brooklyn Society of Etchers, Westport Artists, Darien Guild of Seven Arts, Silvermine Guild, and others. He was awarded the Shaw prize for illustration at the Salmagundi Club in 1920.

Charcoal drawing of "Lincoln with Harriet Beecher Stowe," published by *Harper's Monthly* magazine.

From the Sanford Low Memorial Collection of American Illustration, New Britain, Connecticut, Museum of American Art.

·J·Scott Williams·

JOHN SCOTT WILLIAMS, N.A. (1877-) was born in England, studied composition with Fred Richardson at the Art Institute of Chicago. His first illustrations were done as early as 1905 for *The Saturday Evening Post*. In subsequent years he did work for more than 20 different American magazines (of these only six are now being published). From 1927 to 1934, he contributed covers regularly for the magazine section of the *New York Herald Tribune*.

Williams later became a designer and painter of mural decorations including those for the Indiana State Library and Historical Building, Johns Hopkins University and a huge 72- by 28-foot ferro-porcelain enamel mural in the main concourse of the Union Terminal in Cleveland, Ohio.

Illustration for the story, "Campbell Corot," from *Scribner's* magazine in 1907. Over the original pen-and-ink drawing in black, a yellow-ochre second color was printed, with both solid and benday tint blocks as specified by the artist.

A

Courtesy of *Civil War Times Illustrated* magazine, Gettysburg
Pennsylvania.

N.C.WYETH

NEWELL CONVERS WYETH, N.A. (1882-1945) had a huge zest for life. He carried this enthusiasm through a tremendous number of paintings, more than 3,000 illustrations, numerous vast murals, and a great many still life and landscape paintings.

Howard Pyle was his teacher and idol. Wyeth emulated Pyle's approach as nearly as possible, painting much of the same kind of subject matter — medieval life, pirates, Americana. To this he added his own dramatic picture concepts and rich, decorative color. Outstanding in this phase of his work were the more than twenty-five books he illustrated for Charles Scribner's Sons' Classics series. The popularity of these books is such that, even after decades, most of them are still in print.

After painting in oils for many years, Wyeth turned to the egg tempera medium and also began to paint more for exhibitions. He encouraged an interest in the arts in his children, giving them every opportunity for self-expression. His daughters, Henriette and Caroline, are both accomplished painters; Ann, a composer, and his son Andrew is famous as a painter in his own right. The October, 1965 issue of *American Heritage* contains an excellent article by Henry C. Pitz about the career of Wyeth and his family.

At the time of his tragic death in a railway crossing accident, N. C. Wyeth was one of America's best loved illustrators.

A. With but a few figures revealed through the smoke of gunfire, Wyeth has dramatically symbolized the whole Civil War in his painting, "The Battle."
B. "The Silent Burial," one of five pictures of "The Solitude Series," for the Outing Publishing Company, 1907 (here cropped as used for magazine cover).
C. Illustration for "Arizona Nights," by Stewart Edward White, *McClure's* magazine, March, 1906.
D. "One More Step, Mr. Hands," from *Treasure Island*, by Robert Louis Stevenson, published by Charles Scribner's Sons. From the Collection of the New Britain, Connecticut, Museum of American Art.

B

C

D

EDWARD ARTHUR WILSON, A.N.A. (1886-   ) was elected to the Society of Illustrators' Hall of Fame in 1962 in recognition of his long and distinguished career as an illustrator. He was born in Glasgow, Scotland, spent his childhood in Rotterdam, Holland, and later came to America where he studied at the Chicago Art Institute and with Howard Pyle in Wilmington, Delaware.

Wilson's first commissions were for advertising, and he was most active in this field for many years. During this time he won many awards and honorable mentions in annual exhibitions of the Art Directors Club in New York. Notable among the campaigns he contributed to were: LaSalle-Cadillac, Coral Gables Corporation, and Victrola. He also illustrated for most of the major magazines during this period.

His first book illustrations were done as woodcuts for a collection of sea chanteys entitled *Iron Men and Wooden Ships*. It was a labor of love as well as a great artistic success. He'd always been most interested in nautical subjects and this book established his reputation as an authority. Over the next several years he illustrated *Fall and By*, a collection of drinking songs, *The Pirate's Treasure*, which he also wrote, *Robinson Crusoe*, *Two Years Before the Mast*, *Treasure Island* — altogether well over 60 books, many of them for the Limited Editions Club and The Heritage Press.

Water-color illustration, for reproduction by stencil, *The Man Without a Country*, published in 1936.

Reprinted with permission of The Limited Editions Club.

F. C. YOHN

FREDERICK COFFAY YOHN (1875-1933) is most noted for his illustrations of historical and battle subjects. The picture reproduced here is of a cavalry drill at Chickamauga for the War with Spain in 1898, one of his many reportorial paintings of this conflict. He also did a fine series of historical illustrations to accompany Henry Cabot Lodge's *The Story of the Revolution*, published by *Scribner's* magazine.

Yohn was born in Indianapolis, attended the Indianapolis Art School and the Art Students League in New York where he studied under H. Siddons Mowbray. At 19, he made his first illustrations for *Harper's* periodicals. This was followed by a long career in illustration with most of the major magazine and book publishers.

A permanent collection of his work is in the Cabinet of American Illustration at the Library of Congress in Washington, D.C.

From *The Story of the War of 1898*, published by P. F. Collier and Son in 1900.

1920-1930

ILLUSTRATORS 1920-1930

Maginel Wright Barney
Walter Biggs
Charles Edward Chambers
René Clark
Thomas Maitland Cleland
Dean Cornwell
Harold Thomas Denison
Walter H. Everett
Maude Tousey Fangel
Clark Fay
Laurence Fellows
Anton Otto Fischer
John Richard Flanagan
Ernest Fuhr
Arthur D. Fuller
Gordon Hope Grant
William Heaslip
John Held, Jr.
Albin Henning
Frank B. Hoffman
Lynn Bogue Hunt
Lyle Justis
William Henry Dethlef Koerner
Robert L. Lambdin
William Andrew Loomis
Neysa Moran McMein
Harry Morse Meyers
William Oberhardt
Russell Patterson
Herbert Paus
James Moore Preston
May Wilson Preston
William Meade Prince
Grant Tyson Reynard
Norman Rockwell
Tony Sarg
John E. Sheridan
Frank Street
Dudley Gloyne Summers
Donald Teague
Earle Grantham Teale
Saul Tepper
Adolph Treidler
Loran F. Wilford
Charles David Williams

DRAWING BY DEAN CORNWELL

The Decade: 1920-1930

by Norman Rockwell

I am not sure that I should be writing about this decade. As a student at the Art Students League, my idols were of an earlier day — Abbey and Howard Pyle. As a matter of fact, after all these years, they still are. However, I guess that my own career did sort of blossom out in the 'twenties.

A lot of the old timers were still going strong then. James Montgomery Flagg was riding high. Coles Phillips was doing the most fashionable and elegant young females of the day. The Leyendecker brothers were working from the seclusion of their château in New Rochelle. Howard Chandler Christy was still capturing the headlines with his Christy Girl and was a judge of feminine pulchritude at the Miss America contests at Atlantic City.

The 'twenties were years of extravagance and experimentation; all the emphasis was on trying something different. Jazz was discovered; the sax and the uke were newly popular. Prohibition created the speakeasy and the hip flask. John Held, Jr. caught the essence of the times with his short-skirted flappers and frat men with their bell-bottom trousers.

Paris became the gravitational center for many artists. Not only were Picasso and the Cubists leading the avant garde, but French artists — Drian, Brissaud, Cassandre and Bernard Boutet De Monvel — were influencing a new look in American publications.

Dean Cornwell was coming into his own as the leading exponent of the Pyle school. He'd studied under Harvey Dunn, who was a student of Howard Pyle, and then with the English mural painter, Frank Brangwyn. Dean did the swashbuckling romantic costume stories that were popular then, but probably the best pictures he ever made were done for *Good Housekeeping*, a series on the Life of Christ and of the Holy Land made after a painting and sketching trip to the Middle East.

Walter Biggs was using color in a brilliant and poetic way. Charles Chambers, too, was a good influence; his pictures were in the Academy tradition, soundly painted, with good taste and sensitive characterization.

A new patron for the illustrator became a powerful influence in the field at this time — the advertising agency. Its influence was a mixed blessing. To many illustrators, including myself, I feel that it was a corrupting one. The temptation of their big budgets took away the kind of integrity that earlier artists like Howard Pyle had brought to their work. One could easily become too busy or too dependent on the income from painting for one product after another to afford to take on more worthy projects, such as a mural or an important book.

On the other hand, many artists (and art directors) had the ability to translate a commercial theme into more lofty concepts and their work was and is still, important. Franklin Booth and Harvey Dunn were such examples. The agencies also provided a whole new school for the development of talent; almost every illustrator of note from that time on has done advertising illustration.

So many influences, both old and new, were part of the development of illustration in the 'twenties that it is hard to pick a predominating one. Because it was a boom period and the economy of America was expanding in all directions, there seemed to be room for all of them — including mine.

If I were to try to summarize the decade, I'd say it was generally a healthy one — a lot of new ideas were tried and a lot of good pictures painted. If some of them look a little dated, well, look at today's pictures 40 years from now!

Norman
Rockwell

B

C

WALTER BIGGS, N.A. (1886-   ) represents the South at its best, both as a gentleman and as an artist who has painted the South with sensitive artistry and poetic nostalgia.

Biggs was born in Elliston, Virginia, and spent his boyhood there. He arrived in New York to study art at the Chase School, later renamed the New York School of Art. Among his teachers were Edward Penfield, Lucius Hitchcock and Robert Henri. Henri was an especially inspiring teacher who instilled in the students a real desire to work. Biggs was in an unusual class which included Clifton Webb, Eugene Speicher, Edward Hopper, George Bellows, Guy Pène Dubois, Rockwell Kent, and W. T. Benda, all of whom became famous in their respective ways.

Biggs himself became a famous illustrator and teacher at the Art Students League and the Grand Central School of Art in New York.

His illustrations over the years have appeared in *Harper's*, *Scribner's*, *Century*, *Ladies' Home Journal*, *Women's Home Companion*, *Good Housekeeping*, *McCall's*, *Cosmopolitan*, and others.

He has exhibited regularly at the National Academy, Salmagundi Club, American Water Color Society and Philadelphia Water Color Society, winning many awards. In 1963, the Society of Illustrators elected him to the Hall of Fame, "For distinguished achievement in the art of illustration."

A

A. Biggs' use of color is rich and brilliant as demonstrated in this illustration for the *Woman's Home Companion*, November, 1922.
B. "Deep South," published by *The American Legion* magazine, 1934.
C. Illustration from *Woman's Home Companion*, September, 1932.

TMCleland

THOMAS MAITLAND CLELAND (1880-1964), "achieved three or four distinct reputations. He is known to large groups of people as the foremost decorative designer in America; to others, as a great printer; to still others as a great typographer. . . . T. M. Cleland is not only an illustrator, he is a master in the world of graphic arts. When he accepts a commission every detail of it bears the touch of his genius." This was said of Cleland by George Macy, his host at a dinner given in his honor at the Grolier Club.

At 16, Cleland became a printer's apprentice; at 20, he had designed a typeface with ornaments and gone into the printing business for himself. For two years prior to World War I, he was art director of *McClure's* magazine.

Combining printing with designing and illustration, Cleland was one of the first to invest institutional advertising with the mantle of fine art. His clients included Locomobile, Cadillac and Rolls-Royce. One notable project was the "Grammar of Color" which he wrote, designed, and printed for the Strathmore Paper Company.

His sojourns in Paris confirmed his preoccupation with 18th-century subjects. His first commission for the Limited Editions Club was a two-volume *Tristram Shandy*. He spent three years on more than 62 color drawings for a masterful interpretation of the times. Two Fielding books followed — *Jonathan Wilde* and *Tom Jones*, relating text and illustrations in the finest tradition of the art of printing.

Cleland was a member of The Players, Century and the Coffee House Club; also of the Architectural League of New York, and the American Institute of Graphic Arts.

"The Celebration," copyright 1936 by West Virginia Pulp & Paper Company.

MAGINEL WRIGHT BARNEY

MAGINEL WRIGHT ENRIGHT — later BARNEY — (1882-1966), was the youngest of three children; the eldest Frank Lloyd Wright, always encouraged his sister's talent for drawing and painting. When her school days were over, she attended the Chicago Art Institute. Then she worked for several years at an advertising agency before her marriage to Walter J. Enright, another young artist. They soon came to New York where, eventually, both became successful illustrators.

Maginel's earliest efforts were pictures for some fantasies by one Laura L. Bancroft, later unveiled as that *Wizard of Oz*, L. Frank Baum. Maginel illustrated young classics — *Heidi*, *Hans Brinker of the Silver Skates* — and innumerable fairy tales. She was largely responsible for revolutionizing the quality of illustration in children's readers (till then fairly deadly) and over the years painted cover designs for many magazines, as well as illustrations in *McClure's*, *Everybody's*, *Woman's Home Companion*, *Ladies' Home Journal*, *Woman's World*, and others.

When work became scarce during the Depression, she took up "painting in wool," landscapes and flower pictures. There were two exhibitions of these at the Marie Sterner Gallery and one, as recently as 1962, at the Sagittarius Gallery, in New York.

Illustration for "The Littlest Mouse," by Margery Williams Bianco which appeared in the *Delineator*, March, 1928.

C. E. Chambers

CHARLES EDWARD CHAMBERS (1883-1941) was born in Ottumwa, Iowa, studied at the Chicago Art Institute and later at the Art Students League in New York with George Bridgman.

His illustrations were extremely competent, marked by subtlety of value and color. He early learned to adapt his method of painting for the best possible reproduction and to insure fidelity of printing, he often followed the assignments through to the hands of the platemaker.

Chambers divided his time almost equally between editorial and advertising assignments. Among his advertising commissions was an outstanding series of portraits of musicians for Steinway & Sons. He also did a great number of distinctive illustrations for twenty-four-sheet, outdoor posters, notably for Chesterfield and Palmolive Soap which set high standards for that field.

He illustrated stories in most of the major magazines, for such authors as Pearl Buck, Louis Bromfield, Faith Baldwin, and W. Somerset Maugham; worked under exclusive contract for *Cosmopolitan* magazine for many years.

Among his numerous awards was the second Altman Prize at the National Academy of Design Exhibition in 1931, for his portrait of water-colorist and fellow-illustrator, John Alonzo Williams.

Illustration for a serial in *Harper's* magazine, "The Price of Love," by Arnold Bennett in 1913-14.

R.C.

RENÉ CLARKE (1886-   ) began life in Eustis, Florida, as James Alfred Clarke. He grew up in Springfield, Massachusetts, studied art briefly at the Connecticut League of Art Students in Hartford, Connecticut. While working on a number of printing and advertising jobs, he came under the influence of a fellow-artist, the French illustrator René Vincent. Later, he joined the advertising firm of Calkins & Holden, Inc., where he talked so much about his friend that the name René became transferred to him, and remained.

Although Clarke did some editorial illustration for *Woman's Home Companion*, *Collier's*, *McCall's*, and *Judge*, the greater part of his work was concerned with advertising. His drawings and high-key water-color renderings for such clients as Wesson Oil, Snowdrift, Crane Paper Company, and the Hartford Fire Insurance Company, were distinguished by artful simplicity and taste.

His work was awarded four gold medals and numerous other awards from 1920 to 1950 in annual Art Directors Club exhibits.

As art director, and later president, of Calkins & Holden he had a considerable and constructive influence in maintaining high artistic standards in the field of advertising art.

Courtesy of Black, Starr and Frost, Ltd.

In this illustration for the cover of a booklet for Black, Starr and Frost in 1925, Clarke makes masterful use of simple black-and-white pattern in dealing with a complex subject.

A

DEAN CORNWELL

DEAN CORNWELL, N.A. (1892-1960) was a brilliant, left-handed painter who dominated the illustration field for many years. As a student of Harvey Dunn, he inherited much of the teachings of Howard Pyle and later studied under Frank Brangwyn, the British muralist. To these influences Cornwell added his own monumental style, almost rococo in manner.

Cornwell was an untiring worker who made a great many preliminary studies and compositions before attempting a final painting, usually in oils. These drawings have great interest in themselves for the beauty of their draughtsmanship.

Prolific, and in great demand, he illustrated for a wide variety of magazines and advertisers, but found time as well to paint several important murals. Notable among them were those for the Los Angeles Public Library, The Lincoln Memorial in Redlands, California, The Tennessee State Office Building, Eastern Airlines in Rockefeller Center, and the Raleigh Room at the Hotel Warwick in New York City.

Dean was president of the Society of Illustrators from 1922-1926, taught illustration at the Art Students League in New York, and by example created a whole new "Cornwell School."

A. Vignette, illustration for *Cosmopolitan* magazine, 1935.
B. Painting commemorating the 300th anniversary of the founding of New York City. Courtesy of the New York Life Insurance Co.

B

C

C. "A Copper Shop in Jerusalem," from *The City of the Great King*, published by Cosmopolitan Book Corporation, 1926.

D. "Thomas Edison's Greatest Invention," advertising illustration reproduced by permission of General Electric Company.
E. "The Race of the Natchez and the Robert E. Lee." Reproduced through the courtesy of the Boatmen's National Bank of St. Louis where it may be seen as part of their permanent collection.

HAROLD THOMAS DENISON (1887-1940) came from Richmond, Michigan, studied at the Chicago Academy of Fine Arts and the Art Students League in New York. His illustrations, often in line with a color overprinted, are strong and straightforward and appeared regularly in most of the major periodicals for many years, beginning with the old *Life* magazine.

An enthusiastic etcher, as well as illustrator, Denison was a member of the Society of Illustrators, the Salmagundi Club, and the Philadelphia Society of Etchers. His work is represented at the University of Nebraska in Lincoln and at the M. H. DeYoung Memorial Museum in San Francisco, California.

Illustration for the *Country Gentleman* magazine.

W.H. Everett

WALTER H. EVERETT lived on a farm in southern New Jersey and, as an art student, used to bicycle from home to the Wilmington ferry, cross the Delaware, and ride up to Howard Pyle's composition class on Franklin Street. He also worked his way through the School of Industrial Arts in Philadelphia where he later taught illustration for many years.

Everett developed a highly personal approach to illustration. His paintings were almost like posters, with flattened shapes and unmodeled forms, relying largely on color and value changes to delineate the objects. Unfortunately, most of his pictures were reproduced only in black and white, but those which did appear in color, particularly in the *Ladies' Home Journal*, were brilliant and impressionistic.

Illustration for the *Ladies' Home Journal*.

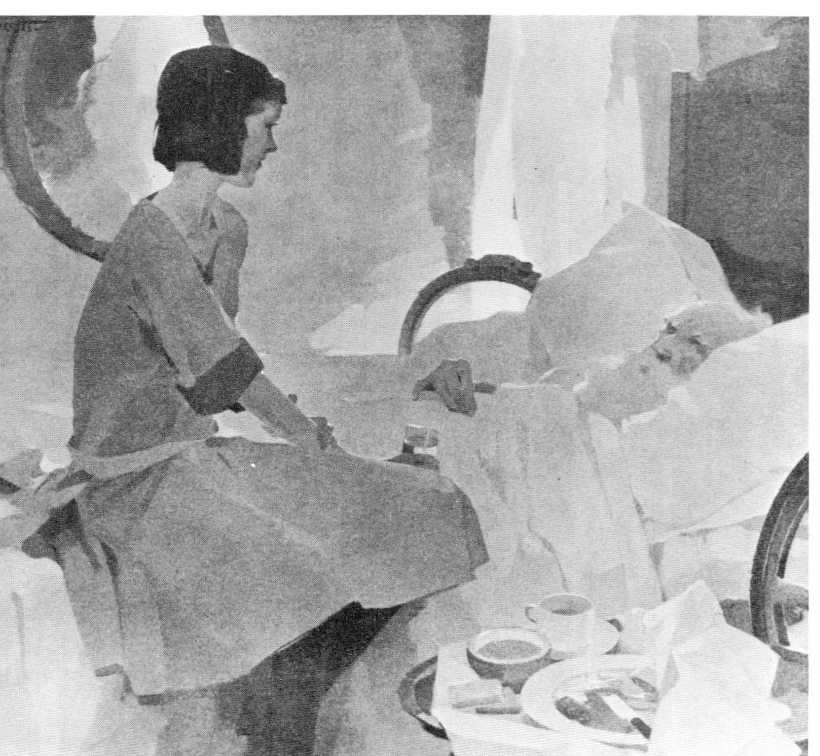

MAUD TOUSEY FANGEL has a special knack of drawing and painting babies that is both artistic and extremely appealing. Because she has always insisted on drawing directly from life, her pictures reveal an extra insight and understanding of baby characteristics that could only have been gained in this way. Much of her work has been done in pastels, appropriate to her subjects in range of color and softness of texture.

For many years she was very productive as a cover designer for the *Ladies' Home Journal*, *McCall's*, *Woman's Home Companion*, and many other magazines, as well as illustrator for national advertising of the Cream of Wheat Corporation, Swift & Company, Squibbs Cod Liver Oil, and other products for babies.

Born in Boston, Mrs. Fangel attended the Massachusetts Normal Art School, Cooper Union, and the Art Students League in New York. She has also done many portraits in addition to her illustrations.

Illustration for the Earnshaw Sales Company, 1924.

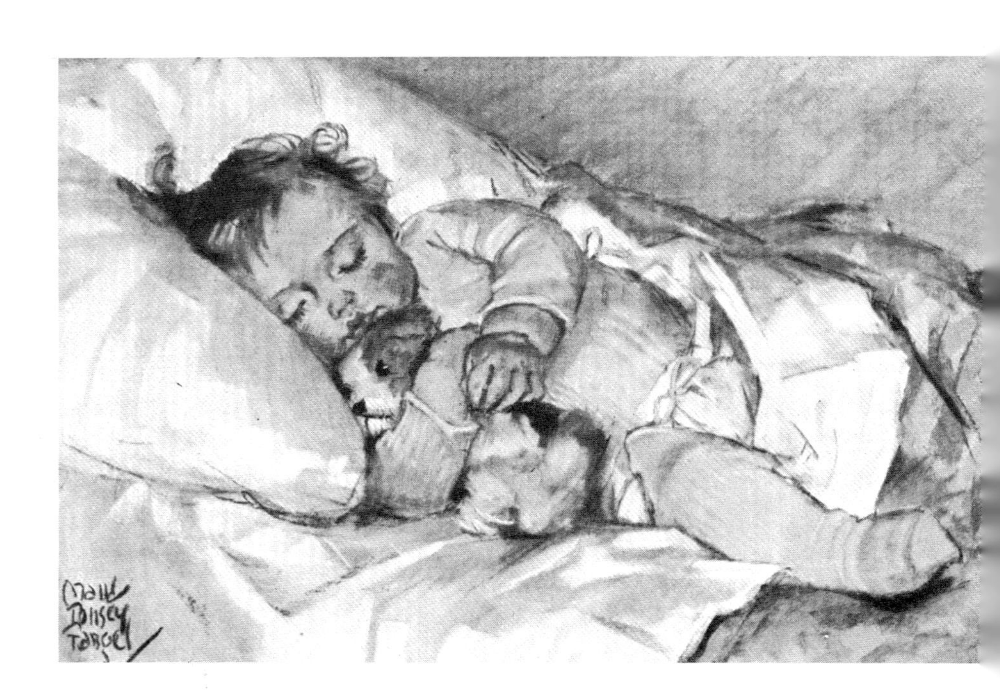

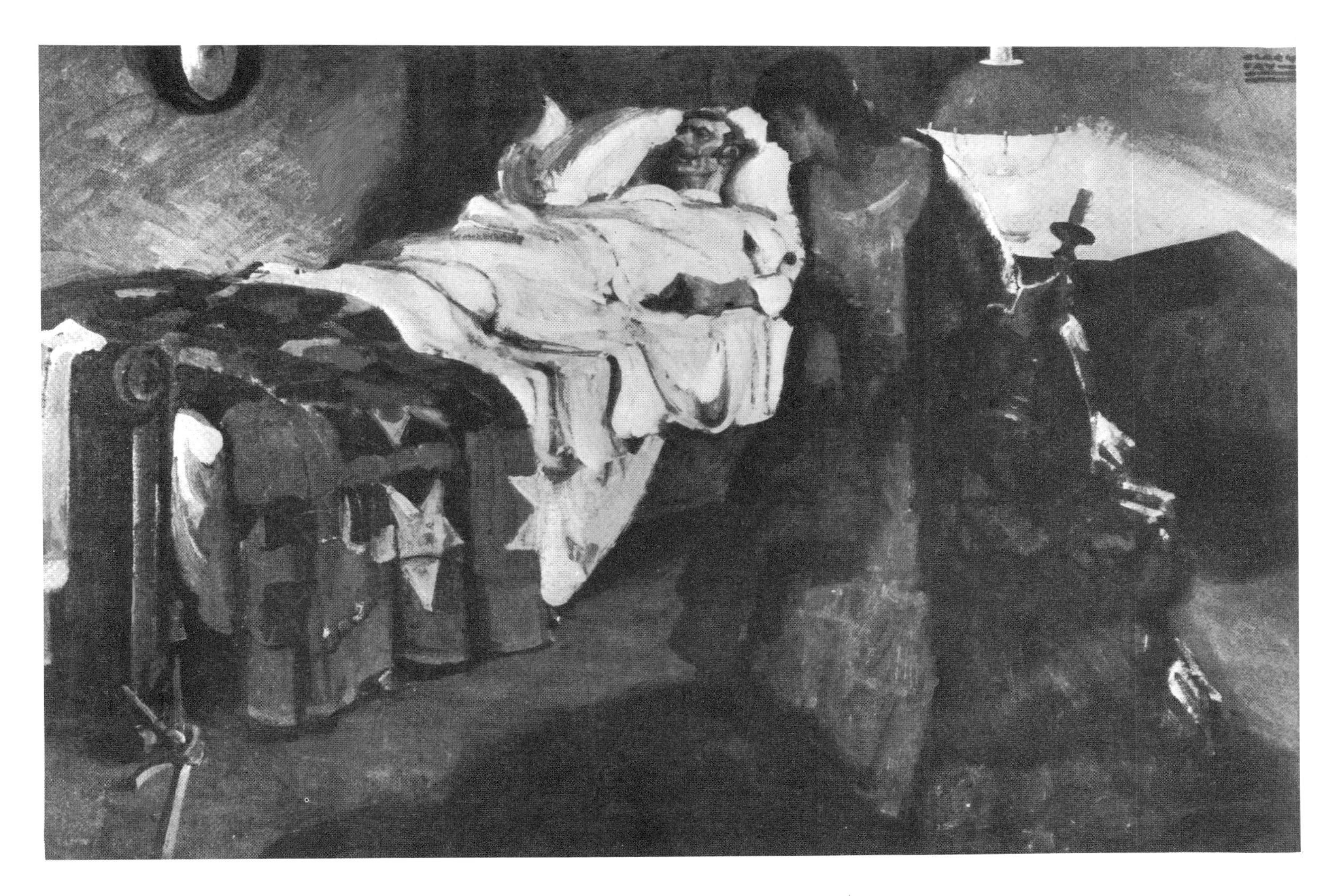

CLARK FAY traveled East from Denver, Colorado, and studied illustration with N. C. Wyeth and Harvey Dunn. Most influenced by Dunn, Fay's work is bold and direct, with emphasis placed on the broad picture concept.

Fay's success came early. He illustrated for *The Saturday Evening Post*, *Delineator* and other major publications for several years, then moved abroad to the village of Chamant, outside Paris; later he lived in London, where he has continued to pursue his career in illustration.

Illustration for *Delineator* magazine, October, 1928.

L·FELLOWS.

LAURENCE FELLOWS (1885-1964) is probably best remembered for his outstanding series of illustrations for Kelly-Springfield Tire advertisements in the 'twenties. The drawings were in black and white with large areas of white space and an economy of line, combined with good taste and a restrained sense of humor.

Fellows was a native of Ardmore, Pennsylvania, and studied at the Philadelphia Academy of the Fine Arts. This was followed by a stay in England and France where he continued his studies. By the 'twenties he had returned to America and did a great many humorous drawings for *Judge* and the old *Life* magazine.

His technique was ideally suited to fashion illustration; his work also appeared regularly in *Vanity Fair*, *Apparel Arts*, and *Esquire*.

Early illustration for Kelly-Springfield Tires.

Arthur D. Fuller 1964

ARTHUR D. FULLER (1889-   ), an ardent sportsman all his life, he has been identified with hunting and fishing pictures for the major part of his career. The accuracy of detail in his covers and story illustrations for *Field and Stream* won him a large following among sharp-eyed and critical readers for many years.

Earlier in his career, Fuller had illustrated more general subject matter for nearly all of the major magazines, including *Greenbook*, where he started, *Redbook*, *The Saturday Evening Post*, *Collier's*, *Ladies' Home Journal*, *Cosmopolitan*, *The American Legion*, and *McCall's*.

Fuller was born in Exeter, New Hampshire, and educated at Harvard, the Fenway School of Illustration in Boston, and the Chicago Academy of Fine Arts. He also studied with Harvey Dunn. He is a member of the Animal Artists' Society, the Salmagundi Club, the Westport Artists, and the Society of Illustrators in New York.

Illustration for *The Saturday Evening Post* serial, "Con."

ERNEST FUHR (1874-1933), a pupil of William Chase, also studied in Paris, but was most influenced by the point of view of Frederic R. Gruger.

The majority of Fuhr's illustrations were in black and white, and although he depicted a wide range of story backgrounds, he was at his best with small-town or rural subjects. His characters were never glamorous or fashionable; they were ordinary people presented plainly, and, therefore, most convincingly.

He began his career as a newspaper artist for the *New York Herald* and the *New York World* and for many years was associated with *The Saturday Evening Post*. His work also appeared in numerous other publications, including the juvenile magazines, *Youth's Companion*, and *American Boy*.

Illustration for "The Lantern on the Plow," by George Agnew Chamberlain for *The Saturday Evening Post*.

JOHN RICHARD FLANAGAN (1895-1964) carried on the tradition of Joseph Clement Coll in his pen-and-ink technique. For many years, he was associated with the same kind of subject matter in illustrating the "Dr. Fu Manchu" stories by Sax Rohmer for *Collier's* magazine. His renderings were much more "controlled" than Coll's but, as demonstrated here, he employed a richly varied pattern of textures and values.

Flanagan was born in Sydney, Australia, and apprenticed to a lithographer at the age of 12. At the same time he enrolled in art school. When he completed his art training, he came to the United States where he obtained his first illustration assignment from *Every Week* magazine to do a story concerning a Chinese episode. This and subsequent stories established him as an authority on the Orient, although he did not visit there until many years later on an assignment for the French Line.

Actually, Flanagan did a wide variety of illustration, in full color as well as with pen and ink or scratch board. In later years he designed stained-glass windows and also served as an instructor at the York Academy of Arts in York, Pennsylvania, from 1954 until the time of his death.

Illustration for *Bluebook* magazine story, "The Man with Nine Souls," July, 1942.

ANTON OTTO FISCHER

The marine paintings by ANTON OTTO FISCHER (1882-1962) are as authentic as only a working sailor could make them. Born in Munich, Germany, but orphaned as a boy, Fischer ran away to sea at 16 and spent eight years before the mast on a variety of sailing ships. Paid off in New York, he stayed to apply for American citizenship and to teach seamanship on the school ship, "St. Mary's." He later served as a hand on racing yachts on Long Island Sound and worked as a model and handyman for the illustrator, A. B. Frost.

When he had saved enough money, he spent two years at the Académie Julian in Paris under Jean Paul Laurens.

Returning to the United States, Fischer sold his first picture to *Harper's Weekly*, and its success led to more commissions. *Everybody's* magazine sent him the first of several Jack London stories. In 1910, he began a 48-year association with *The Saturday Evening Post* which included illustrating for such story series' as Peter B. Kyne's "Cappy Ricks," Norman Reilly Raines' "Tugboat Annie," Guy Gilpatrick's "Glencannon," as well as serials for Kenneth Roberts and Nordoff and Hall.

In 1942 he was given the rank of Lieutenant Commander as "Artist Laureate" for the United States Coast Guard and was assigned North Atlantic convoy duty on the Coast Guard cutter "Campbell" during the winter of 1943. The "Campbell" was disabled during a successful attack on a German U-boat, and Fischer's dramatic series of paintings of this experience was published by *Life* magazine. The pictures are now in the Coast Guard Academy at New London, Connecticut.

In 1947, Fischer wrote and illustrated a book about his earlier sailing years, entitled *Fo'cs'le Days*, published by Charles Scribner's Sons.

A. "Midnight Sailing," by Fischer, in 1943, effectively illustrates the assembly of freighters for a convoy during World War II, used to promote the purchase of War Bonds. Reproduced by courtesy of Swift & Co., Inc.
B. Illustration for *The Saturday Evening Post*.

 →

193
ANTON OTTO FISCHER

Gordon Grant

GORDON HOPE GRANT, N.A. (1875-1962) was born in San Francisco. His father sent him to school in Scotland in order to maintain ancestral ties. The voyage of four-and-a-half months, from San Francisco, was made around the Horn, in a full-rigged Glasgow sailing vessel. Grant's life-long interest in the sea began with this early experience. After graduation from school in Fifeshire, he studied art in London at the Heatherly and Lambeth Schools.

On his return to America, Grant served on the Mexican Border with the Seventh Regiment National Guard and, as a war correspondent, contributed pictures to newspapers in New York and San Francisco. Early in his career, he made illustrations of a great variety of subject matter but gradually, as his reputation grew, restricted himself to nautical subjects.

His painting of the "Constitution" was used by the Navy Department to raise funds for the preservation of "Old Ironsides." The picture is now in the President's office in the White House. Grant is represented in many collections, including The Metropolitan Museum of Art, the Library of Congress, Annapolis Naval Academy, International Business Machines, New Britain Museum of American Art. He also painted a mural for the Post Office in Kennebunkport, Maine.

Grant illustrated a number of books, was both author and illustrator of *Ships under Sail,* 1941; *The Secret Voyage,* in 1943; and other marine stories.

Courtesy of the Grand Central Art Galleries

HEASLIP

WILLIAM HEASLIP (1898-) was born in Toronto, Canada. As a boy, he decided to become an artist. He was apprenticed to a lithographer at 50 cents a week, (the amount to be raised 50 cents, semi-annually for five years!)

World War I provided an opportunity for him to enlist in the Royal Flying Corps, and he has been interested in flying and depicting aviation subjects ever since.

After the war, Heaslip came to New York to study at the Art Students League and the National Academy of Design where he won the Suydam Medal. He has since illustrated widely for *The Saturday Evening Post*, *Collier's*, *Boy's Life*, and many other national magazines.

Illustration for the *American Boy-Youth's Companion*, December 1931.

Albin Henning

ALBIN HENNING (1886-1943) is best remembered for his spirited illustrations of World War I; after the war he researched the battlefields to confirm the authenticity of his work.

His special forte was adventure, and in addition to illustration for the major magazines he did many assignments for boys' stories, with subjects ranging from the French Foreign Legion to polar exploration, for *Boy's Life* and *American Boy*.

Henning was born in Oberdorla, Germany, but was reared in St. Paul, Minnesota. He studied at the Art Institute of Chicago and with Harvey Dunn at the Grand Central School of Art in New York.

Illustration for *The Saturday Evening Post*.

A

John Held Jr

B

JOHN HELD, JR. (1889-1958), more than anyone else, expressed in his pictures the brash spirit of the 'twenties with his famous flappers and collegiate capers, bootleg gin, jazz bands, and necking parties. His drawings, highly stylized, are fragile and delicate, yet entirely appropriate to the artificiality of the era.

As a youth, Held had made a number of linoleum cuts styled after the early, crude, wood engravings. Harold Ross, the *New Yorker* editor, encouraged Held to develop this second approach; it became a very popular feature, usually as a vehicle for satirical parody of the Victorian era.

All of Held's work was tremendously successful throughout the 'twenties and appeared copiously in the old *Life, Judge, Liberty, College Humor, Cosmopolitan,* and the *New Yorker.*

With the onset of the Depression, such frivolity was no longer appropriate, and Held quietly turned to the more serious career of breeding and sculpting horses, working with ceramics and wrought iron. He was also artist in residence at Harvard in 1940 and at the University of Georgia in 1941.

C

E

A. Doublespread in *Cosmopolitan* magazine, "Some call it Love . . . but I call it Spinach."
B. Spot drawing from the old *Life* magazine.
C. Cover illustration for the old *Life* magazine, January 14, 1926.
D. Typical Held linoleum cut, reproduced from *The Works of John Held, Jr.*, published by Ives Washburn, 1931.
E. Cover design for *McClure's* magazine, August, 1927.

D

HOFFMAN
NEW MEXICO

The father of FRANK B. HOFFMAN (1888-1958) raced horses in New Orleans, and young Frank spent all of his spare time working and sketching around the stables.

Through the interest of a family friend from Chicago who admired Frank's drawing of horses and other animals, he was given a job on the old *Chicago American* newspaper. Here he had an opportunity to draw a great variety of subjects, from opera to prize-fights; he eventually became head of the art department. Meanwhile he acquired a more formal art training by studying privately with J. Wellington Reynolds for five years.

In 1916, having been rejected for military service because of an eye defect, Hoffman went west to paint, and eventually was drawn to the art colony in Taos, New Mexico. His bold, broad brush work and striking color attracted the attention of advertisers. He painted for national campaigns for many corporations, including Great National Railroad, General Motors, General Electric, and others. This was followed by illustrations for the leading national magazines for which he specialized in Western subjects. His ranch in New Mexico was convenient for keeping live models, not only of cow ponies and thoroughbred horses, but also longhorn steers, several breeds of dogs, eagles, a bear, and burros.

From 1940 on, Hoffman was under exclusive contract to Brown and Bigelow and painted over 150 canvases of the West which were used as calendar subjects.

B

A. From *The Saturday Evening Post.*

B. Hoffman's dry-brush drawings, as typified by this vignette for *Cosmopolitan*; inspired countless imitators among pulp magazine illustrators who found the technique ideally suited to reproduction in line.

C. Reprinted by permission of *McCall's*. Published in 1929.

C

← A

LYNN BOGUE HUNT

LYNN BOGUE HUNT (1878-1960) painted pictures of wildlife almost exclusively. Although he occasionally included human figures in his illustrations, he felt more at home with the animals, fish, or birds, which he painted with great authority and dramatic use of color.

Born in Honeoye Falls, New York, Hunt became interested in wildlife at an early age, studied the anatomy of birds and animals, and learned taxidermy. Some of Hunt's first illustrations were done for the old *Outing* magazine. He subsequently worked for a wide range of publications and manufacturers of arms and ammunition but for many years was closely identified with *Field and Stream* magazine.

"Wild Turkey," one of a series of "Game Birds of America," published by *Field and Stream* magazine in 1948 and later as a special portfolio of prints.

LYLE JUSTIS

LYLE JUSTIS (1892-1960) displays in this lively illustration for *Treasure Island* his unique approach to pen drawing. Self-taught, Justis evolved a method of developing his drawings and compositions by means of a series of warm-up work sheets, covered with exploratory characters and poses. They were done without preliminary penciling-in or any prior planning. With these drawings as a guide, he was able to retain much free informality and vigor in his finished renderings. As an illustrator, Justis was at his best with historical subjects crowded with figures, especially rough frontier types, his flexible pen line perfectly adapted to reproduce their roistering gusto.

Justis was born in Manchester, Virginia, and obtained his first art work doing music titles. Eventually he illustrated for many books, magazines, advertising campaigns and motion pictures. For several years he was an active member of the Sketch Club and the Pen and Pencil Club of Philadelphia; his pictures won several awards in exhibitions of the Philadelphia Art Directors Club.

"Signing on of the Crew for the Hispaniola," from a special edition of Robert Louis Stevenson's *Treasure Island*, published by Grosset & Dunlap in 1930.

W. H. D Koerner

WILLIAM HENRY DETHLEF KOERNER (1878-1938) came from Clinton, Iowa. His first art job, when he was 15, was with the *Chicago Tribune* where he later became assistant art editor. After a brief stint as the art editor of a Midwest magazine and an attempt to free-lance in New York, he realized his need for further study.

By this time Howard Pyle was no longer carrying on his school, but Koerner went to Wilmington where Pyle gave him special help. Pyle's pupils — Dunn, Wyeth, Arthurs, and Schoonover — were still in the area and provided much helpful criticism.

With this background Koerner was able to achieve his ambition to become an illustrator. He was identified with *The Saturday Evening Post* for most of his long career, specializing in Western and other outdoor subjects. He also illustrated a number of books including *Covered Wagon*, and *North of 36*, by Emerson Hough.

Illustration for "Wolf Dog," by Hal G. Evarts, *The Saturday Evening Post.*

R. L. LAMBDIN

ROBERT L. LAMBDIN (1886-   ) is one of the many illustrators who came out of the training school of the newspaper art department. Born in Dighton, Kansas, he studied for a year at the Read Art School in Denver. His first job was with the *Rocky Mountain News*; he then worked for the *Denver Republican*, and eventually the *Kansas City Star* where he became an illustrator of feature stories.

From this training ground he came to New York, in 1917, and obtained his first story manuscript from the old *Greenbook* magazine. In subsequent years he illustrated for nearly all the major magazines, did advertising commissions, and illustrated many books.

Much of Lambdin's early work was done in pen and ink, later as line went out of vogue, he worked in halftone washes and oils.

A member of the National Society of Mural Painters, he has done a series of murals for the Saugatuck and Bedford Elementary Schools in Westport, Connecticut, The Beekman Downtown Hospital in New York City, the Bridgeport Brass Company, the Post Office in Bridgeport, and several other murals.

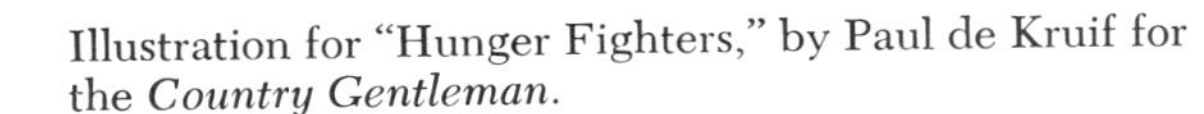
Illustration for "Hunger Fighters," by Paul de Kruif for the *Country Gentleman*.

Copyright 1937 by Newspaper Enterprise Association.

As a youngster WILLIAM ANDREW LOOMIS (1892-1959) loved to draw pictures, but it was a visit to the nearby studio of Howard Chandler Christy that made him decide to seek for himself an artist's career.

Loomis was born in Syracuse, New York, and grew up in Zanesville, Ohio. At 19 he went to New York to attend the Art Students League where he studied under George Bridgman and Frank Vincent DuMond.

In 1915 he got a job in Chicago with the art organization of Charles Daniel Frey; he also attended classes at the Chicago Art Institute. This was interrupted in 1917 when he enlisted in the Army and served 20 months, half of them overseas, in France.

After the war, Loomis returned to Chicago to work at the Charles Everett Johnson Advertising Art Studio, then for Bertch and Cooper. He finally opened his own studio as a free-lance artist. Equally at home in either editorial or advertising illustration, Loomis had a long career in both and also painted many outdoor twenty-four-sheet posters.

This broad experience especially qualified him as a teacher at the American Academy of Art in Chicago. Countless other art students who could not study with him personally have benefited from his several art books, including *Fun with a Pencil, Figure Drawing for All It's Worth,* and *Creative Illustration,* published by The Viking Press.

The Dionne Quintuplets with Dr. Allan Roy Dafoe. Advertising illustration for the Colgate Palmolive Co.

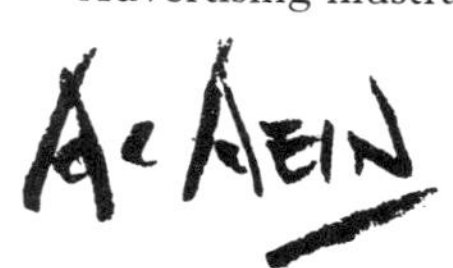

NEYSA MORAN McMEIN (1890-1949) — in private life Mrs. John Baragwanath — wanted, as a girl in Quincy, Illinois, to be a musician. Although she changed her mind and attended the Art Institute of Chicago, she paid her way through school by writing music and playing piano in a ten-cent store.

She painted her first *McCall's* magazine cover in 1923 and for many years made pastel portraits of beautiful or notable young women for *McCall's* monthly issues, as well as occasional covers for the *Woman's Home Companion* and *The Saturday Evening Post.* She also regularly contributed her drawings for the annual *New York Times'* "Hundred Neediest Cases."

Neysa was equally noted as a hostess and friend of such notables as Alexander Woollcott, Irving Berlin, Marc Connolly, Bea Lillie, Irene Castle, Richard Rodgers, Dorothy Parker, Jascha Heifetz, and George Abbott, who visited at her studio or home. As young models, Kay Francis and Fredric March posed for her.

Eventually she turned to portraiture and painted most of the country's prominent women. The Whitney Museum of American Art has established a memorial fund in her honor, which is used to purchase work by living American artists.

Pastel cover design for *McCall's* magazine, June, 1934.

HARRY MORSE MEYERS.

HARRY MORSE MEYERS (1886-1961) was a collector of antique arms and armor which he displayed on two carved oak screens that had belonged to the curator of arms at the Tower of London. Since he illustrated many period stories, these authentic objects frequently served as props for his characters.

Meyers was from New Orleans, Louisiana; attended Tulane University there, followed by classes at the Art Students League in New York and further study with Harvey Dunn.

With a few years' interruption during World War I, as an Army airplane pilot, he had a long and successful career as an illustrator for the Crowell-Collier publications, particularly *Collier's* magazine.

Illustration for a *Collier's* story, "Appointment in Martinique," by William A. Krauss.

Oberhardt

WILLIAM OBERHARDT, A.N.A. (1882-1958) early in his career as an illustrator found his greatest interest in delineating the human head. Over the years he developed a remarkable faculty for presenting the special qualities revealed by the sitter's character. An important factor in this ability came from his own warm personality which relaxed and charmed his subjects.

"Obie" would never draw from photographs, but always insisted on working directly from the model, earning added respect from editors and his fellow-artists for his refusal to lean on the photograph for help in getting a likeness.

His sitters comprised a veritable *Who's Who.* He said that most of them were people he would have paid willingly for the privilege of portraying. Among these famous subjects were Presidents Taft, Harding, and Hoover; Thomas Edison, Sergei Rachmaninoff, Luther Burbank, Ezio Pinza, Cardinal Spellman, Bernard Baruch, and Walter Lippmann.

During World War II, Oberhardt contributed a great number of portrait sketches at various centers and hospitals for men of the armed services from many nations.

Lithograph portrait of Joe Cannon, Speaker of the House of Representatives, used for the cover of the first issue of *Time* magazine.

FIFTEEN CENTS

TIME

The Weekly News-Magazine

Oberhardt

VOL. 1, NO. 1 MARCH 3, 1923

Reprinted by permission of *TIME* The Weekly Newsmagazine; copyright *TIME*, Inc., 1923 and 1956.

PAUS

HERBERT PAUS (1880-1946) was a native of Minneapol and got his first job as a cartoonist for the St. Paul *Pioneer Press.* Ambitious to become an illustrator, he enrolled in the Fine Arts School there, later found employment in a Chicago art studio.

Later he moved to New York where he became a free-lance illustrator. Paus had a strong sense of design, ideally suited to the many effective posters he painted during World War I. This approach, combined with a striking us of color was carried over into his magazine illustrations and cover designs.

Paus painted for such advertisers as Victor Records, Hart, Schaffner & Marx, and for several years was under exclusive contract to do all of the covers for *Popular Science* monthly.

Illustration for *Everybody's* magazine.

Wm Meade Prince

WILLIAM MEADE PRINCE (1893-1951) was born in Roanoke, Virginia and grew up in Chapel Hill, North Carolina. He could not choose between West Point and architecture at Georgia Institute of Technology, settled it by going north to study art at the New York School of Fine and Applied Arts.

After five years of advertising work in Chicago, he settled in Westport, Connecticut, where he could combine his illustration work for the magazines in New York with his interest in riding and in maintaining fine Arabian horses. When Westport eventually became too urban for riding, Prince returned to Chapel Hill, where he built his own studio and stables and continued to do illustration. He was particularly noted for his spirited and sympathetic interpretations of Roark Bradford's Negro stories for *Collier's* magazine.

For several years Prince also taught illustration and figure drawing at the University of North Carolina and was the head of the Art Department there from 1943-1946.

Illustration for *The Saturday Evening Post.*

Illustration for an article by O. O. McIntyre for *Cosmopolitan* magazine in 1928.

Russell Patterson.

RUSSELL PATTERSON (1896-   ) has been very influential not only as an illustrator (in the 'twenties his flappers were as famous as those of John Held, Jr.), but also has been equally successful in many areas outside illustration.

Patterson was born in Omaha. The family moved to Canada, where he spent one year studying architecture at McGill University. When financial reverses terminated that study, Patterson tried various newspaper jobs, finally doing a comic strip in French, "Pierre et Pierrette," for *Là Patrie* in Montreal.

He next went to Chicago and attended the Chicago Art Institute and the Academy of Fine Arts. His early work was for department stores: Carson, Pirie, Scott and Company, and Marshall Field, where he became noted for his interior designs.

A year of painting landscapes in France followed. When he returned to America in 1921 the Jazz Age was just beginning. Patterson began to draw flappers, and they were an immediate success when they appeared in *College Humor.* With his flair for clothes, Patterson also became a pacemaker in setting styles. The raccoon coat and galoshes were among his contributions to collegiate garb; and his drawings were followed eagerly for what was *right* to wear.

Commissions for the theatre followed. Patterson did both the costumes and set designs for the Ziegfield Follies of 1922 and a number of other Broadway shows, including George White's Scandals.

Patterson spent the 'thirties in Hollywood doing set and costume designs for the movies, mostly elaborate musicals, similar to his Broadway shows.

In the late 'thirties, he returned to New York, again to the department store field. He designed coats for I. J. Fox, Christmas toy windows for Macy's, and resumed advertising illustrations.

During World War II he designed the Women's Army Corps uniforms, train interiors, did a comic strip, and has since designed hotel lobbies and restaurant interiors. No one, including Patterson himself, knows quite what he'll be doing next.

JAMES MOORE PRESTON (1873-1962) studied at the Philadelphia Academy with fellow students Henri, Luks, Sloan, and Shinn, and had then gone to Paris to complete his training. There he met May Wilson; they were married in 1903 upon their return to the United States. The success of their union can be seen in the similarity of styles, reflecting their influence on each other.

For many years both were active contributors to nearly all of the major magazines.

Cover painting for *Woman's Home Companion.*

MAY WILSON PRESTON (1873-1949) came to New York to attend the Art Students League after graduating from Oberlin. This was followed by study in Paris with Whistler at the World's Art center. She first came to the master's notice when he discovered black on her palette. "There is no such color . . . scrape it off!" Such was Whistler's prestige that other students eagerly offered him their lace handkerchiefs for his use as a paint rag — to be treasured later as mementos.

May Wilson's first magazine illustrations were published by *Harper's Bazaar* as early as 1901. For the next thirty years she illustrated stories for *McClure's, Scribner's,* and particularly *The Saturday Evening Post,* including a number of serials by Mary Roberts Rinehart. A prolific painter, her illustrations were airy and witty reflecting her own energy and good humor.

Illustration for *Ladies' Home Journal* serial story by Alice Duer Miller.

REYNARD

GRANT TYSON REYNARD, A.N.A. (1887-) attended the Chicago Art Institute and the Chicago Academy of Fine Arts, paying his own way by doing odd jobs, including piano playing for sheet music sales, in his home town of Grand Island, Nebraska.

His first job was as art editor of *Redbook* magazine, then in Chicago. There he met and worked with many of the top writers and illustrators and had his first opportunity to do his own illustrations.

After three years Reynard decided to come East to study further with Harvey Dunn in Leonia, New Jersey, with the hope of working for the larger magazines. Within a year he had made it and had begun illustrating for *The Saturday Evening Post, Harper's Bazaar, Cosmopolitan, Good Housekeeping,* and *Collier's.* During this time most of his illustrations were done in charcoal with a full range of values.

He began experimenting with other media for exhibition pictures and gradually turned to an independent career as painter and etcher. Study with Mahonri Young and Harry Wicky, with a year of travel and sketching in Europe, furthered this ambition. Reynard's pictures and prints now hang in many major museums including The Metropolitan Museum of Art, Addison Gallery of American Art, Fogg Museum in Boston, Newark Museum, and the Library of Congress. He has won a number of prizes.

Over the years, Reynard has taught at various art schools and universities and lectured widely. At present, Grant Reynard is president of the Montclair Art Museum and Chairman of its Art Committee.

Illustration for the *Ladies' Home Journal.*

TONY SARG

The interests of TONY SARG (1882-1942) were as diversified as his background. Sarg was born in Guatemala, sent to school in Germany. With no formal art training, he did his first professional work in London, for *Sketch* magazine and also did advertising drawings.

In London he became fascinated with marionette performances by the great Holden and for months followed the troupe from one engagement to another to learn the secrets of the craft.

When Sarg came to America in 1914, he successfully organized his own marionette workshop and also experimented with early animated cartoons for the movies.

Among Sarg's first illustration assignments was one for Irvin Cobb's "Speaking of Operations," in *The Saturday Evening Post.* The humor of his drawings matched Cobb's, delightfully. He eventually illustrated for a great number of publications and advertisers. Sarg also wrote and illustrated several books for children; designed textiles, wallpapers, boxes, rugs, glass and pottery, toys, and the monster balloons for the annual Macy parades on Thanksgiving Day in New York City.

"The shopping hour on the busy East Side," from *Tony Sarg's New York,* published by Greenberg, 1926.

A

A. "Saying Grace." A readers' poll named this picture Rockwell's best and most moving *Post* cover.

Norman Rockwell

The pictures of NORMAN ROCKWELL (1894-) are recognized and loved by almost everybody in America. The cover of *The Saturday Evening Post* was his showcase for over 40 years, giving him an audience larger than that of any other artist in history. Over the years he has depicted there a unique collection of Americana, a series of vignettes of remarkable warmth and humor.

In addition, he has painted a great number of pictures for story illustrations, advertising campaigns, posters, calendars, and books.

As his personal contribution during World War II, Rockwell painted the famous "Four Freedoms" posters, symbolizing for millions the war aims as described by President Franklin Roosevelt. One version of his "Freedom of Speech" painting is in the collection of The Metropolitan Museum of Art.

Since that time he has been occupied with other serious subjects, among them a large painting illustrating the "Golden Rule." One of his most recent is an effective commentary on the segregation problem, reproduced here from *Look* magazine.

Rockwell left high school to attend classes at the National Academy of Design and later studied under Thomas Fogarty and George Bridgman at the Art Students League in New York. His early illustrations were done for *St. Nicholas* magazine and other juvenile publications. He sold his first cover painting to the *Post* in 1916 and has since done over 300 more. Presidents Eisenhower, Kennedy, and Johnson sat for him for portraits, and he has painted other world figures including Nasser of Egypt and Nehru of India.

In 1957 the United States Chamber of Commerce in Washington cited him as a Great Living American, saying that . . . "Through the magic of your talent, the folks next door — their gentle sorrows, their modest joys — have enriched our own lives and given us new insight into our countrymen."

His work and career are described more fully in "Norman Rockwell, Illustrator" by Arthur L. Guptill; in his autobiography, "Norman Rockwell: My Adventures as an Illustrator," as told to his son, Thomas Rockwell; and "The Norman Rockwell Album," the last two published by Doubleday and Company.

© Copyright Cowles Communications, Inc.

B

B. "The Problem We All Live With." *Look* magazine, January 14, 1964.
C. Cover for *The Saturday Evening Post*.
D. Rockwell has painted annual *Boy's Life* covers since 1913. Reproductions of the paintings for calendars have been the all-time most popular subjects with the public.
E. "Freedom of Speech," one of the famous "Four Freedoms" paintings, originally published in *The Saturday Evening Post*.

C

© 1924 by The Curtis Publishing Company.

D

Reproduced by courtesy and copyright of *Boy's Life* and Brown and Bigelow.

E

© 1943 by The Curtis Publishing Company.

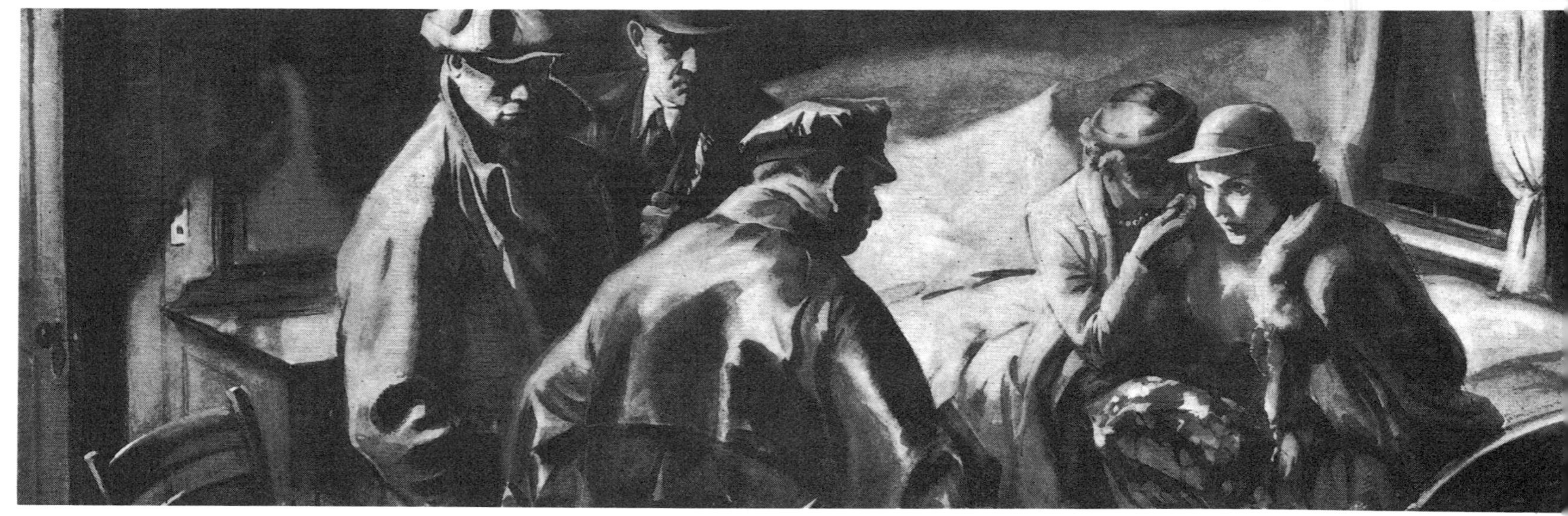

DUDLEY GLOYNE SUMMERS

The illustrations of DUDLEY GLOYNE SUMMERS (1892-) are straightforward and rendered with great economy of means, characteristic of the composition for a mystery story, shown here, in which he has concentrated on the essentials to establish setting and characters.

Summers was born in Birmingham, England, educated there and in America. He attended the New School of Art in Boston, and the Art Students League in New York, studying under Thomas Fogarty, Charles Chapman, and F. R. Gruger.

His first illustrations were made in the early 'twenties for MacLean's magazine in Canada and were followed by work for most of the American magazines.

Illustration for an Erle Stanley Gardner story, "The D.A. Holds a Candle," *Country Gentleman.*

A

B

ADOLPH TREIDLER

ADOLPH TREIDLER (1886-) was born in Westcliffe, Colorado, studied at the California School of Design in San Francisco and with Robert Henri in New York. He first illustrated for *McClure's* magazine in 1908, then made pictures or cover designs for *Harper's, Century, Scribner's, Collier's, The Saturday Evening Post, Woman's Home Companion,* and many national advertisers.

Posters have been his particular forte. During World War I, he designed numerous Liberty Loan and recruiting posters and was Chairman of the Pictorial Publicity Committee for the Society of Illustrators during World War II.

Travel subjects are his favorites. For many years he painted posters for the Bermuda officials, the Furness Bermuda and the French Lines, and through these associations has traveled the world over.

Treidler is a member of the Art Directors Club, Charter Member of the Artists' Guild, and life member of the Society of Illustrators.

A. "The Farragut Statue," New York. Linoleum cut.
B. Poster for the United States Marines during World War I.

Sheridan

JOHN E. SHERIDAN (1880-1948) was at his best as a poster and cover artist as exemplified in his paintings for the *Ladies' Home Journal, The Saturday Evening Post, American, Collier's* and in the posters he made for the Bureau of Public Information during World War I. He was also noted for his advertising illustrations for Hart, Schaffner & Marx and the Bosch Magneto Company.

Sheridan was born in Tomah, Wisconsin, and earned his tuition for Georgetown University in Washington, D.C., by painting posters for sports events. He also spent a year at the Colorossi School in Paris. He next became art editor of the *Washington Times* and later helped to produce the first Sunday supplement in color for the *San Francisco Chronicle*.

He was an active member of the Society of Illustrators, The Players, Dutch Treat Club, and taught at the School of Visual Arts in New York from 1945-48.

Cover illustration for *The Saturday Evening Post.*

Illustration for "Some were Brave," by Ernest Haycox in *Collier's* magazine, 1940.

Teale

EARLE GRANTHAM TEALE (1886-1924) was tragically killed while standing in the darkened interior of a garage when a driver coming in from the bright sunlight failed to see him in time.

At the time of his death he was one of the country's foremost automobile artists having painted a brilliant series of advertisements for the White Motor Car Company. Teale's style was decorative and influenced by both his admiration for Japanese prints and his interest in murals.

He had attended the Art Students League in New York and later studied architectural design at Stanford University as a preparation for mural painting. He painted several murals during his career including a year's project for the Panama-Pacific Exposition in 1915.

Illustration for the White Motor Truck as included in the First Annual Exhibition by the New York Art Directors Club in 1921.

Frank Street

FRANK STREET (1893-1944) came from Kansas City, Missouri, to study at the Art Students League in New York and at the Charles Chapman-Harvey Dunn School of Illustration in Leonia, New Jersey.

Dunn, who carried on the Pyle tradition, was the dominant influence in Street's work. He also helped him to obtain his first illustration commission from Walter Dower, then art editor of *The Saturday Evening Post.* Street had a long career of illustration with the *Post* and with many other publications, including the *Ladies' Home Journal, Cosmopolitan, Collier's* and *The American Legion* magazines.

Although he did not exhibit them formally, Street painted many landscapes and portraits, between illustration commissions, and also conducted private classes in his own studio for the last five or six years of his life.

A

B

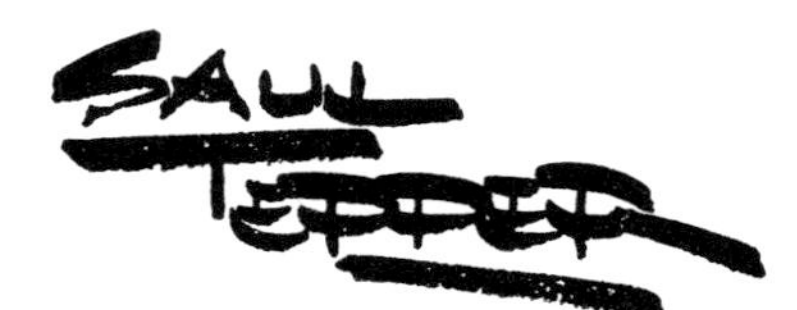

SAUL TEPPER (1899-) was born on the lower East side of New York City and has remained a New Yorker all his life.

As a youngster, Tepper won a correspondence course in the Landon School of Art. He studied also at Cooper Union, the Art Students League and at the Grand Central School of Art, under Harvey Dunn.

He worked as a letterer in a fashion catalog studio before establishing himself as an illustrator. Tepper has since illustrated almost equally for fiction and advertising assignments for most of the magazines and for many national accounts, such as Mobiloil, Texaco, Packard, General Motors, and Coca-Cola.

Among his many honors are the Harvard Award (1929), the Newspaper Award (1936), Annual Advertising Award (1940), and the Laskinlamb Institute Award (1943).

For many years, Tepper has also been an active teacher and lecturer at: Pratt Institute, Cooper Union, the New York Art Directors Club, and the Society of Illustrators.

Music has been a parallel interest with him. Saul has written many popular songs which have been recorded by Nat (King) Cole, Ella Fitzgerald, Ezio Pinza, Glenn Miller, Harry James, and others. He is a member of ASCAP and AGAC and has written sketches, lyrics and music for 15 annual Society of Illustrators' Shows.

A. The influence of Harvey Dunn's teaching is apparent in this powerful advertising illustration for Lysol Disinfectant, 1931.

B. Illustration for *The Saturday Evening Post.*

A

DONALD TEAGUE

DONALD TEAGUE, N.A. (1897-) is respected by his fellow-illustrators as a thorough craftsman whose pictures are composed and painted with great professional competence.

Teague begins a picture with many thumbnail sketches in black and white, followed by small full-color studies of the most promising approaches. After a composition has been evolved, models are posed for further sketching and photographing (for factual information). Photostats, reduced in scale from the rather large figure studies, are then projected and traced on water-color paper, free from any corrections or erasures, ready to render in water color or gouache.

Research, for authenticating every detail, is equally important in his picture-making. Teague, who lives in California near the motion picture studios, has had the advantage of using their props for Westerns. He can obtain cowboy actors, a stage coach complete with horses, and even use the Western Town movie sets. The Pacific Ocean is equally accessible for his sea illustrations. Air express has made it possible for him to keep deadlines with publishers in the East.

Teague was born in Brooklyn, New York, studied at the Art Students League in New York under Bridgman and DuMond. After serving in the Navy during World War I, he went to England and studied under Norman Wilkinson, P.R.I. Back in America, he found Dean Cornwell most helpful while he was getting started as an illustrator.

Besides his work for publications, Teague has exhibited regularly. His prizes and awards, too numerous to list, include the Gold Medal of Honor, American Water Color Society in 1953, and the S. F. B. Morse Gold Medal, National Academy, 1962. He is also represented in many museums and private collections, including the Virginia Museum of Fine Arts in Richmond; Frye Museum, Seattle, Washington; and Collection of the State of California in Sacramento.

A. "Wagons West," from a series entitled "Masterpieces of the Old West," reprinted by permission of and copyrighted by Brown and Bigelow, St. Paul, Minnesota.
B. Vignette for a *Collier's* story, "Tavern at Powell's Ferry," under the pseudonym of Edwin Dawes. Because of rivalry between the two publications, Teague used his own name for *The Saturday Evening Post*; "Dawes" at *Collier's*.

B

C. D. Williams

CHARLES DAVID WILLIAMS (1875-1954) worked in pen and ink in the early part of his career; especially notable were his sensitive line drawings for Booth Tarkington's *Monsieur Beaucaire*. He later worked in charcoal with great control and subtlety in this difficult medium.

Williams, who was from Pittsburgh, had had a brief career in the 'nineties, as a professional lightweight boxer.

Gregarious and hard-working, he spent much of his time on behalf of the programs of the Society of Illustrators and served as its president from 1927 to 1929.

Illustration for *Cosmopolitan*, November, 1924.

L. F. Wilford

LORAN F. WILFORD (1893-) is at present teaching at the Ringling School of Art in Sarasota, Florida. Prior to this he taught at the Grand Central School of Art in New York City and has had a long career of painting for exhibition and illustrating for newspapers and magazines.

Born in Wamego, Kansas, Wilford studied at the Kansas City Art Institute and was soon doing feature illustrations for the *Kansas City Star*.

Ambitious, he gravitated to the East for further study with Jonas Lie and George Pearce Ennis. Soon he began a career working for such publications as *Cosmopolitan*, *Everybody's*, *McCall's*, and *Hearst's International*. His early illustrations were done in dry brush; later he became very much interested in water colors which he soon began to exhibit.

He has since become one of our outstanding water colorists and has won many honors for both his water colors and oils, has painted several murals and is represented in the permanent collection of the Toledo Museum of Fine Art, the High Museum of Atlanta, Georgia, and many private collections.

Dry-brush illustration for the *Ladies' Home Journal*.

1930-1940

ILLUSTRATORS 1930-1940

Constantin Alajálov
James E. Allen
Harold N. Anderson
Boris Artzybasheff
Ernest Hamlin Baker
Lowell Leroy Balcom
McClelland Barclay
Cecil Calvert Beall
Harry Beckhoff
Frank C. Bensing
Earl Blossom
Vladimir Bobritsky
E. Melbourne Brindle
Elmore J. Brown
Paul Brown
Pruett A. Carter
Frederick Trench Chapman
Benton Clark
Matt Clark
Ralph Pallen Coleman
Roy Huse Collins
Grattan Condon
Dan Content
Mario Ruben Cooper
Bradshaw Crandell
William Galbraith Crawford
John Henry Crosman
Robert W. Crowther
Floyd MacMillan Davis
William James Dufault
Nick Eggenhofer
Carl Oscar August Erickson
John J. Floherty, Jr.
Harland Frazer
John Russell Fulton
Edwin A. Georgi
Jules Gottlieb
Ruth Sigrid Grafstrom
Roy Frederic Heinrich
Wilmot Emerton Heitland
Clarence Peter Helck
David Hendrickson
Edwin Henry
E. Everett Henry
R. John Holmgren
George Howe
Rockwell Kent
Stephen R. Kidd
Walter Charles Klett
Clayton Knight
Larry B. Kritcher
John LaGatta
Charles Louis LaSalle
Manning deVilleneuve Lee
Philip Lyford
Orison MacPherson
Ronald Norman McLeod
Frederic Kimball Mizen
Irving Nurick
Robert Patterson
Garrett Price
William Reusswig
Martha Sawyers
Mead Schaeffer
Oscar Frederick Schmidt
James W. Schucker
Howard Scott
Henry J. Soulen
Roy Frederic Spreter
Herbert Morton Stoops
Haddon Hubbard Sundblom
Dan Sweeney
Harry Laverne Timmins
Rico Tomaso
Edmund F. Ward
William P. Welsh
Howard W. Willard
James W. Williamson
Denys Wortman

The Decade: 1930-1940

by Floyd Davis

DRAWING BY WALT REED

We thought of ourselves not merely as illustrators but also as fine artists and took our work very seriously. We believed that the field of illustration was eminently worth while and that our goal was to paint the best pictures we knew how. Of course, we were subject to the particular limitations of the subject matter, the policy of the publication, the mechanics of working for good reproduction, and so forth. However, these restrictions, if different, were perhaps no greater than those placed on the painters of pictures in the past by awkward architectural settings, poor lighting, or dogmatic interpretation of religious subjects by church officials.

A good illustration should be able to stand on its own as a picture. If it has merely been a "photograph" of an incident in a story, its usefulness will be as transient as the sentences it illustrates. However, if it is a picture true to human behavior or motivation as revealed by the manuscript — and done with artistry and integrity — it has a chance of being worth-while. To make a great picture requires a combination of many qualities, plus good luck. It is rare good fortune to feel, even once in a lifetime, that you are joining hands with Rembrandt.

Good art directors, too, had their share in making illustration important. The best of them, men like Bill Chessman of *Collier's*, Pete Martin of *The Saturday Evening Post*, and Henry Quinan of the *Woman's Home Companion*, brought out the best in us with their stimulation and encouragement. We were challenged to try new approaches in our own individual ways, without the restraint of contrived layouts or predetermined situations in the manuscript. Whenever possible, we were allowed to take the extra time necessary to interpret the assigned story creatively.

There were a great many talented and dedicated men in the illustration field in the 'thirties: John Gannam, Henry Raleigh, Frank Hoffman, Harold Von Schmidt, Albert Dorne, Rockwell Kent, Lynd Ward, Edward A. Wilson, Wallace Morgan, Eric, and many others. Some are still active. I admire the work of all the good ones. These artists raised the position of American illustration to international preëminence, both in technical excellence and in the scope of their influence.

The Depression had some effect on the illustration field then, but since we were in our busy, productive years as artists, we didn't feel the economic pinch as much as did many of the easel and mural painters, some of whom needed the relief assistance of the Federal Government to survive at all as artists.

Denys Wortman, in his syndicated "Metropolitan Movies," "Mopey Dick and the Duke," and "Mrs. Rumpel's Boarding House," made poignant and wry commentary on this period in his humorous newspaper drawings. The pulp magazine, inexpensive and printed on cheap, uncoated paper, became very popular during this time. The covers were generally lurid in color and subject, although some, such as *Adventure* magazine and *Bluebook*, were "quality" pulps which showed better taste and better art. Inside illustrations were almost invariably done in a dry-brush technique which reproduced inexpensively in line, often styled after Frank Hoffman's earlier, sparkling black-and-white drawings. Devoted to special subjects, such as Westerns, detectives, and aviation, the pulps provided an excellent market for upcoming authors and young illustrators. Amos Sewell, John Clymer, Walter Baumhofer, John Falter, and Tom Lovell were among those who were active in this field and later graduated to eminence in the slicks. (The quality magazines were printed on coated, or slick, paper.)

By the end of the 'thirties, the Depression was over and, with it, an era. As war came to Europe in 1939, great changes were taking place in the United States, too. The effects of war mobilization were felt throughout the economy, including the art field. The insular hill-billy disappeared, and subsequently we all became involved with the war effort.

F. W. Davis

J.E. ALLEN

JAMES E. ALLEN (1894-   ) has been a student and serious experimenter all his life. Born in Louisiana, Missouri, he attended the Art Academy in Chicago, the Art Students League, the Grand Central School, and the Hans Hoffman School in New York. He also studied in Paris and London.

Among his instructors were Frank Stick, Joseph Pennell, Robert Brackman, Robert Philipp, William Auerbach-Levy, Arshile Gorky, Sigurd Skou, and Harvey Dunn.

He began illustrating for the *Peoples' Popular Monthly* in 1913. Assignments from nearly all of the major magazines followed. Most of his pictures were painted in oils, but he was also interested in lithographs and etchings which have been exhibited widely in the United States and abroad.

Allen has been a member of the Salmagundi Club, the Society of American Etchers, the Chicago Society of Etchers, Philadelphia Society of Etchers, and New Rochelle Art Association. His work has won many awards and he is represented in several collections, including the Brooklyn Museum, the Cincinnati Museum, Cleveland Museum of Art, Seattle Art Museum, Philadelphia Museum of Art, and the Library of Congress.

Illustration for *Good Housekeeping* magazine, November, 1927.

HAROLD ANDERSON

HAROLD N. ANDERSON (1894-   ) studied at the Fenway Art School in his native Boston. Among his instructors were Chase Emerson, Harold Brett, and Arthur Spear.

His first illustrations were made for *Boy's Life* in 1919 and were followed by work for most of the leading publications, many national advertising campaigns, and billboard twenty-four-sheet posters.

He has won numerous poster awards and exhibited in Art Directors Club shows in 1937, 1940, 1942, 1946, 1950, and 1951. Anderson is a member of the Society of Illustrators, The Old Greenwich Art Society, the Artists' Guild and the Westport Artists. He had a one-man show at the Society of Illustrators in 1942.

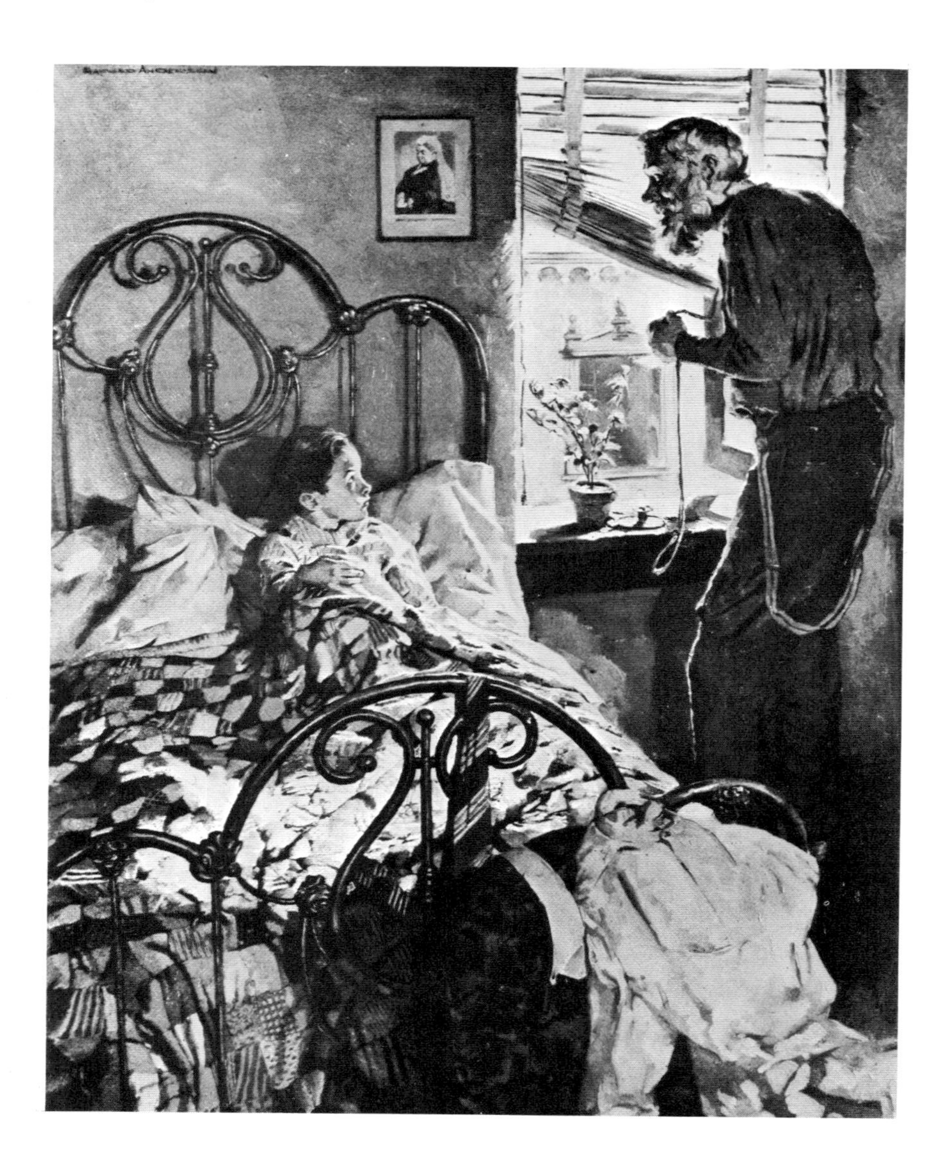

Illustration for "The Green Years," by A. J. Cronin in *Redbook* magazine, 1944.

alajálov

CONSTANTIN ALAJÁLOV (1900-) sold his first cover to *The New Yorker* magazine in 1926 and has since painted a long and colorful series of satirical vignettes of American life for *The New Yorker* and *The Saturday Evening Post*.

Alajálov was born in the Russian town of Rostov-on-the-Don. The Revolution came when he was 17 and a student at the University of Petrograd. He survived this period by working as a government artist, painting huge propaganda pictures and portraits, and eventually made his way, in 1921, to Constantinople, which was an international refugee haven.

Although largely self-taught as an artist, Alajálov earned a precarious living by sketching portraits in bars or painting sidewalk advertisements for movie houses. He eventually progressed to doing murals for night clubs, taking most of his payment in food. After two years of this, he saved enough to pay his passage to America.

Once here, Alajálov resumed painting murals, in Russian night clubs, and within three years had sold that *New Yorker* cover. He has continued to give us a candid and refreshing look at our foibles ever since.

Artzybasheff

BORIS ARTZYBASHEFF (1899-1965) combined a spirit of fantasy with wry humor in his incomparable ability to give human qualities to machines; a meticulous rendering made his most imaginative creations entirely convincing. His designs were always carefully planned — there is not an accidental stroke in them — and he mastered every technical problem by thoughtful preliminary studies.

Artzybasheff was born in Kharkov, Russia, and was graduated from the Prince Tenisheff School in St. Petersburg. After the Revolution he escaped the country on a freighter. When he arrived in America in 1919, he had only a few Turkish coins, the equivalent of 14 cents.

Befriended by a Russian Orthodox priest, he found work in an engraving shop doing lettering, borders and ornamental details. He first gained a reputation as an artist by illustrating over 40 books, several of which he also wrote or edited. The best known of these, perhaps, are his *Aesop's Fables, Seven Simeons,* and *Balzac's Droll Stories.* Advertising and cover painting assignments followed. He was a regular contributor of incisive and penetrating cover portraits for *Time* magazine for 24 years, painting over 200 covers. His work was also well known abroad; he did commissions for firms overseas as well as many advertising campaigns for leading companies in the United States.

During World War II Artzybasheff served as an expert adviser to the U.S. Department of State, Psychological Warfare Branch.

During his long career, he was the recipient of many awards, including the Newberry Medal and citations from the American Institute of Graphic Arts.

"Imperturbable tank and anti-tank guns," one of a series of illustrations that appeared in *Life* magazine, November 3, 1941.

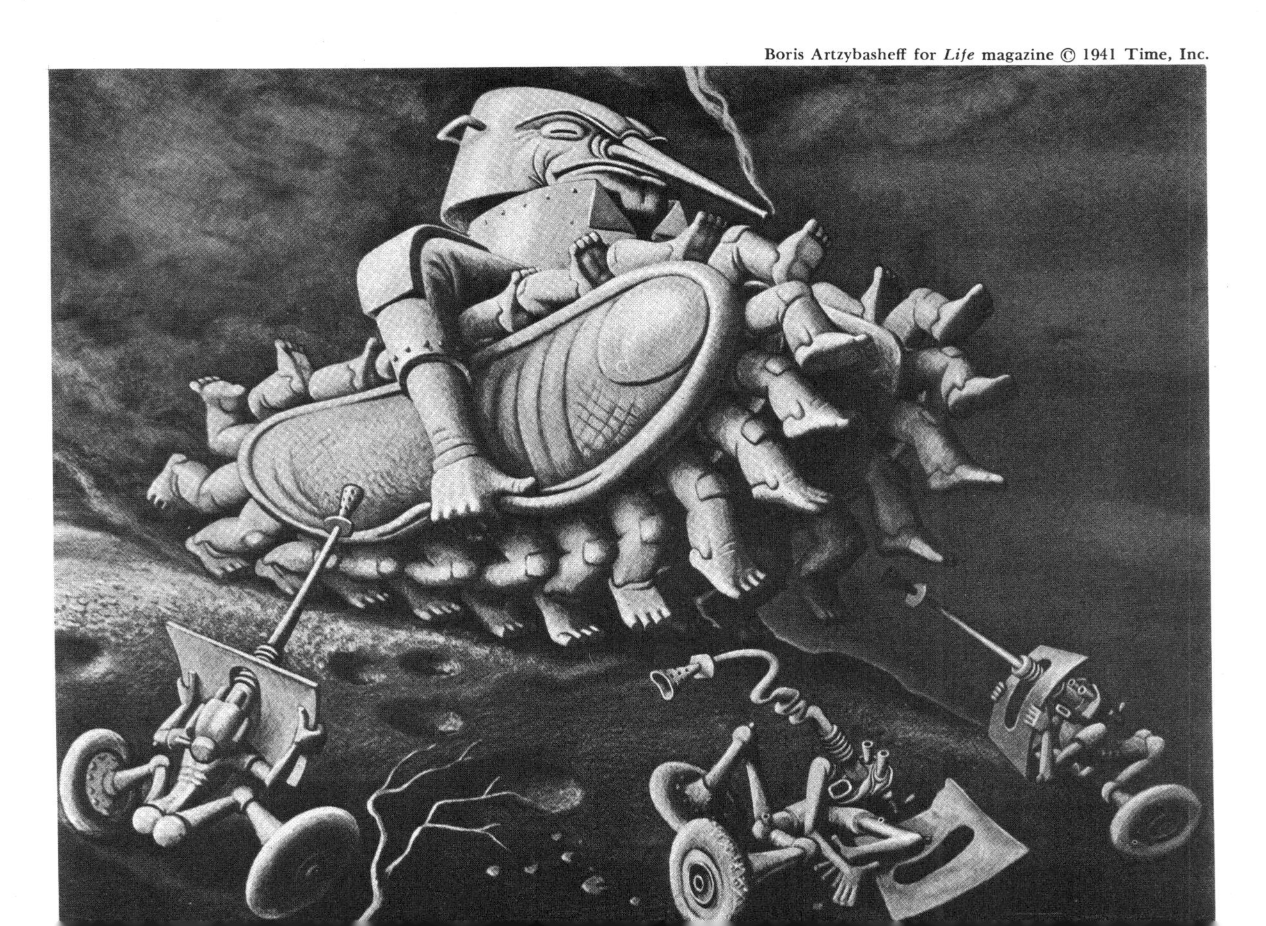

Ernest Hamlin Baker for *Time* magazine © 1942 by Time, Inc.

Ernest Hamlin Baker

ERNEST HAMLIN BAKER (1889-) is a self-taught artist who has evolved his own personal, and painstakingly intricate, approach as typified by nearly 400 cover portraits he has painted for *Time* magazine.

The portraits are painted from photographs of the subjects taken from all possible angles, with different light sources, and then studied minutely — even with a magnifying glass — to give him a knowledge of the whole face and head.

Baker then makes a highly detailed preliminary pencil study or "facial guide-map." Every wen, wart, indentation, or vein is factually and honestly depicted. It is from a careful analysis of these "facts" and their relationship to each other that a faithful likeness emerges, a likeness that reveals character.

His painting process is equally detailed, beginning with a tracing from the pencil drawing on illustration board. The portrait is gradually built up with repeated strokes of diluted tempera color allowing the drawing beneath to show through. From time to time this pencil drawing is reinforced to retain it clearly. Values are thus built up from light to dark with minute strokes, even for the large areas (never broad, flat washes), each stroke successively blotted to remove any excess of color. This unique process, laborious as it is, gives the artist complete control of the painting right up to the final stroke.

Cover portrait painting of Chief of Staff George C. Marshall.

BALCOM

LOWELL LEROY BALCOM (1887-1938) was born in Kansas City, Missouri, and got his start there. He studied privately with John D. Patrick and at the Kansas City Art Institute with Charles Wilimovsky. His first job was as an artist for the *Kansas City Star*. In the Army, during World War I, his duties consisted largely of drawing and painting portraits of officers.

After the war, Balcom visited the Virgin Islands to paint in water colors and oils. He made his first experiments there with linoleum cuts which he was later to develop as his own personal medium.

Balcom's first break came when he did a series of illustrations for the U. S. Shipping Board which also provided him an opportunity to travel to the Orient and the Mediterranean. Subsequently, he did illustrations for numerous magazines such as *The American Legion* and *Hearst's International* and for advertisers including Exide Batteries and Bridgeport Brass.

He was a member of the Artists' Guild in New York and active in the Silvermine Guild in Norwalk, Connecticut, up to the time of his death.

Cover illustration for the December, 1930, issue of *The American Legion* magazine, tinted linoleum block.

A

B

McClelland Barclay/USNR

McCLELLAND BARCLAY (1891-1943) was appointed a Lieutenant Commander, U.S.N.R., during World War II and contributed many posters, illustrations, and officer portraits for the Navy before being reported missing in action, in the Pacific theatre, aboard an L.S.T. which was torpedoed.

Before the war Barclay was most noted for his ability to paint strikingly beautiful women, as best exemplified by his series for General Motors illustrating the slogan, "Body by Fisher."

Born in St. Louis, Missouri, Barclay was a student of H. C. Ives, George Bridgman, and Thomas Fogarty. He was a member of the Artists' Guild, the Art Students League of New York, and the Society of Illustrators.

In 1946, on the third anniversary of his death, a foundation was established in his name, The McClelland Barclay Fund for Art, "to aid the thousands of American Artists who have never had a fair opportunity."

A. This illustration by Barclay for an advertisement for the Koppers Company was awarded The Art Directors Club Medal posthumously in 1944, "in recognition of his long and distinguished record in editorial illustration and advertising art and in honor of his devotion and meritorious service to his country as a commissioned officer of the United States Navy, which lists him as missing in action in the South Pacific."

B. One of a series of illustrations for Fisher Body which appeared in the late 'twenties and early 'thirties.

© 1964, The Lincoln National Life Insurance Company.

C.C. Beall

CECIL CALVERT BEALL (1892-) has traveled far since leaving his birthplace of Saratoga, Wyoming.

He studied at the Art Students League under George Bridgman and at Pratt Institute. His early illustrations were done in bold poster style in water color marked by a strong pattern of light and shadow, favored by a number of illustrators of the *Collier's* "school."

In 1936 Beall did a composite portrait of President Franklin D. Roosevelt for a *Collier's* cover which so pleased the President that he appointed Beall art director for the National Democratic Committee.

During World War II, Beall painted the portraits of a number of decorated heroes as covers for *Collier's* magazine. At the close of the war, Beall was one of the privileged few to witness the surrender ceremony aboard the U.S.S. Missouri. His painting of the event was made the official one by President Harry S. Truman.

Beall is a member of the Society of Illustrators; won their Award of Excellence in the 1961 exhibition; also belongs to the American Water Color Society, the Overseas Press Club, the Hudson Valley Art Association, and the Salmagundi Club.

His pictures are included in many collections, including the Air Force Academy Museum in Colorado Springs, Colorado, and the Marine Museum at Quantico, Virginia.

Illustration of President Lincoln posing for the famous photographer, Mathew Brady.

Harry Beckhoff

HARRY BECKHOFF (1901-) begins his pictorial compositions with small sketches that are almost literally thumbnail in size. These tiny drawings contain all of the information needed for the final rendering — even down to facial expressions. He then pantographs the drawing, about five times larger, and inks in the outlines. The tone or color areas are painted in with flat washes.

Beckhoff describes his work as having been influenced by the French illustrators, Martin, Brissaud, and Marty. He also cites his teachers, George Bridgman, Dean Cornwell, and Harvey Dunn for their encouragement and training.

Country Gentleman published his first magazine illustrations in 1929. He subsequently worked for many of the other periodicals, but Beckhoff is most closely associated with the wonderful Broadway characters he drew to illustrate Damon Runyon's famous stories which ran for many years in *Collier's* magazine.

Here is a typical, odd assortment of Beckhoff types for the *Collier's* story, "Man Meets Metronome," in 1940.

Earl Blossom

EARL BLOSSOM (1891-   ) had no formal art instruction but received his training in the practical school of advertising. Some of his early work included drawings for men's fashions, newspaper illustration for the *Chicago American* and a stint as a bull-pen artist in the old Charles Daniel Frey studio in Chicago.

Many of today's largest advertising agencies were getting started in the 'twenties and Blossom, who worked at one time or another for most of them, was kept busy almost day and night during the hectic period of their expansion. He also spent some time promoting the land boom in Florida — wrote and illustrated full-page advertisements for Boca Raton.

Blossom had known Pete Martin earlier in Chicago and under his art direction at *The Saturday Evening Post*, Blossom began to do fiction illustration. He was not entirely happy at the *Post*, however, where "everyone was supposed to imitate Arthur William Brown," and when Martin left the *Post*, Blossom switched to *Collier's* magazine.

William Chessman who was art director at Collier's, encouraged Earl to develop his own humorous bent. Said Chessman, "He is a masterful artist. You never have to tell him what to do. Just give him a good story and let him alone." Blossom responded with that wonderful blend of comedy and realism that has since been his specialty.

Illustration for *Collier's*, "The Worm that Eats its Tail," by Joe Coogan.

FRANK BENSING

FRANK C. BENSING (1893-   ) was born in Chicago, Illinois, and received his art training there at the Art Institute. Among his teachers were De Forrest Schook, Wellington Reynolds, Charles Schroeder, and Walter Biggs.

Bensing's first illustrations were made in 1926 for *Redbook*, an association which continued for many years; he also worked for *McCall's*, *Country Gentleman*, *The Saturday Evening Post*, *American*, *Pictorial Review*, *The American Legion*, and *This Week* magazines.

Bensing has combined his illustration for periodicals with exhibitions of his oils and water colors at the National Academy of Design, the American Water Color Society, Allied Artists, and others. In recent years he has turned increasingly to portraiture.

Bensing is a member of the Dutch Treat Club, Artists and Writers, Allied Artists, Salmagundi Club, the American Water Color Society and the Society of Illustrators.

Illustration for *Pictorial Review*, 1937.

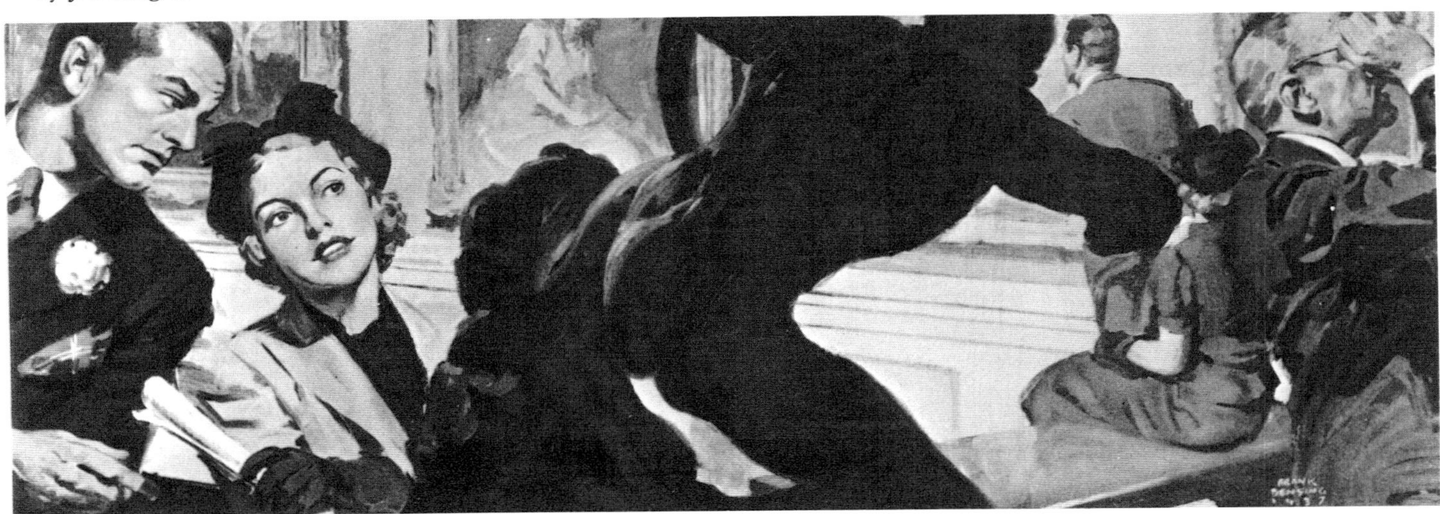

VLADIMIR BOBRITSKY (1898-   ) was a student at the Kharkov Imperial Art School in the Ukraine before the Revolution and had begun to design sets for the Great Dramatic Theatre of Kharkov.

Swept up in the conflict, he fought in several armies, on both sides and eventually, with a passport he forged for himself, managed to escape to Constantinople.

Several years of varied art activities followed — painting Greek icons and playing guitar in a gypsy chorus before Bobri was able to come to America.

His experiences here have been no less varied, ranging from the operation of a textile printing business, to art direction for Saks Fifth Avenue. His newspaper and magazine layouts represented a fresh departure. Bobri soon found himself with enough clients to embark on a free-lance art career, largely for advertising illustration, and strongly influenced by his background of classical training and theatrical designing.

He also has continued his serious study of the guitar both as a composer and performer, is president of the Society of the Classic Guitar in New York and serves as editor of the *Guitar Review*. In recent years he has illustrated a great many children's books.

Illustration for Saks Fifth Avenue advertisement which appeared in *Vogue* magazine, 1934.

Melbourne Brindle

E. MELBOURNE BRINDLE (1904-   ) who was named for his birthplace in Australia, has made a reputation for himself in the United States with his precise and fastidious illustrations.

With no formal training, Brindle progressed through a number of jobs in the San Francisco area, from show-card writing to a department store art department, to affiliation with a large advertising agency.

Although now at home in every medium, he first developed a brilliant black-and-white technique which won him medals in the New York Art Directors Club annual shows in 1935 and 1938.

Brindle began to do editorial illustration for *Woman's Home Companion* in 1940, followed thereafter by commissions from most of the other national magazines. He is especially expert in depicting antique automobiles since he also collects and restores them as a hobby.

Illustrâtion for Sanderson & Porter, Inc., 1939. This pen-and-ink drawing displays the artist's combination of good taste with technical excellence.

Paul Brown

PAUL BROWN (1893-1958) began to draw horses at the age of six; they continued to be his favorite subject to the end of his life. During this time, he wrote 33 books of his own and illustrated over 100 more by other authors.

Brown's knowledge of horses was acquired through continuous study and sketching at polo matches and races until he became so familiar with them that he could draw entirely without models. His specialty was painting horses in sports or in violent action.

He began doing catalog and sporting illustrations for Brooks Brothers in 1920, continuing with them for nearly 40 years. He also illustrated for many of the major magazines, including *Cosmopolitan*, *Collier's*, *Spur*, *Polo*, *Harper's Bazaar*, *Liberty*, *Elks*, and *The American Legion*.

Polo illustration for *Liberty* magazine.

Elmor Brown/64

ELMORE J. BROWN (1899-) illustrated Ernest Hemingway's first published short story, "A Matter of Color," in the *Tabula*, an annual for the Oak Park (Illinois) high school where both were students in 1916.

Brown went on to study at the Chicago Art Institute and the Art Students League in New York. Among his instructors were John Norton, George Bellows, Leopold Seyffert, Leon Kroll and Eugene Speicher.

His first major illustrations, done for the *Ladies' Home Journal* in 1931, were soon followed by work for most of the other magazines. However, his work appeared most regularly in *Collier's* magazine, from 1933 to 1949.

Brown, who has been a keen student of the technical problems of painting, once determined that to obtain Munsell's neutral #5 gray requires .01 of an ounce of black and .3904 of an ounce of white! He also reverses the usual procedure of the traditional school and works from light to dark in accord with his own scientific analysis of the problems of painting.

He is a member of the Artists and Writers Association and a life member of the Society of Illustrators.

Collier's illustration for the story, "Strange Honeymoon," by Octavus Roy Cohen.

A

B

PRUETT CARTER

PRUETT A. CARTER (1891-1955) once described the role of the illustrator in this manner:

> "The illustrator may be likened to the director of a motion picture, or a spoken stage-play. He must know his characters — their emotions and desires — he must set the stage and direct the arrangement and action and conflict of drama. He must live the part of each actor. He must do the scenery, design the costumes and handle the lighting effects. His illustration must be deeper than a poster, for he must make his characters live and breathe and react to each other as the author intended."

For nearly 40 years, Carter fulfilled this role in his work for the leading magazines. Especially, he had the ability to paint women sympathetically; his heroines were noted for their gentle, patrician beauty. Walter Biggs had taught him the use of color; Pruett used his palette with brilliance and taste.

Carter was born in Lexington, Missouri and was reared on an Indian reservation in Wyoming where his father ran a trading post and his mother taught school. The family moved on to California so that Pruett could go to high school there. Upon graduation Carter was encouraged in his art ambitions by James Swinnerton, the cartoonist, creator of "Little Jimmy."

Carter went to the Los Angeles Art School and got his first job on the Hearst *New York American*, was later transferred to the *Atlanta Georgian*.

As a step toward his ambition to become a magazine illustrator, Carter next became art editor for *Good Housekeeping* magazine and, eventually, was able to assign one of the story manuscripts to himself. From then on he worked as a free-lance illustrator.

A vacation trip to California in 1930 became a permanent move. Taking along an assignment from Henry Quinan, art editor of *Woman's Home Companion*, Carter air-mailed the pictures back. He found this to be a practical arrangement, with the addition of long distance telephone conferences.

Carter taught many of today's illustrators, some at the Grand Central School of Art in New York, others at the Chouinard Art Institute in Los Angeles, where he headed the Illustration Department for several years. He is remembered with great affection and respect by all of them.

A. *Woman's Home Companion*, 1935, illustration for "Lucy Gayheart," by Willa Cather.
B. Illustration for *McCall's* magazine, October, 1929.

C. "Nancy Hanks' Lullaby," color illustration for *Ladies' Home Journal.*

A

FREDERICK TRENCH CHAPMAN (1887-) has a strong sense of line and pattern which has logically led to his present eminence in the field of book illustration. He is an acknowledged master of the figure in action and specializes in period costume subjects for which he can utilize his love of historical research.

Notable examples of this talent are seen in his illustrations for the *History of America*, published by D. C. Heath and Company; *Virginia: History, Government, Geography*, published by Charles Scribner's Sons; plates drawn for *The Quarterly, The Company of Military Collectors & Historians*, and the many historical juvenile novels he has illustrated for various publishers.

Chapman is a Californian who studied at the Art Students League of New York with George Bridgman. Some of his early art work was done in collaboration with the Czech artist, Vojtech Preissig, who was an expert printmaker and exponent of the use of the linoleum block.

For a number of years Chapman illustrated for magazines, such as *Everybody's*, *Harper's Bazaar*, *Collier's*, *Liberty*, and *Woman's Home Companion*, but it was the success of his first book, *Voyages to Vinland*, published by Alfred A. Knopf in 1942 that led to his eventual specialization as an illustrator of books.

B

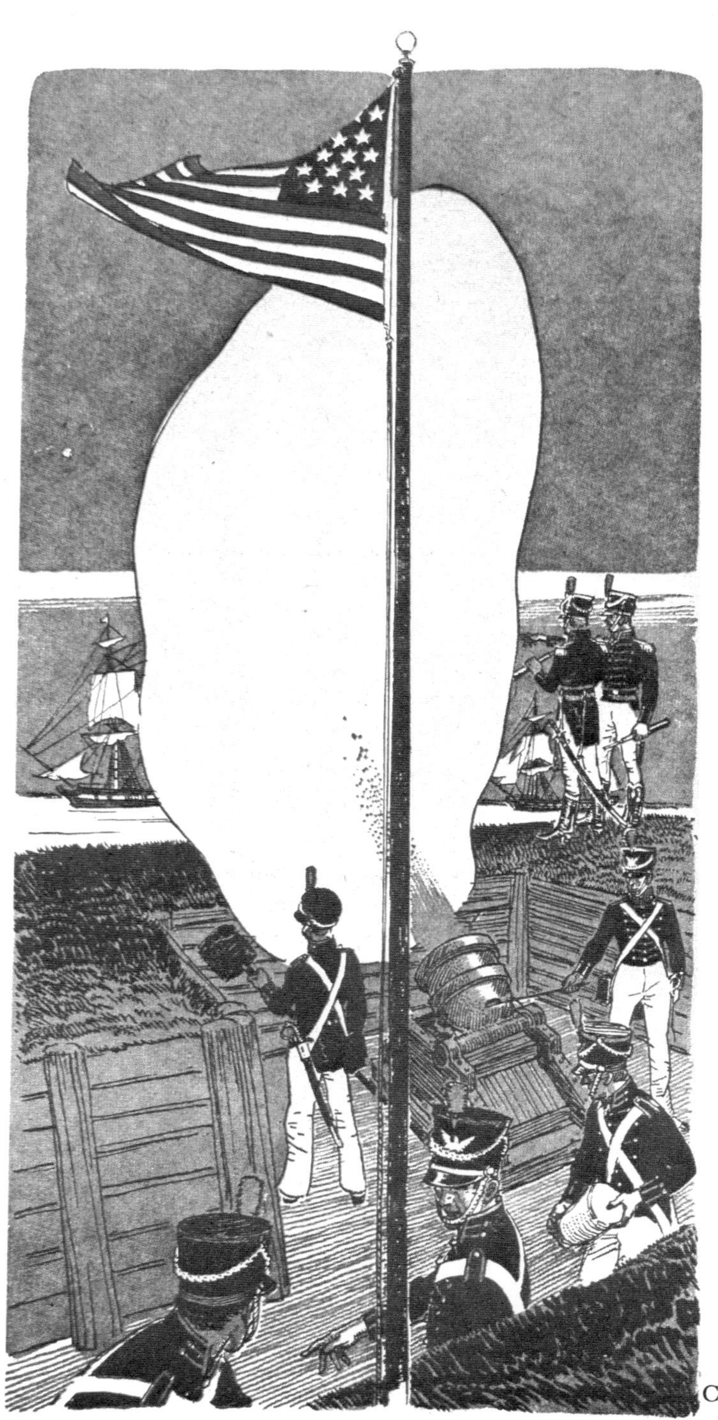

C

A. Line and color illustration for *Woman's Home Companion*.
B. Two color cover illustration, "King John and the Magna Charta," for *American Artist* magazine, March, 1947.
C. Illustration for "Hamilton's Battery," *Bluebook* magazine, July, 1950. Originally printed in red and black ink.

© 1939 by The Curtis Publishing Company.

RALPH PALLEN COLEMAN

Over his long career, RALPH PALLEN COLEMAN (1892-) has illustrated stories by many famous authors, including Somerset Maugham, Rex Beach, F. Scott Fitzgerald, Louis Bromfield, and Clarence Buddington Kelland, for most of the major magazines.

Coleman, who was educated at the Philadelphia Museum School of Industrial Art, has also found time in his busy career to paint many portraits and a number of murals in churches in Jenkintown, Lancaster, and Montoursville, Pennsylvania, and in Wilmington, Delaware. He did a series of paintings depicting the Life of Christ for the George Washington Memorial Park in White Marsh, Pennsylvania.

Illustration for the *Country Gentleman*.

ROY HUSE COLLINS (1883-1949), born in Stone Mills, New York, began early in life to draw animals. Although he illustrated a variety of subjects, editors tended to associate him most with animal stories.

This authority made him a logical choice for the long series of illustrations he did for Calvert Distillers Corporation advertisements. The theme of the pictures, "Nature's Protective Blending," gave Collins the chance to paint a wide variety of animals in settings demonstrating their use of natural camouflage.

Over the years his editorial illustrations appeared in many publications, including *The Saturday Evening Post*, *Collier's*, and *Woman's Home Companion*.

Illustration for "In Coldest New England," by Frederic F. Van de Water in *Woman's Home Companion*, 1936.

Illustration for *The Saturday Evening Post.*

Benton Clark

BENTON CLARK (1895-1964) owed much, as have all subsequent painters of the Old West, to Frederic Remington and his original recording of the period. Benton also greatly admired Harvey Dunn and Frank Hoffman for their work in this locale.

Clark's own contribution is in dramatically synthesizing the era in a robust and colorful way. His illustrations make the past alive and convincing; the picture reproduced here exemplifies his work at its best.

Benton was trained at the Art Institute of Chicago and the art school of the National Academy of Design in New York. His early work was in the Art Department for M.G.M. in Culver City, California; for the Stevens, Sundblom studio and the Kling Studio, both in Chicago.

He first illustrated for *Liberty* magazine in 1927, subsequently for most of the other major magazines, including *The Saturday Evening Post*, *McCall's*, *Cosmopolitan*, and *Good Housekeeping*.

A

B

MATT CLARK (1903-), like his older brother Benton, was born in Coshocton, Ohio. He, too, attended the National Academy Art School in New York and is also an expert in depicting the Old West, particularly horses and their accoutrements, harnesses and buggies. Matt's subjects are in no way restricted to the Old West, however; he is equally at home with contemporary subjects from the farm to urban society.

Although Benton worked almost exclusively in oils, Matt is noted for his masterful use of dry brush, often combined with water color. This medium, because of the underlying black-ink drawing, reproduces exceptionally well, whether in full color or in black and white.

His first illustrations were published by *College Humor* in 1929; he, too, has added nearly all of the other magazines to his list of clients.

A. Here is an example of Matt's expert use of shapes in designing the edges of a vignette. Published by *The Saturday Evening Post*.

B. This illustration in dry brush and water color was originally published in full color by *The Saturday Evening Post* for the story, "Red Wheels Rolling," by Walter D. Edmonds.

Dan Content

The illustrations of DAN CONTENT (1902-) retain the strong stamp of his teacher, Dean Cornwell. A precocious student, Content also studied at Pratt Institute and the Art Students League of New York. He sold his first illustration at the age of 21 to *McCall's* magazine.

Stories of high adventure predominate among his illustrations for such magazines as *Cosmopolitan, Good Housekeeping, Liberty, Ladies' Home Journal, Collier's,* and *Woman's Home Companion.*

Content taught at the Work Shop School of Art in 1947-48 and in recent years has been affiliated with an advertising marketing firm in New York City.

Illustration reprinted by permission of *Good Housekeeping* magazine, © 1933 by the Hearst Corporation.

Grattan Condon

GRATTAN CONDON (1887-1966) is perhaps best-known for his illustrations of stories of World War I although he could draw other subjects equally well. Many of his illustrations were rendered in charcoal and have a freely drawn effect as though done directly at the scene; it is this quality that makes his war subjects convincing.

Condon was born in Eugene, Oregon, and studied at both the Los Angeles School of Art and Design and the Art Students League of Los Angeles. Among his teachers were Walter Biggs and Lewis Daniel.

An illustrator, painter, and educator, Condon was a member of the Society of Illustrators and the Salmagundi Club in New York City.

Illustration for the story, "Under Arrest," by Franklin M. Reck, *American Boy-Youth's Companion*, May, 1931.

Illustration for *Collier's story*, "Beautifully and Bravely," by Harry Sylvester in 1939.

MARIO
COOPER

MARIO RUBEN COOPER, N.A. (1905-   ) has had several careers in the field of art, each pursued with great enthusiasm and marked by excellence.

Born in Mexico City of Mexican-American parentage, he was reared in Los Angeles and received his education there at the Otis Art Institute and Chouinard Art Institute. He later attended the Grand Central School of Art and Columbia University in New York. Among his teachers were Pruett Carter and Harvey Dunn – Dunn especially influencing his philosophy and point of view.

Cooper was at various times employed in an engraving house, and as a visualizer for Batten, Barton, Durstine and Osborne; as art director for Lord and Taylor, and as an expert layout man and letterer, before finally obtaining his first commission for an illustration from *Collier's* magazine.

As an illustrator, Cooper is noted for the dramatic concepts of his pictures combined with a meticulous rendering, usually in colored inks on illustration board. His work has appeared in many national magazines but is most closely identified with *Collier's* and other Crowell-Collier publications.

Cooper himself has taught illustration at the Grand Central School of Art, Columbia University, National Academy, Art Students League, City College of New York, and a class for returned veterans after World War II at the Society of Illustrators.

He has also been an active water colorist, President of the American Water Color Society and is the author of a book, *Flower Painting in Water Color*, published in 1962 by Reinhold.

A parallel interest of his has been sculpture. He studied under Oronzio Maldarelli, and has executed a number of commissions for churches and other institutions.

A long-time member of the Society of Illustrators, and National Sculpture Society, he is also a past president of the Audubon Artists.

© 1934 by The Curtis Publishing Company.

Robt. W. Crowther

ROBERT W. CROWTHER (1902-) works in charcoal from which he obtains a full range of values from rich blacks to crisp whites. Note how effectively, in the illustration here, he has used maximum contrasts to center the viewer's attention on the burning document.

Crowther was born in Philadelphia and attended both the Pennsylvania Museum School of Industrial Art and the Pennsylvania Academy of the Fine Arts, then also studied under Thornton Oakley. He taught at the Pennsylvania Museum School of Industrial Art from 1926-1928.

His first illustrations appeared in the *Lutheran Young Folks* magazine in 1924; eventually he worked for most of the major publications, including *The Saturday Evening Post, Country Gentleman, Farm Journal, Liberty, Cosmopolitan, Pictorial Review, McCall's* and *Good Housekeeping.*

Illustration for a J. P. Marquand story, "Davy Jones," in *The Saturday Evening Post.*

Bradshaw Crandell

BRADSHAW CRANDELL (1896-1966) took over the *Cosmopolitan* cover where Harrison Fisher left off. For a period of twelve years, in the 'thirties and 'forties, he did a continuing series of beautiful girls' heads in pastels for their monthly covers. Many top Hollywood stars and young starlets of that time were his models.

Crandell was born in Glens Falls, New York, educated at Wesleyan University and the Chicago Art Institute. He sold his first cover to *Judge* magazine in 1921 and from then on concentrated on cover designs for such other publications as *Collier's, Redbook, American, Ladies' Home Journal,* and *The Saturday Evening Post.*

For several years he had confined his work to portraiture, painted the governors of various states and many prominent society figures.

He was a member of the Society of Illustrators, the Artists and Writers Association and the Dutch Treat Club.

Cover design in full-color pastels for *Cosmopolitan* magazine in 1936.

J. H. CROSMAN-

JOHN HENRY CROSMAN (1897-) began his career in illustration in the 'twenties as a brilliant performer in pen and ink. In the 'thirties, however, tastes in illustration changed considerably, and the pen-and-ink medium was no longer popular with the magazine reading public. Crosman then successfully changed his technique to half-tone, working occasionally in water color or wash, but usually with Russian charcoal.

For over 20 years Crosman illustrated for most of the major publications including *Collier's*, *Woman's Home Companion*, *Ladies' Home Journal*, *The Saturday Evening Post*, *American*, and *Good Housekeeping*, but now confines his work to portraiture.

Born in Swampscott, Massachusetts, he attended the Massachusetts Normal Art School in Boston studying under Richard Andrew and Ernest Major. He has also done some teaching and is a member of the Guild of Boston Artists.

Illustration in pen and ink, published as a halftone with a tint block of yellow in the *Woman's Home Companion*, 1928.

N. EGGENHOFER

NICK EGGENHOFER (1897-) was born in Gauting, Bavaria. As a young boy he was fascinated by stories of Buffalo Bill and other heroes of the American Wild West. He also greatly admired the drawings and paintings of Frederic Remington and Charles Russell which were reproduced in German publications.

By the time he arrived in the United States at the age of 16, he had decided to become a Western artist himself. He studied nights at Cooper Union and thoroughly immersed himself in the subject by making exact scale models of wagons, stagecoaches, harnesses, and other authentic props.

In *Western Story*, pulp magazine of Street & Smith, he found a ready and voracious market for all the drawings he could produce for years. He illustrated for other magazines, also, and many books to which his dry-brush black-and-white drawings are ideally suited. He wrote and illustrated his own book, *Wagons, Mules and Men*, published by Hastings House in 1961.

Eggenhofer now makes his home in Wyoming and paints Western subjects which have been exhibited widely in the West and in the Kennedy Galleries in New York.

Reprinted from Street & Smith's *Western Story* magazine.

A. Typical gallery of hill-billy characters for a *Saturday Evening Post* story.

B. This painting tellingly epitomizes the British spirit under the ordeal of bombing during World War II.

B

C

D

FLOYD MACMILLAN DAVIS (1896-1966) gives much of the credit for the success of his pictures to the critical judgment of his wife, painter Gladys Rockmore Davis. Floyd Davis' point of view, however, is uniquely his own. His visual world is peopled by a gallery of wonderful characters depicted with poetic realism and warm humor. The wealth of detail in his pictures would seem to have required much study from models or photos of them. In fact, Davis does not use models at all but relies instead on his remarkably retentive memory and lively imagination.

In his early years he did a lot of advertising illustration notable for the fragile beauty and lofty hauteur of the society types he drew.

In the 'thirties, however, Davis began to illustrate stories of humbler subjects. His pictures of southern rural and hill people for such authors as William Faulkner, Sigman Byrd, Glenn Allan, and MacKinlay Kantor became immensely popular. He loved these assignments and filled the pictures not only with a fascinating cast of individuals, but added the special Davis touches, a cat crouched in the corner ready to leap out at a rival, a fly on an old man's head, a small lizard hiding behind a tree while a dice game is in progress. None of these details intrude on the picture story itself — they are there for the perceptive viewer to discover. Readers responded enthusiastically; his pictures were admired as much as the stories themselves.

With the outbreak of World War II, Davis was selected as a correspondent-artist for the War Department and painted in various war theatres. Many of these distinguished paintings were reproduced by *Life* magazine as part of a pictorial record of the war and now hang in the Pentagon building in Washington, D. C.

Over the years, Davis has won several Art Directors Club medals and other awards, but more important than this, his work has had the admiration of his whole profession. Floyd Davis is one of the great figures of American illustration.

C. *Saturday Evening Post* illustration for "Last Act, Last Scene," by Almet Jenks.
D. Early Davis illustration for Hupmobile advertisement, 1929.

B

Eric

A

CARL OSCAR AUGUST ERICKSON (1891-1958) dominated the field of fashion illustration for over 35 years. His virtuosity of line and tone was combined with innate elegance and taste. Eric's work looks deceptively effortless, but dozens of preliminary attempts often were discarded before a final direct and spontaneous effect was ready for his signature.

Eric's birthplace was Joliet, Illinois; his formal art training limited to two years at the Chicago Academy of Fine Arts. This was followed by work for Marshall Field, Lord & Thomas, and other advertising accounts in Chicago until 1914, when he moved to New York City.

In New York, he continued advertising illustration, and did his first fashion drawings for the *Dry Goods Economist*. In 1920, Eric made his initial trip to Paris where he felt a total rapport; for the next 20 years it was his second home. During that period he illustrated for French publications, and did society portraits. Beginning in 1923, he became a staff illustrator for *Vogue* magazine. In 1940 he returned to America, continuing his work for Condé Nast, and began illustrating for American, rather than French, advertisers.

Himself the personification of his elegant world, Eric wore a bowler and carried a walking stick, directly participating in the fashionable life of the international set.

His drawings and paintings are authentic because he knew his subjects and their world; his taste and beautiful draughtsmanship reveal him to be an artist of permanent importance.

The Brooklyn Museum held a retrospective show of his drawings in 1959 shortly after his death.

A. Cover illustration for *Vogue* magazine.

B. "Paris Side Show — Bal Tabarin," for *Vogue* magazine.

© 1935 by The Curtis Publishing Company.

Harland Frazer

HARLAND FRAZER, a very talented painter, was a member of the St. Louis Art Guild, winning the Mallinckrodt Portrait Prize in 1921 and the First Figure Prize in 1922.

Frazer's illustrations for magazine editors and advertisers were also painted in the full richness of academic style and color. Influenced by the work of Frank Brangwyn, Edwin Austin Abbey and Henry Raleigh, Frazer's work exemplifies many of the best qualities of each. Some of his most notable pictures were painted for the Packard Motor Car Company, as a series depicting the history of transportation.

Frazer was equally at home in other media, as demonstrated by this charcoal illustration for *The Saturday Evening Post* story, "Stocketeer," by Thomas McMorrow.

FLOHERTY JR

JOHN J. FLOHERTY, JR. (1907-), as a World War II combat artist, covered the initial invasions of Iwo Jima and Okinawa and did over 350 pictures in three years as a Chief Petty Officer in the U. S. Coast Guard. He also produced many Coast Guard posters for the U. S. Treasury Department.

Born in New York City, educated at St. Paul's School and Columbia University, Floherty got his art training at the Art Students League and the Grand Central School of Art with Harvey Dunn.

His first illustrations were for *The New Yorker* magazine in 1931, followed thereafter by a long list of commissions for national magazines and book publishers. In addition, he has done much work for Paramount Pictures; made reportorial drawings of Army life as a member of the Seventh Regiment, New York; drawings of life at sea and in port as a freighter seaman. He also has exhibited drawings of prison life in Arkansas, sketched during an Ozark painting trip.

Floherty is a life-member of the Society of Illustrators, and artist-member of the Coast Guard Advisory Committee.

Illustration for a *Collier's* magazine story, 1951

Drawing by Galbraith; Copyright © 1935, 1963, The New Yorker Magazine, Inc.

John Fulton

JOHN RUSSELL FULTON was a studio artist who did advertising illustrations for several years but is best remembered for his association with two periodicals, *Redbook* and *Blue Book*.

His *Redbook* illustrations in oils, were in the manner of Harvey Dunn, strong and well composed, but it was in *Blue Book* that he developed his own individual approach. *Blue Book's* masculine, swashbuckling subject matter gave Fulton an opportunity to use dramatic action and a much freer technique. He developed a method of working back and forth in black and white on a rough white ground which allowed good reproduction in line, yet produced a rich halftone quality. Oftentimes he used a second color, also in line, to heighten the dramatic effect.

Illustration for a Sax Rohmer story, "Kiss of the Scorpion," *Blue Book* magazine, 1951.

Galbraith

WILLIAM GALBRAITH CRAWFORD (1894-) is best known for the humor and drawings of his widely syndicated panel cartoon, "Side Glances," which he drew for 23 years. A prolific and facile draughtsman, Galbraith had extensive experience prior to this as an illustrator for such publications as *The Saturday Evening Post*, *Vanity Fair*, *The New Yorker*, *Harper's Bazaar*, *Cosmopolitan*, and *Delineator* magazines.

Crawford was born in Salt Lake City, Utah, and attended Brigham Young University for two years. This was followed by instruction at the New York Art Students League, the Los Angeles School of Art and Design, and the University of Mexico. Among his teachers were Mahonri Young, Thomas Fogarty, Edward Dufner, and Henry Wolf.

"Of course, if the worst comes to the worst, I can always fall back on my art or on Mr. Bergstrom." Drawing for *The New Yorker* magazine.

Georgi

EDWIN A. GEORGI (1896-1964) was studying civil engineering at Princeton when World War I broke out. He volunteered and served as a pilot in the U.S. Air Force.

After the war, Georgi took his first job doing paste-ups in an advertising agency art department and began his practical training as an artist.

His early illustrations were for advertisers. Over the years, he did a number of notable series for such clients as Hartford Fire Insurance, Crane Paper Co., Hockanum Woolens, and Yardley & Co.

Georgi's ability to depict beautiful women and sumptuous settings also brought him story manuscripts; he was soon illustrating for most of the national magazines. His use of color was lavish and dramatic, giving his pictures great impact on the printed page.

Illustration for a *Saturday Evening Post* mystery story, "Date with Death," by Leslie Ford.

Grafstrom

RUTH SIGRID GRAFSTROM (1905-) was born in Rock Island, Illinois, and studied at the Art Institute of Chicago and at the Colorossi Academy in Paris, with Henri Morriset.

A fashion artist for *Vogue* magazine from 1930 to 1940 in the New York, Paris, and London offices, she has also done free-lance advertising illustrations for Saks Fifth Avenue, the Matson Line, and various fabric, cosmetic, and clothing manufacturers.

This work led to fiction assignments for magazines such as *Delineator, Cosmopolitan,* and *Woman's Home Companion,* involving fashionable people and backgrounds. Miss Grafstrom's work is marked by sophistication and good drawing which won her many awards and citations in annual exhibitions of the New York Art Directors Club. She has also been a member of the Society of Illustrators in New York.

"The Beaux Arts Ball," an illustration in pastels for Spud cigarettes, 1932.

GOTLIEB

JULES GOTLIEB (1897-   ) has traveled in many out-of-the-way parts of the world, from North Africa to the jungles of Dutch Guiana, collecting background material for his illustrations. He has also accumulated a library of over 2,000 volumes for reference in doing historical illustrations for nearly every national magazine, including *Collier's, Cosmopolitan, Redbook, American, Woman's Home Companion, Liberty, This Week, Ladies' Home Journal,* and for several books.

A native New Yorker, Gotlieb studied at the National Academy School of Fine Arts, the Pennsylvania Academy at Chester Springs and the Art Students League. Among his teachers were George Bridgman and Harvey Dunn. He later taught at the League himself from 1932 to 1934.

Illustration for "Conqueror," by Arthur Howden Smith for *Redbook* magazine, 1933.

Reproduced, courtesy of National Life Insurance Co., Montpelier, Vermont.

RFH

ROY FREDERIC HEINRICH (1881-1943) was best known for his series of Vermont historical illustrations and had completed exactly 100 of them at the time of his death. The drawings, made with litho-crayon, are noted for their authenticity of detail and spirit, as well as originality of concept.

Heinrich was born in Indiana, reared in New York State; studied at the Connecticut League of Art Students under Charles Noel Flagg. His first work was for a small Sunday newspaper. In 1910 he moved to Detroit, as one of the earliest automobile illustrators, where his clients included Graham-Paige, Packard, Ford, Chevrolet, Buick, Dodge, Chrysler, and Cadillac. He also illustrated for many other advertising accounts.

Of all his assignments, however, Heinrich most enjoyed doing the pictures of early Vermont. These were exhibited widely in galleries in New York and New England, shown at the Vermont building at the New York World's Fair (1939-40). They were published in book form, of which several hundred thousand were furnished by the advertiser to fill requests from schools and individuals all over the country.

"French and Indians prepare to sack Deerfield, Mass., 1704."

W EMERTON HEITLAND

WILMOT EMERTON HEITLAND, N.A. (1893-) is a master water colorist — his paintings of Barbados, particularly, rival the directness and vigor of Winslow Homer.

His illustrations also have the same quality of strength, the water color reinforced by a bold outline, with emphasis on composition and rich color.

Heitland was born in Superior, Wisconsin, studied at the Pennsylvania Academy of the Fine Arts, won the Cresson traveling scholarship in 1913, attended the Colarossi School in Paris, and the Art Students League in New York. His teachers included Arthur Covey, Harvey Dunn, and Walter Biggs.

He first illustrated for *Collier's Weekly* in 1922. This was followed by work for *Cosmopolitan, McCall's, Woman's Home Companion, Delineator*, and other magazines. Both his illustrations and exhibition water colors have won many awards, and his work is represented in several museums, including the Brooklyn Museum, Art Institute of Chicago, and Philadelphia Museum of Art. He has also taught at the Art Students League, Pennsylvania Academy Summer School, and the Philadelphia Museum School of Art.

This illustration for *Woman's Home Companion* in 1936 shows Heitland's typical use of line and pattern.

D.H.

DAVID HENDRICKSON (1896-), born in St. Paul, Minnesota, won a scholarship there to attend the St. Paul Institute of Art. He later studied at l'Ecole des Beaux-Arts at Toulouse, France, Grand Central School of Art, and the Art Students League of New York. Among his teachers were Harvey Dunn, Dean Cornwell, and George Bridgman.

Beginning in 1913 with his first art job for the *St. Paul Dispatch & Pioneer Press*, Hendrickson has since had a long and varied career, illustrating for periodicals, advertisers, book publishers, and has exhibited widely.

Hendrickson's special ability is to portray the rural American scene, sympathetically, truthfully and without artifice. His direct, vigorous pictures are, basically, in line, sometimes with washes of tone or color added.

He has been a member of the Artists' Guild, Society of American Etchers and Graphic Artists, Society of Illustrators, Phillips Mill Artists, New Hope, Pennsylvania, and the Palo Alto Art Club in California, where he also taught from 1948 to 1951.

Illustration for *The Three Black Pennys*, by Joseph Hergesheimer. Published by Alfred A. Knopf Inc., 1930.

A. Painting for General Electric calendar 1947 showing copper-mining in Utah. Selected for New York Art Directors Club Exhibition, 1947.

B. Helck's spectacular painting shows the Bessemer "blow" as impurities are burned away in a furious burst of gas and flame. Reproduced, courtesy of National Steel Corporation.

C

C. This painting for *True* magazine of the 1908 French Grand Prix shows Helck's ability to recreate authentically the setting and excitement as well as the mechanical details of the early days of racing.
D. Illustration for a *Saturday Evening Post* story.

D

Peter Helck

CLARENCE PETER HELCK, N.A. (1893-) has spent his life painting a record of man's work. He has made this basic theme a monumental one in his pictures, whether it be a giant foundry, an open pit mine, or a dramatic moment in an historic automobile race.

Peter came by his love for automobiles as a boy when he saw some of the early racing competitions. He eventually came to know many of the drivers and their giant racing cars intimately. These later became the inspiration for his illustrated book, *The Checkered Flag*. He himself owns a number of old automobiles, including "number 16," the famous Locomobile which won the Vanderbilt Cup Race in 1908.

Helck studied at the Art Students League of New York and privately with many distinguished teachers, including Frank Brangwyn in England. In addition to a complete artistic competence, he has a great capacity for hard work, as evidenced in the preliminary, thinking stages of his pictures. The nature of his subject matter demands a thorough mechanical knowledge, including the parts that do not appear in the picture itself. His working drawings which precede the finished paintings are completely worked out even down to the placement of bolts or rivets. The endpapers of this book reproduce one of his preliminary studies for a painting to illustrate the dismantling of a steam locomotive for scrap — a sad theme for Helck who has great nostalgic love for their now obsolete construction.

Helck's rare combination of artistry and factual know-how has for many years made him the dominant figure in this field. He has won very many medals and awards in art directors' exhibitions. He has illustrated for almost every national magazine; his advertising clients have been the industrial giants, General Electric, Chevrolet, Mack Trucks, National Steel Corporation, and numerous others.

Helck makes no distinction between the pictures he paints on commission from magazines or advertisers and those for exhibition. During his whole career, he has exhibited regularly and won awards. His pictures are owned by collectors and museums, including The Metropolitan Museum of Art, The Carnegie Institute of Technology, and the Library of Congress. He is a member of the founding faculty of the Famous Artists Schools in Westport, Connecticut.

Edwin Henry

EDWIN HENRY was primarily an advertising illustrator, his career coinciding with the tremendous growth of advertising art in the 'twenties and 'thirties. As a partner in the Chicago advertising art service of Stevens, Sundblom and Henry, he did illustrations for many of the largest national accounts, including Studebaker, Packard, Procter & Gamble, Camel and Chesterfield cigarettes, Kohler of Kohler, Graybar Electric, Postum, Quaker Oats, and others. He painted editorial illustrations for most of the major magazines as well, his work marked by sensitivity and very effective use of color.

Henry was born in Mt. Sterling, Kentucky, and studied at the National Academy of Design in New York. He later taught illustration at the Studio School and the American Academy in Chicago as well as at the Grand Central School of Art in New York. He was also a member of the Artists' Guild and the New York Society of Illustrators.

Although not reproduced in color here, this advertising illustration from the 'twenties displays Henry's full command of oil technique.

Everett Henry

E. EVERETT HENRY (1893-1961) was an advertising artist during much of his career, which began in the 'twenties, and illustrated for many advertising campaigns.

Henry brought to his work a thorough academic training through study at the Art Students League, the School of Fine and Applied Art, New York University, and Columbia University. He also did some teaching at the School of Fine and Applied Art in New York.

In 1935 he painted murals for the Ford Company Building at the San Diego Fair. This led to many other mural commissions, several of which he executed in collaboration with Allen Saalburg and Louis Bouché. These included decorations for 12 clubcars for the Pennsylvania Railroad, designs in the Westinghouse Building, the U. S. Government Building, and the Building Service Center at the New York World's Fair of 1939-40. He has also painted both murals and easel pictures for private collectors, and is represented in the permanent collection of the Whitney Museum.

One of Henry's book illustrations for *Frankenstein*, published by The Limited Editions Club in 1934.

The illustrations of R. JOHN HOLMGREN (1897-1963) were characterized by a fresh, youthful outlook and bright color. He managed, over a long span of years, to keep his fiction heroines looking contemporary, beginning with the pert flappers on his first cover illustrations for the old *Life* and *Judge* magazines in the 'twenties.

Holmgren was born in St. Paul, Minnesota, and studied at the St. Paul Art Institute before going to New York in 1919 to study at the Art Students League under C. O. Woodbury, George Bridgman, Robert Henri, and Frederic R. Gruger.

His illustrations appeared in most of the national magazines and for many advertisers, including Chevrolet, Ford, Alcoa, White Rock, and Cunard Lines.

A long-time member of the Society of Illustrators, Holmgren was its president from 1941 to 1944. He was also a member of the Dutch Treat and Artists and Writers Clubs.

Reproduced from a full-color illustration for *Collier's* magazine in 1945.

G H

GEORGE HOWE, originally HAUTHALER, (1896-1941) was born in Salzburg, Austria. He ran away from home at the age of 14, visited the United States, then went to France where he studied art for two years before returning to America to stay.

He had to work at all kinds of jobs, from dishwashing and chauffeuring to painting scenery for a motion picture studio, before he was eventually able to realize his ambition of illustrating for the magazines.

Howe painted almost exclusively with water color, treated in a flat, poster style, similar to that of Ludwig Hohlwein of Munich, Germany. For many years his work was associated with the Crowell-Collier publications: *Collier's, American*, and *Woman's Home Companion,* although he also illustrated for others, such as *Elks,* and *Good Housekeeping.*

From one of George Howe's last major projects, a series of paintings commissioned by Norman Bel Geddes, used as posters for the Barnum and Bailey Circus.

A

WILLIAM JAMES DUFAULT (1892-1942) was born in Great Falls, Montana, of French-Canadian parentage. His mother died when he was a year old, and his father was killed by a rampaging steer three years later. Thus Will was orphaned at the age of four and was brought up by a Montana fur-trapper, who taught him to read and write. The trapper drowned when Will was 13 and from that time on he took care of himself, hiring out as a cowhand and rodeo rider.

Will James' introduction to art was quite by chance. Harold Von Schmidt was conducting a painting class at the California School of Fine Arts in San Francisco and advertised for a cowboy model. James, just then in the city with a shipment of cattle, answered it and was hired. During the course of posing sessions, Will brought in some of his own crude drawings, and Von Schmidt recognized in them an observation and knowledge of animal anatomy which showed great promise. Through the encouragement and criticism of both Von Schmidt and Maynard Dixon, another fine painter of the West who was a co-instructor, James was able to sell his first drawings to *Sunset* magazine.

A year later he sold a short story with his own illustrations to *Scribner's* magazine. The combination of true-to-life Western story and drawings was an immediate success and was followed by several more. His first book appeared in 1924. He was awarded the Newberry medal by the American Library Association for his book, *Smoky*. Both *Smoky* and another book, *Lone Cowboy*, were made into films. Altogether he wrote and illustrated 20 books and many short stories.

A. No one could dramatize the explosive, twisting action of horses better than James who learned his subject from the saddle, in competition as a rodeo rider. From *Scorpion – A Good Bad Horse*.
B. Spot illustration for *Smoky*.

B

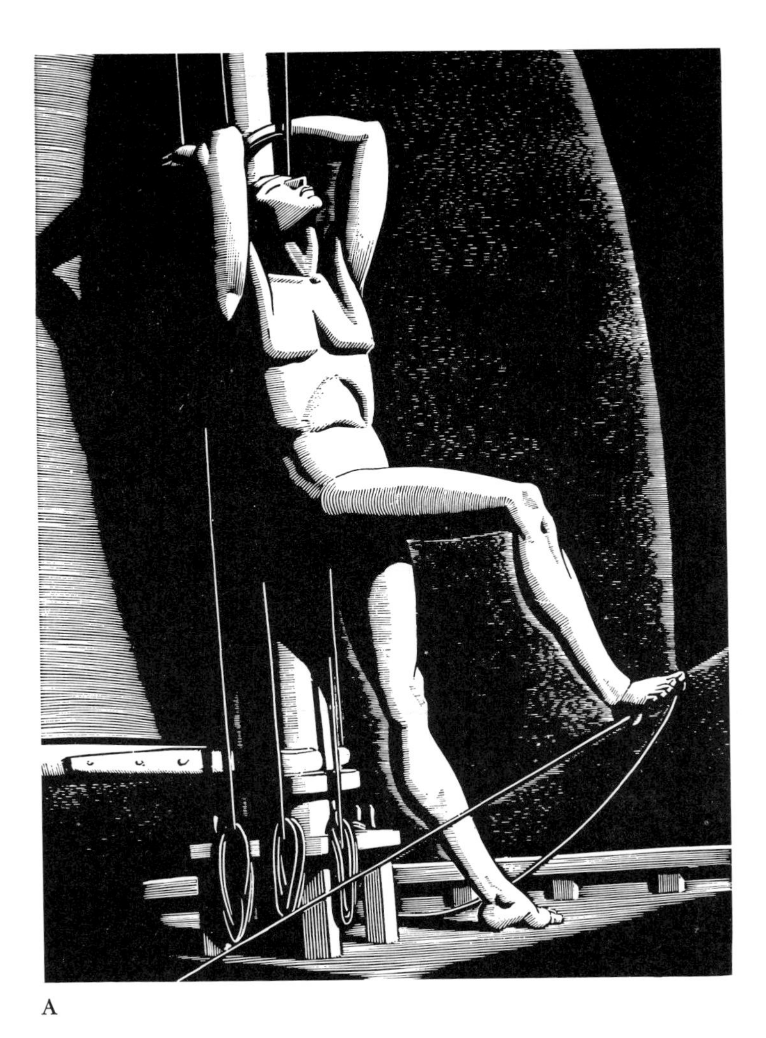

A

Rockwell Kent

ROCKWELL KENT, A.N.A. (1882-   ) has won fame outside of illustration, as an engraver, lithographer, mural painter, writer, and lecturer.

As an illustrator; Kent is equally noted for his own books, *Wilderness, Voyaging, N. by E., Salamina, This is My Own,* and for those of others, such as *Candide, Moby Dick, Leaves of Grass,* and *Canterbury Tales.*

Kent has also made a great many distinguished illustrations for advertisers, among them Marcus & Company, Jewelers; Steinway & Sons; Rolls-Royce, and American Car and Foundry Company. Some of his advertising and humorous pictures are signed "Hogarth, Jr."

Born in Tarrytown Heights, New York, Kent studied art with Robert Henri, Abbott Thayer, and William Chase. Much of his work is based on personal experiences in his travels to such remote areas as Greenland, Alaska, and Patagonia.

A. An Art Directors Club Medal was awarded to Kent in 1931 for this striking line drawing for A.C.F. Industries, Inc.
B. Illustration for *Moby Dick,* published by Random House, 1930.
C., D. Chapter headings from Kent's *N. by E.* published by Brewer and Warren in 1930.

B

C

D

STEVEN R. KIDD (1911-   ) has illustrated for the Sunday fiction page of the *New York News-Chicago Tribune*, coast-to-coast syndicate, for over 30 years. Despite their transitory life, Kidd lavishes on these illustrations the same artistry and design that distinguish his work for magazine and book publishers.

Kidd's versatile pen line can be decorative or realistic, bold or delicate. Over the years he has successfully coped with every possible pictorial subject and historical period, his conceptions always original and arresting.

Kidd was born in Chicago, Illinois, and attended the Chicago Art Institute there. Coming to New York, he studied at the Art Students League with George Bridgman and, for ten years, with Harvey Dunn at the Grand Central School of Art. He was only 18 when he did his first illustrations for a pulp magazine, *Two Gun Western Stories*.

During World War II, he was an official Army war artist, illustrated leaflets for psychological warfare and covered the occupation of Korea for the Historical Section of the War Department. Many of these oil- and water-color paintings hang in the Pentagon, have been on exhibit in the White House and in traveling shows, and were reproduced in *Life* magazine at the outbreak of the Korean War. He has since painted illustrations of United States air activities in the West for the Air Force Historical Museum.

Kidd is a member of the Society of Illustrators, has taught for three years at the Newark School of Fine and Industrial Art in New Jersey and currently teaches at the Art Students League in New York.

Newspaper illustration in 1936 for *New York News* Syndicate Co., Inc.

Klett.

WALTER CHARLES KLETT (1897-   ) specializes in painting glamorous women for the reason, as he puts it, that Rubens, Velasquez, or Botticelli preferred to paint beautiful females rather than ugly ones. He has painted portraits of many celebrated women including Gladys Swarthout, Mrs. William Woodward, Mrs. Jansen Noyes, Alicia Markova, Vera Zorina, and Bidu Sayao.

Klett, who has been a painter for both magazine illustration and for the galleries, brings a contemporary approach to each. His fiction illustrations have appeared in most of the national magazines, and he has designed and executed numerous campaigns for national advertisers. He has also exhibited in many museums and galleries, including the Pennsylvania Academy, Farargil Gallery, Reinhardt Gallery, The Metropolitan Museum of Art, Grand Central Art Galleries, and at shows of the Art Directors Club of New York.

Born in St. Louis, Klett attended the St. Louis School of Fine Arts, Washington University, and made study trips to France, England, Italy, Switzerland and Germany.

He is the author of a popular book, *Figure Painting*, published by Watson-Guptill and has taught portrait and figure painting for ten years at Pratt Institute in Brooklyn, New York. For two years he taught an advanced class in illustration.

Alicia Markova, reproduced from *Collier's* magazine.

CLAYTON KNIGHT

CLAYTON KNIGHT (1891-) brings a lifetime of knowledge and authority to his aviation illustrations. During World War I, he joined the U. S. Army Air Service which was attached to the Royal Flying Corps in France, was shot down and taken prisoner by the Germans, and spent many months in hospitals recovering from his wounds.

After the war, Knight returned to an illustration career for books and magazine stories or articles about flying. To keep pace with the rapid changes in aviation, he made frequent flying junkets of his own and was a guest of the Army and Navy during their annual maneuvers.

Prior to United States' entry into World War II, Knight headed a committee which assisted American flyers in joining the Canadian and Royal Air Force during the critical Battle of Britain. He himself was combat historian for the 8th, 11th, and 20th Air Forces, covered the Aleutians, Alaska, and the Pacific. He also attended the historic ceremony of Japan's surrender on the U.S.S. Missouri, at the end of the war.

Knight was born in Rochester, New York, and studied at the Art Institute of Chicago. Among his teachers were Robert Henri and George Bellows. He is married to Katherine Sturges, a well known advertising artist; their son, Hilary Knight, is a contemporary illustrator of children's books.

"The Top Man Wins." Illustration from Knight's book, *Pilot's Luck*, published by David McKay Co. 1929.

LARRY B. KRITCHER (1900-) spent 11 years on the editorial side of the desk as a *Saturday Evening Post* associate art director assigning manuscripts to other illustrators, only an occasional one to himself. In 1943, he turned to a full-time, free-lance illustration career and was subsequently kept busy by the *Post* and other publications.

Kritcher was born in McKeesport, Pennsylvania, studied at Carnegie Institute of Technology in Pittsburgh and the Pennsylvania Academy of the Fine Arts in Philadelphia where he was awarded a Cresson Scholarship to study and travel in Europe for two years.

Kritcher returned to America just in time for the 1929 stock market collapse and found that the art market had disappeared with it. Newly married, he and his wife tried to sit out the Depression in southern France, but after a year they returned to the United States, determined to find work, and in 1932 he joined the *Post* staff. This was valuable experience for gaining an insight into the requirements of illustration from the magazine's point of view; Kritcher's illustrations are always directly to the point, explicit and competent.

Illustration for *The Saturday Evening Post*.

C. Here LaGatta managed to keep his heroine glamorous even while illustrating "I was a Homely Girl," for the *Ladies' Home Journal.*

JOHN LAGATTA (1894-) shows a full appreciation of the female figure in his illustrations. In even the most decorously dressed of his models, the clothes appear to reveal the figure rather than to hide it. Millions of readers would have had it no other way. Probably no illustrator in the 'thirties was more popular or did a greater number of pictures, both for advertising and editorial.

In spite of his emphasis on the figure, there is no overtone of suggestiveness in LaGatta's work. The women are painted in frank admiration of their beauty — colorful, curvaceous, vital — in the same spirit as Rubens' more buxom, but very female, nudes.

LaGatta, was born in Naples, Italy, but received his education in America, studying under Kenneth Hayes Miller and Frank Alvah Parsons at the New York School of Fine and Applied Art. His first work was in advertising and much of his early work shows the influence of Drian, the famous French illustrator.

Later, as he developed his own personal style, LaGatta's work was in tremendous demand. He worked for nearly a decade to the limit of his capacities in supplying all the magazines that competed for his pictures. Since the 'forties, LaGatta has continued to do a curtailed amount of illustration but has found a new career in his enthusiasm for teaching at the Art Center School in Los Angeles, California.

A. Advertising illustration for Chase and Sanborn Coffee.

Courtesy of Standard Brands.

B. Illustration for *The Saturday Evening Post*.

CHARLES LASALLE

Illustration in charcoal for *The Saturday Evening Post* story, "To Stay the Night," by Dorothy Thomas.

Illustration for "Dan'l Come to Judgment," by Ben Ames Williams in *The Saturday Evening Post*.

CHARLES LOUIS LASALLE (1894-1958) was a classmate of Harold Anderson and of Arthur Fuller at the Fenway Art School in Boston. He and Anderson later had studios together at the Beaux Arts Studio in New York and then in New Rochelle.

LaSalle who was born in Wakefield, Massachusetts, first worked as a bull-pen artist in the Snow Advertising Agency in Boston. His early work, in emulation of F. R. Gruger and Henry Raleigh, was in Wolfe pencil. He later began to use charcoal and developed a mastery of the medium in his own style. His first magazine illustrations were for *Boy's Life*, and he was soon working for *The Saturday Evening Post*, *Collier's*, *Redbook*, and others. Advertising clients included Ford, General Motors, and General Electric.

After many productive years he moved to Arizona where he followed a new career, painting Western subjects for galleries and exhibitions, until the time of his death.

LYFORD

PHILIP LYFORD (1887-1950) painted one of the best known posters of World War I as an illustration for the poem, "In Flanders Fields." It was also used as a flyer for the fifth Victory Loan, and a reproduction of it, 150 feet high, was lighted in San Francisco Bay. The painting, made while he was a young artist in a Chicago studio, helped to launch his own career; he became one of Chicago's top advertising illustrators. He also illustrated for such publications as *Redbook*, *Collier's*, *College Humor*, *Country Gentleman*, and *The Saturday Evening Post*.

Lyford was born in Worcester, Massachusetts, and studied for four years at the Boston Museum of Fine Arts under Frank Benson, Edmund C. Tarbell, and Philip Hale.

M. de V. Lee

MANNING DEVILLENEUVE LEE's (1894-) art education was interrupted by two stints of Army duty. The first was on the Mexican border in Texas as a member of the Virginia Field Artillery in 1916. This was promptly followed by service in World War I as a Lieutenant at the front in France with the anti-aircraft artillery.

Following the war, Lee resumed his studies at the Pennsylvania Academy of the Fine Arts, won the Cresson Scholarship for travel in Europe in 1921. The following year he won the Second Toppan Prize at the Pennsylvania Academy and with this encouragement began his long career as a free-lance illustrator.

Over the years, Lee has illustrated for a great many magazines and advertisers, and for more than 200 books for 27 publishers. He has made film strips and designed several series of postage stamps for the Republics of Liberia, Indonesia, and Guinea.

Book illustration for *Knight of the Revolution*, published by Macrae-Smith Co., 1941.

ORISON MACPHERSON

ORISON MacPHERSON (1898-1966) spoke with the Scottish accent of his Pictou, Nova Scotia, birthplace. His art education was acquired partly at the Ontario Art School in Toronto, and at the Art Students League in New York under John Sloan. He learned most, however, from the helpful advice of his friends, J. W. Schlaikjer, Franklin Booth, and the artist whose work he admired above all others, F. R. Gruger.

MacPherson got his start in the art field, after the usual odd jobs to keep alive, as an assistant to the art director of the old Hearst's *International* magazine. Within a short time he started his career in illustration with an assignment from the *Country Gentleman*, followed soon by others from *The Saturday Evening Post*, *Good Housekeeping*, and several Canadian publications, MacLean's magazine and *Chatelaine*. He also did a long series of advertising illustrations for the Jones and Laughlin Steel Corporation.

Illustration for *The Saturday Evening Post*.

IRVING NURICK

IRVING NURICK (1894-1963) took a trip to France in 1928 for a chance to study art, and to make a change from the advertising drawing and layout work he had been doing in New York. He fell in love with Paris, and it became his second home.

His Paris paintings and sketches provided an entrée into the field of magazine illustration. Mrs. Nurick showed them to various editors who were impressed and began sending him manuscripts.

Although Nurick did many pictures with Continental settings, he eventually became best known for his ability to depict young people sympathetically — teen-agers and sub-debs. The young responded with enthusiasm, wrote him for suggestions about clothes, and hair styling; Irving Nurick fan clubs came into existence as far away as New Zealand and Australia.

Nurick also continued his painting for exhibition, had one-man shows in New York and Paris; won the Ranger Prize in 1957, and the Samuel Finley Breese Morse Medal in 1960, in exhibitions at the National Academy of Design.

Illustration for Georges Simenon story "The Crime at Lock 14," in *Harper's Bazaar*, February, 1934.

Frederic Mizen

FREDERIC KIMBALL MIZEN (1888-1965) was a dominant figure in the outdoor advertising field for several years, many of his paintings doubling as magazine advertisements. He also did fiction illustration for magazines, such as *Cosmopolitan* and *The Saturday Evening Post*, but is probably best known for his long and distinguished series of advertising paintings for the Coca-Cola Company in newspapers, magazines, and billboards.

A Chicagoan, Mizen attended Smith's Art Academy from 1904-06 and obtained his first employment with the Gunning System, a predecessor to General Outdoor Advertising. Meanwhile, he continued to study in evening classes at the Art Institute of Chicago under John Vanderpoel, DeForrest Shook, and Walter Marshall Clute.

He later conducted his own school, the Mizen Academy of Art, for several years, but eventually restricted himself to portraiture.

Illustration in water color for the story, "Home Boy," in *Cosmopolitan* magazine, October, 1934.

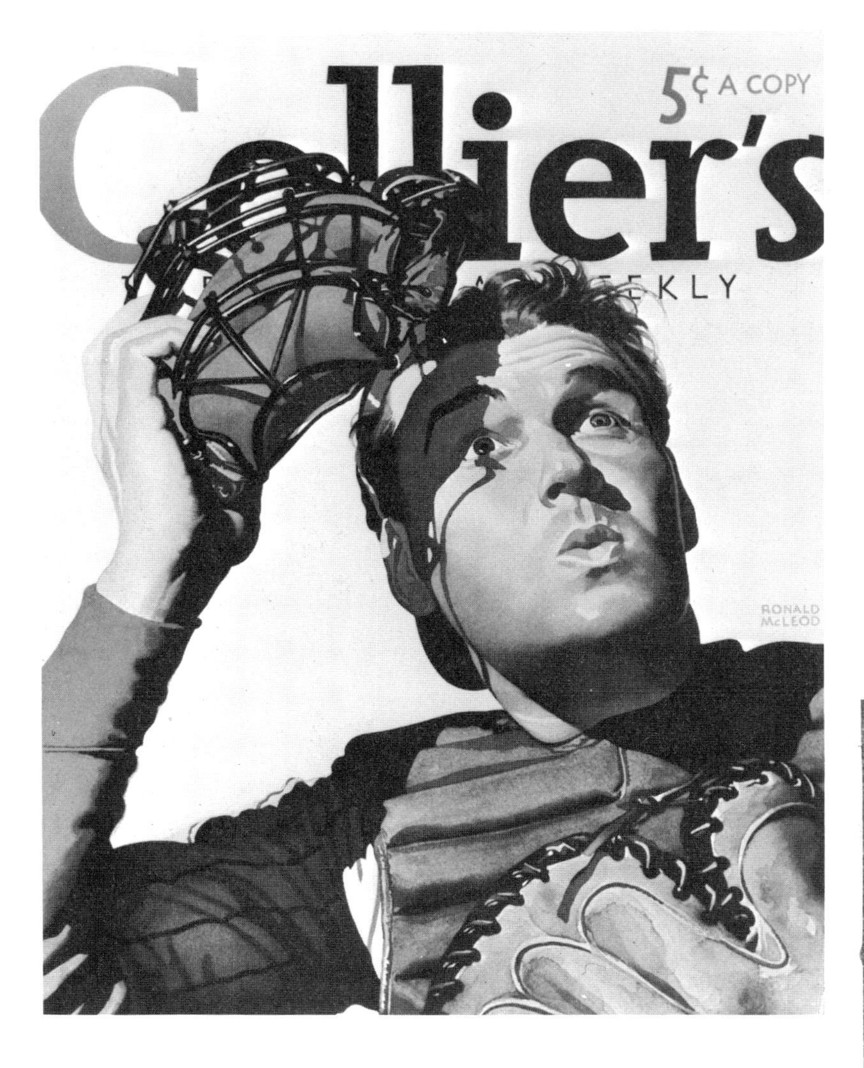

RONALD McLEOD

RONALD NORMAN McLEOD (1897-) was born in St. Paul, Minnesota, and was educated at the University of Chicago. He never had formal art training but made up for it by arduous self-education and observation.

In the process, McLeod developed a bold poster style in transparent water color, an unusual use of a medium that is traditionally somewhat muted.

Beginning in 1928, McLeod illustrated for *Collier's* regularly for twenty years; also worked for many other periodicals including *American, Cosmopolitan,* and *Pictorial Review*. Over this same period, he did an immense amount of advertising and poster illustration, several times had his work included in "100 Best Posters of the Year."

Cover illustration for *Collier's* magazine.

Garrett Price

GARRETT PRICE (1896-) has made it a lifetime habit to carry a small sketch pad with him. Many of his best picture ideas have been generated from these on-the-spot notes, sometimes coming to light years afterward.

Although Garrett has had a long career as an illustrator, he is best known for the original humor and incisive renderings of his *New Yorker* covers.

Price was born in Bucyrus, Kansas, attended the University of Wyoming, and the Art Institute of Chicago. His earliest art job was in 1916 with the *Chicago Tribune* where he first carried his sketchbook on assignments for news stories. Later he made the transition to illustrating for magazine stories for *College Humor, Collier's, Scribner's,* and other major magazines.

Garrett has exhibited widely — at The Metropolitan Museum of Art, Philadelphia Academy of the Fine Arts, American Water Color Society, Chicago Art Institute and others. He is an active member of the Society of Illustrators in New York, the Westport Artists, and the Mystic Art Association in Connecticut.

Drawing by Garrett Price. Copyright © 1947 *The New Yorker* Magazine, Inc.

Reproduced courtesy of the owner, E. Edward Cerullo.

Reusswig

WILLIAM REUSSWIG (1902-) is a fine illustrator, and married to an equally fine one, Martha Sawyers (below). They have traveled the world together and, in collaboration, have written and illustrated two books about the Far East, published by Grosset and Dunlap. They have a New York apartment with two studios where each can pursue individual assignments.

William was born in Somerville, New Jersey, studied at Amherst College and the Art Students League in New York. He was only 23 when he made his first illustrations for *Collier's* magazine and has since illustrated for most of the other publications, with masculine subjects of adventure and sports his special forte.

His painting for *True* magazine illustrates the westward ordeal of the Donner Party, nearly half of whom perished in the Sierra Nevadas during the winter of 1846-1847.

MARTHA SAWYERS

MARTHA SAWYERS became an illustrator unintentionally. Her drawings and paintings of China and Indonesia were on exhibition at the Marie Sterner Gallery and happened to be seen by William Chessman, art editor of *Collier's*. Chessman offered her a manuscript with an Oriental setting, which she illustrated with the sensitivity and taste for which her work has since become famous.

Martha is from Cuero, Texas, studied at the Art Students League; has lived and painted in Paris, Bali, Peking, Nepal, and numerous other parts of the world.

During World War II, *Collier's* sent her as an artist-correspondent to the China-Burma-India area and published numerous illustrated articles by her about the armed forces personnel and the native populations. *Life* magazine published a series of her pastel portraits of Orientals in the British Merchant Navy. She also designed posters for China Relief. In addition, Miss Sawyers brought special insight to her illustrations for the writers of fiction, Mona Gardner and Pearl S. Buck.

Illustration for an article, "Dancing Lady," also written by Miss Sawyers, for *Collier's* magazine, 1944.

ROBERT PATTERSON (1898-) was born in Chicago and attended the Chicago Art Institute. Among his teachers there and later were Harvey Dunn, Walt Lauderbach, George Elmore Brown, Ralph Barton, Pierre Brissaud, and Carl Ericson.

Patterson began his professional career in Chicago, and for some time, with his brother Loran, directed the Patterson studios there. In 1922 he came to New York and began doing fashion illustration.

Judge magazine sent him to France in 1924 to do a feature, "Betty Goes Abroad." When *Judge* failed in 1927, Patterson was stranded but managed to obtain a fashion illustration assignment from the Paris office of *Vogue*, where he stayed until 1934.

While in France he also studied further at the Grande Chaumière and l'Académie Julian in Paris, won an honorable mention at the Salon d'automne in 1927.

Upon his return to the United States, he began to do editorial illustrations for the major magazines, including *McCall's, Cosmopolitan, Good Housekeeping, Ladies' Home Journal, Redbook, Collier's, Woman's Home Companion,* and *American* magazine, as well as advertising assignments and book illustration.

He has been a long-time member of the Westport Artists and joined the instruction staff of the Famous Artists Schools in 1964.

Illustration for *Woman's Home Companion*, 1949.

OSCAR FREDERICK SCHMIDT (1892-1957) attended Pratt Institute in Brooklyn and won a scholarship to the Art Students League where he studied under George Bridgman.

During World War I he served in the artillery in France. Following his discharge, he went on an extended tour of the world, including North Africa and the Marquesas Islands, where he remained to carve a tombstone for the unmarked, weed-grown grave of Paul Gauguin.

Schmidt preferred to paint in gouache which he handled with great competence in illustrations for magazines such as *Redbook*, *Liberty*, and *The Saturday Evening Post*.

He exhibited often and was a member of the Salmagundi Club and the Society of Illustrators in New York.

Advertising illustration of a P.T. boat for the Electric Boat Company during World War II.

HOWARD SCOTT

HOWARD SCOTT (1902-) thinks of his twenty-four-sheet poster designs as analogous to one-act plays. He, as the director, must set the scene, cast the characters, and direct the actors. The moral, or message, must immediately be clear to the viewer, who may be traveling 60 miles-an-hour along a highway.

Scott also adds to his work a sparkling water-color technique and an ability to obtain very realistic characterizations in a bold poster treatment.

As an artist, he is a completely regulated and organized performer who keeps his studio as neat and businesslike as a reception room.

Scott has long been associated with Esso, Ford, Schlitz, Heinz, Servel, and other national products, but has also done magazine cover designs, notably for *The Saturday Evening Post*.

Saturday Evening Post cover dramatizing the war production during World War II.

Spreter

ROY FREDERIC SPRETER (1899-) is another of a gifted group of painters who have made advertising art their special province.

Spreter, in particular, is distinguished for the subtlety of his color and values and the good taste which his art conveys to the advertiser's products. He has long been associated with the campaigns of Camay, Campbell's Soups, and Bon Ami and is also in demand as an artist for twenty-four-sheet posters, which require sure control, since the reproduction enlarges the original art from eight to ten times.

His fiction illustration, equally colorful and artistic, has been mostly for the women's monthly magazines where his sensitive and beautiful heroines have found much favor.

Spreter is a Chicagoan, had brief training at the Art Institute there but learned most from Joe Chenoweth, Phil Lyford, Leopold Seyffert, and other members of the Palette and Chisel Club. He is a member of the Art Directors Club and Society of Illustrators in New York.

Illustration for *Pictorial Review*, 1936.

Schucker

JAMES W. SCHUCKER (1903-) was born in Mt. Carmel, Illinois. He received his education at Carnegie Institute of Technology, The Art Institute of Chicago, and studied with Harvey Dunn at the Grand Central School of Art.

His first editorial illustrations were for *Redbook* magazine; over the years, his work appeared in most of the national periodicals. He also did campaigns for advertisers, notably Quaker State Motor Oil, Travelers Insurance Company, and Seagram-Distillers Corporation.

An active painter, Schucker received an honorable mention at the Water Color International show at the Chicago Art Institute, is a member of the Philadelphia Art Alliance, and teaches at his own school in Quakertown, Pennsylvania.

Story illustration for *American* magazine, 1936.

DAN SWEENEY

DAN SWEENEY (1880-1958), a native of Sacramento, California, began his long career as a newspaper illustrator for the *San Francisco Chronicle*.

Sweeney also painted posters for theatre lobbies which led to doing travel posters. He began to specialize in this for various steamship lines and traveled around the world, to many out-of-the-way places, doing background research for unusual poster subjects. One of his most successful series of pictures was of pirate subjects for the Grace Lines.

For many years, Sweeney was a steady contributor of fiction illustrations to *Collier's* magazine, particularly of sea and Western subjects rendered in wash or transparent water color.

Story illustration for "The Drifter," by Ernest Haycox, *Collier's*, 1940.

H. J. Soulen

The work of HENRY J. SOULEN (1888-1965) is richly colored and strongly patterned. Each of his pictures is treated in a manner appropriate to the flat surfaces of a mural painting, and equally, to a magazine cover; he was given a Peabody Award for his magazine cover designs.

Soulen was born in Milwaukee, Wisconsin. He attended the Chicago Academy of Fine Arts and later studied with Howard Pyle. For many years his work appeared regularly in most of the quality magazines and usually in color — even when the use of color was restricted — because of the brilliance of his palette.

During World War II he gave free art lessons at the Valley Forge Military Hospital, a rehabilitation center for veterans.

Illustration for the *Ladies' Home Journal*.

Reprinted by permission of *McCall's*.

A

B

© 1942 by The Curtis Publishing Company.

Mead Schaeffer

The work of MEAD SCHAEFFER (1898-) divides itself into two periods. The early one deals with romantic, swashbuckling, and theatrical subjects. The second, although still strong and dramatic, is based on authentic factual themes and is more reportorial.

Mead, who was born in Freedom Plains, New York, studied at Pratt Institute, and with Harvey Dunn and Dean Cornwell. A brilliant student, he was illustrating for the major magazines while still in his twenties and had begun a series of 16 illustrated classics for Dodd Mead, including *The Count of Monte Cristo*, *Les Miserables*, *Typee*, and *Moby Dick*. Eventually, however, he became dissatisfied with romance and costume stories; he wanted to deal with contemporary subjects that he could personally observe and learn about.

With this in mind, Schaeffer began to paint covers for *The Saturday Evening Post*, which at that time was featuring Americana. The *Post's* artists traveled to various parts of the country to find regional material with national appeal. Schaeffer made an extended trip to the West with his friend and fellow-artist, Norman Rockwell. From this and other trips, many fine covers resulted.

During World War II, Mead painted a notable series of *Post* covers of American soldiers, representative of various branches of the service. The paintings were done with the full approval and cooperation of United States military authorities who provided all the facilities. In researching the pictures Schaeffer rode aboard a submarine, Coast Guard patrol boat, and various aircraft. Later, under sponsorship of the *Post*, the paintings were exhibited in more than 90 cities in the United States and Canada in promoting the war effort.

In other exhibitions Schaeffer won the Salmagundi Show Prize in 1930 and Gold Medal at the Pennsylvania Academy in 1944.

C

A. Early illustration for story by Joseph Vance in 1926.
B. "Paratroopers," the first of the series of *Post* covers illustrating branches of military service.
C. One of a very colorful series of illustrations for the "Captain Blood" stories by Rafael Sabatini. This was for "Out of the Dragon's Jaw," for *American* magazine, 1936.

A

HERBERT MORTON STOOPS (1888-1948) was closely identified with *Blue Book* magazine during his long career in illustration. This periodical published adventure fiction. Its wide variety of subject matter gave Stoops an opportunity to display his expert knowledge of military subjects, the Old West, particularly Indians, animals, and human figures in violent action. Many of his black-and-white dry-brush illustrations were attributed to his pen name, Jeremy Canon. He also painted *Blue Book's* monthly cover illustrations regularly for over 13 years. At the time of his death, he had painted the 17th of a series of covers depicting historical episodes in each of the 48 states.

Stoops, a clergyman's son, was reared in Idaho, attended Utah State College, worked as a staff artist for newspapers in San Francisco and Chicago. In 1917 he enlisted and served as a First Lieutenant with the Sixth Field Artillery of the First Division in France.

After the war, Stoops began his illustration career and his association with *Blue Book*. He did not confine himself to *Blue Book* alone, however, illustrating for *Collier's*, *This Week*, *Cosmopolitan*, and many others, as well as painting for exhibition. His picture, "Anno Domini," won the Isador medal at the National Academy Exhibition in 1940.

Stoops served as president of the Artists' Guild in New York, was a member of the Salmagundi Club, The Society of Illustrators, The American Artists Professional League, and prized highly his honorary membership in the New York Association of Veterans of the French Foreign Legion.

A. Cover illustration for *Blue Book*, October, 1936.
B. Dry-brush drawing for "Kioga of the Wilderness," from *Blue Book* magazine.

B

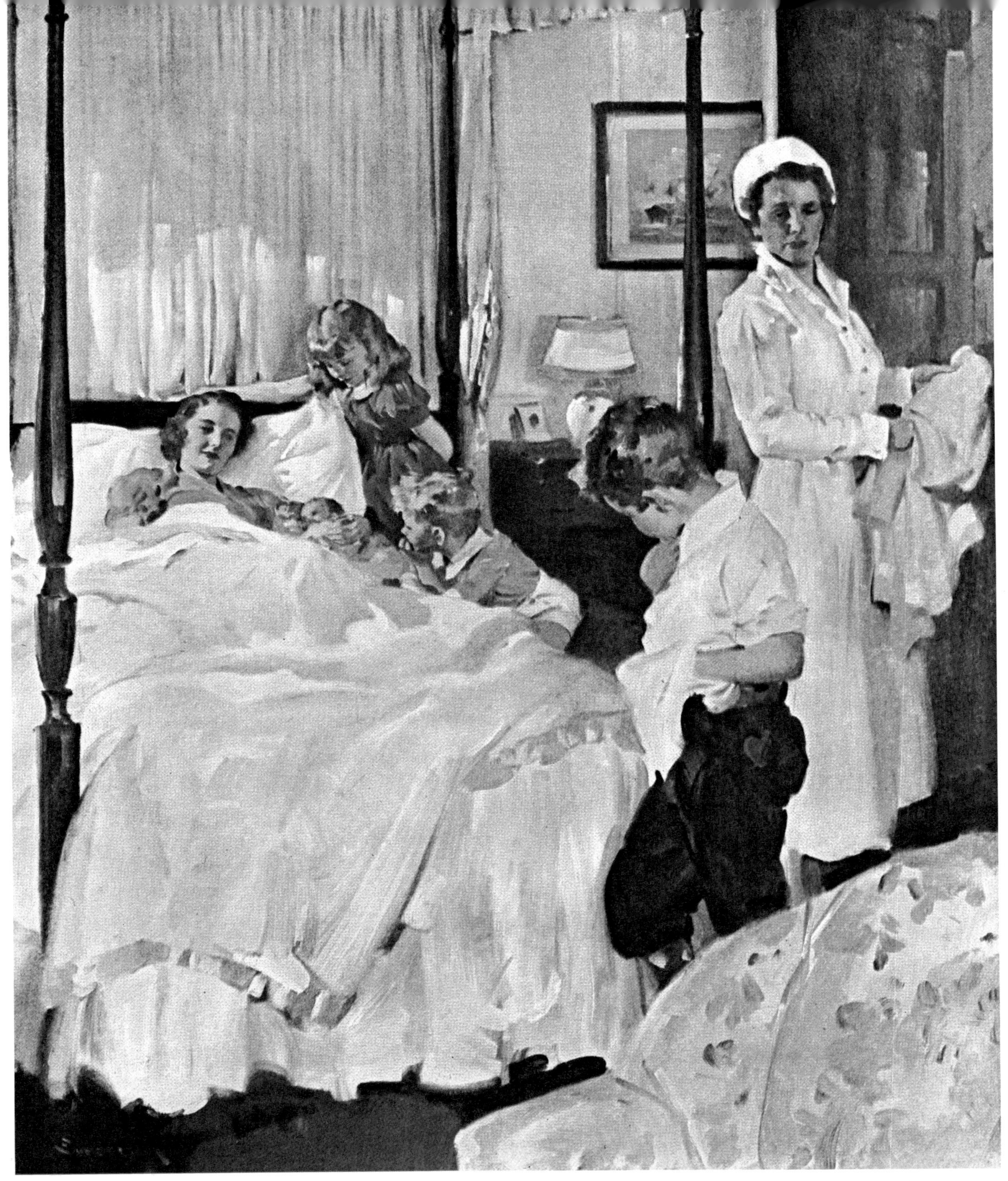

SUNDBLOM

HADDON HUBBARD SUNDBLOM (1899-   ) has dominated the art field in Chicago since the 1920's when he formed a studio partnership with Howard Stevens and Edwin Henry.

The studio, under the artistic direction and influence of Sundblom, attracted a great number of young artists who later, as alumni of the "Sundblom circle," went on to become name illustrators in their own right. Among those, included in this book, are Harry Anderson, Earl Blossom, Matt Clark, Edwin Henry, Walter Richards, James Schucker, Thornton Utz, and Coby Whitmore. Sundblom acknowledges the influence on his own style of many painters including John Singer Sargent, Anders Zorn, Robert Henri, and Sorolla. As amalgamated by Sundblom, it is a brilliant and colorful technique, combined with his own good taste and *joi de vivre*.

These qualities have kept his work in steady demand for nearly 40 years for both magazine stories and advertising campaigns and have won for him many medals and citations. His style became a hallmark for advertisers, such as Coca-Cola, Procter and Gamble, Colgate, Palmolive, Peet & Company, and Maxwell House Coffee.

Sundblom, born in Muskegon, Michigan, left school to work at the age of 13 when his mother died. For many years he attended school at night or took correspondence courses to make up his education. He also studied for four years at the Chicago Art Institute and three-and-a-half years at the American Academy of Art. His art apprenticeship was served at the Charles Everett Johnson Studio in Chicago and, in 1925, the partnership of Stevens, Sundblom and Henry was launched.

Full-color, full-page illustration for the *Ladies' Home Journal*.

HARRY LAVERNE TIMMINS (1887-1963) was an extremely versatile illustrator who was at home in every medium from dry brush to gouache, with a wide variety of subject matter developed from a long advertising and editorial art career.

His pictures appeared in *Ladies' Home Journal*, *Woman's Home Companion*, *Pictorial Review*, *Cosmopolitan*, *American*, *This Week*, *Collier's*, and in several Canadian publications. These and his national advertising illustrations won numerous awards over the years.

Timmins was born in Wilsonville, Nebraska, and studied at the Art Institute of Chicago. He was a co-founder of the American Academy of Art there, where he also taught for several years in the 'twenties. In the last years of his life he painted for galleries in Carmel, Hollywood, and San Francisco, California, and had several one-man shows.

He was a member of the New York Society of Illustrators, the American Federation of Arts and the Palette and Chisel Club of Chicago.

Advertising illustration, 1929.

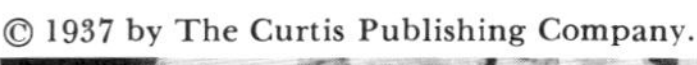

As a young man, RICO TOMASO (1898-   ) played piano in a small dance orchestra — wearing heavy, black woolen gloves as his trademark — (but also to be able to hit harder on the keys to compete with the drummer). The drummer was Dean Cornwell, then just starting his illustration career.

Tomaso, who was encouraged in his art ambitions by a family friend, John T. McCutcheon, the famous cartoonist for the *Chicago Tribune*, studied at the Chicago Art Institute. Among his teachers were Cornwell, Harvey Dunn, Robert Henri, and J. Wellington Reynolds. His work mostly resembled Cornwell's in concept and broad brush style. Tomaso was at his best illustrating mystery stories or those of high adventure in exotic locations as, for example, the Albert Richard Wetjen stories of the South Australian Mounted Police for *The Saturday Evening Post*. He is also known for a series of vigorous, full-color, portrait illustrations for Granger Pipe Tobacco.

For some years, after the Grand Central School of Art was dispossessed from Grand Central Terminal, Tomaso carried on Harvey Dunn's illustration class in Mamaroneck. He now paints for exhibition, has been represented by the Grand Central Art Galleries and by Jean Bohne, Inc., in New York.

Illustration for Erle Stanley Gardner's "The Case of the Lame Canary," for *The Saturday Evening Post*.

EFWARD

EDMUND F. WARD (1892-) made his first illustrations for *The Saturday Evening Post* before he was 20. His early pictures were large, rather somber and serious, painted in oils. Over a period of time he gradually changed to more humorous subjects and began to work in wash and water color. For many years he illustrated the Alexander Botts and Assistant District Attorney Doowinkle stories for the *Post*.

Ward was born in White Plains, New York, and studied at the Art Students League in New York City. Among his teachers were Edward Dufner, George Bridgman, and Thomas Fogarty.

He has spent his professional illustration career in White Plains, where he also painted a mural for the Federal Building. He is a long-time member of the Salmagundi Club, the Guild of Free Lance Artists, and the Society of Illustrators in New York.

Illustration for a *Saturday Evening Post* story by Joel Sayre.

WELSH

WILLIAM P. WELSH (1889-) developed his decorative painting approach through his study at the Julian and Delécluse academies in Paris and at the Art Students League in New York.

Although Welsh has done fiction illustration for numerous publications and advertisers, his poster style is best suited to the many magazine covers he painted, particularly for *Woman's Home Companion*. He has also done several murals, many portraits, has exhibited internationally, and taught at the Chicago Art Institute. In 1945 and 1946 he made paintings in the Far East Theatre of Operations for the Historical Records of the United States Army Air Forces.

Among his numerous awards are: First Prize at the International Water Color Exhibition in 1921; First and Third Prizes, Poster Competition for Chicago World's Fair, and medals from the New York Art Directors Club annual exhibitions of advertising art.

Welsh has been a member of the Tavern Club, Chicago, the Chicago Society of Arts, and the Society of Illustrators in New York. He was elected a Fellow of the British Royal Society of Arts in 1950 and of the International Institute of Arts and Letters in 1962.

Cover painting for the *Woman's Home Companion*, 1931.

Howard Willard

The work of HOWARD W. WILLARD (1894-1960) looks as though it had been dashed off quickly, on the spot. This combination of facility and authenticity resulted in part from his long-time habit of sketching, particularly during his extensive travels in France, England, Italy, Spain, Mexico, Morocco, and, during World War II, in India and China.

Willard was born in Danville, Illinois, moved to California as a boy where direct contact with Chinese, Japanese, and Mexican playmates inspired his lifelong interest in these cultures and in travel.

During World War II his special knowledge was utilized by the Army in producing propaganda literature for distribution in China. Willard served as Art and Design Director of the Department of Psychological Warfare, O.W.I., China theatre.

Willard's use of line and tone was ideally suited to book illustration; he combined his interest in travel and languages in several textbooks. His illustrated *Summer Islands*, by Norman Douglas, was designated as one of the "Fifty Best Books of the Year" in 1931. In recent years he illustrated extensively for the *Reader's Digest* magazine and Condensed Books program.

Illustration for "The China I Knew," condensed from "*My Several Worlds*" by Pearl S. Buck. Courtesy of the Reader's Digest Association.

© 1949 by The Curtis Publishing Company.

JAMES W. WILLIAMSON (1899-   ) has made an immense number of advertising illustrations for such clients as Arrow Shirts, Clicquot Club Ginger Ale, Ford, Paul Jones, and Yardley, all treated with circumspect restraint.

However, in his editorial illustration his sense of humor emerges and becomes his most engaging characteristic. Williamson distills action and renderings down to their essentials; the poses of the figures tell the story without need for captions.

Williamson was born in Omaha, Nebraska; was a graduate of the 1923 class of Yale.

A self-taught artist, he sold his first work to the old *Life* magazine while still in college. This was followed by sales to *Judge, Vanity Fair, Delineator,* and nearly all of the rest of the major magazines, including *The Saturday Evening Post,* where his work appeared for over 30 years.

Williamson currently lives in Puerto Rico and, thanks to the prompt United States Postal System, is able to keep deadlines for his present illustration assignments.

Here Williamson depicts mother-in-law difficulty at its fictional worst in an illustration for *The Saturday Evening Post.*

Wortman

DENYS WORTMAN, N. A. (1887-1958) was a social commentator of penetration and wit. He conveyed much good humor and sympathetic perception in his daily cartoon panel, "Metropolitan Movies." Although his drawings were predominantly concerned with New York characters: frowzy landladies, bums, and hangers-on, the panel was syndicated in 45 newspapers as "Everyday Movies." The common touch and wealth of homely observation made it equally appreciated across the country. His characters, like "Mopey Dick and the Duke," managed to evoke smiles even through the somber period of the Depression.

Wortman was born in Saugerties, New York, educated at Stevens Institute of Technology, Rutgers University, and the New York School of Fine and Applied Art, under Kenneth Hayes Miller. His first art work was done for the old *Herald Tribune,* and he illustrated for many magazines including *The New Yorker, The Saturday Evening Post,* and *Collier's,* but his longest association was with the old *New York World-Telegram and Sun.*

Wortman was equally interested in serious painting. He exhibited at the Armory Show, the National Academy, The Macbeth Galleries, and the Society of Illustrators where he served as president from 1936 to 1938.

His work is represented in the collections of The Metropolitan Museum of Art, and the New York Public Library.

"Mopey Dick and The Duke," reprinted by permission of the *New York World-Telegram and Sun.*

1940-1950

ILLUSTRATORS 1940-1950

Courtney Allen
Harry Anderson
Lyman Matthew Anderson
John Atherton
Warren Baumgartner
Walter M. Baumhofer
Lonie Bee
Robert Benny
Geoffrey Biggs
Gilbert Bundy
John Clymer
Stevan Dohanos
Albert Dorne
John Philip Falter
Robert Fawcett
Fred Freeman
John Gannam
John F. Gould
Hardie Gramatky
Hamilton Greene
Glen Grohe
John Groth
Lealand R. Gustavson
Robert George Harris
George Hughes
Earl Oliver Hurst
Robert F. Kuhn
Robert E. Lougheed
Tom Lovell
Fred Ludekens
John Alan Maxwell
Alfred Charles Parker
Perry Peterson
John Pike
Henry Clarence Pitz
Ben Kimberly Prins
Ray Prohaska
Paul Rabut
Frank Joseph Reilly
Walter D. Richards
Robert Riggs
Nicholas F. Riley
Richard Sargent
Barbara E. Schwinn
Amos Sewell
Edward Shenton
Noel Sickles
Benjamin Albert Stahl
Frederic Varady
Harold Von Schmidt
Lynd Ward
Jack W. Welch
Jon Whitcomb
Mortimer Wilson

The Decade: 1940-1950

by Al Parker

DRAWING BY ROBERT FAWCETT

"Too bizarre!" "Tinsel!" "Gimmicky!"

These were the critical cries heard when venturesome new art saw light of day in the popular women's magazines during the Depression of the 'thirties. The commercial value of this young talent, however, was observed only by a few astute art directors, who decided that here was something to nurture.

In those days, the success of a young artist depended greatly on the capacity of an art director to evoke it. Once evoked, the director expounded its merits to the editor-in-chief of the magazine, who usually asked for a watered-down version — pure innovation being mostly reserved for failing magazines in their dying gasps for attention.

Not until the crisis of World War II did the young artist fully realize his potentialities. It was then that acclaim from reader polls and art awards verified the fact that a minority of art directors had not facilitated a mere fad.

The magazines of the early 1940's concentrated on new formats for entertaining their most important reader: the young housewife and mother. This need was met in editorial art by depicting an idealized world, peopled with handsome men and gorgeous women, bedecked in their best in the most fashionable of settings. The young artist's ingenious execution of this policy established an astonishing rapport with the female reader — still unsurpassed.

Nevertheless, an overplus of taboos accompanied his rewards. He was permitted to paint sautéed mushrooms but not a steak (meat was rationed in World War II); a pair of snakeskin shoes with matching purse but not a snake (too frightening); the mood of a costume story but nary a costume (too old-fashioned); a garaged automobile but not one in motion (gasoline was rationed, too), and never, never, a trace of obesity.

While this hardly created a climate for discovery, the young artist gratified his creative impulse by concentrating on adornment, design, and layout of pages. Further, the wartime shortage of art supplies became an asset by inducing him to experiment with substitute materials, adding unusual techniques to his endeavors.

Illustration had become a commodity. Chic accessories with which he peppered his pictures provided a sustained involvement for the reader. Each illustration that featured these props produced letters from near and far. A chair covered in needlepoint, placed in a composition because of its interesting texture, brought inquiries about the availability of its pattern. A flowering epiphyllum incited requests for sources of rooted cuttings.

The illustrator also received letters of praise from the authors of the manuscripts he illustrated — but not for the above accessories. Instead, they praised the magic of his layouts which schemingly transformed the page-flipper into a reader.

Fan mail from adoring teenagers, superscribed with x's for kisses, told of their love for the heroine's hairdo or for her glamorous wardrobe. Art students wrote, seeking advice, especially: "What size brush do you use?" Mothers of America and their daughters wore matching dresses inspired by the mother-and-daughter paintings which for fourteen years graced the covers of the *Ladies' Home Journal*. Communication was the illustrator's *raison d'être*, and he made the most of it.

The dynamic simplicity that produced these fresh illustrations also affected reproductions, since the paper shortage had foisted inferior stock on the magazines. It was advantageous to employ clean, flat colors from a high-keyed palette, leaving plenty of white areas for vignetting the composition. Large close-ups of the hero's and heroine's heads eliminated unwanted clutter from the background.

Contrasty subject matter was *verboten*, as, for example, a prominently displayed zebra rug, for it was sure to stripe the art and text on the reverse side of the page. Thin paper held no secrets.

As these exercises flowed from the illustrator's brush he took time to join in the war effort. Planned trips of portrait sketching were arranged by the Red Cross and other organizations, for visits to veterans' hospitals around the country. The lifesize likenesses brought joy to convalescing service men and women, and to their folks back home.

Some patients were encased in plaster casts. The variety of matte white shapes made ideal surfaces for the painting of whatever was deemed appropriate — a blonde, brunette or redhead. The hospital wards resembled galleries of Environmental Art as the proud patients, propped in bed, exhibited their decorative conversation pieces.

Meanwhile, the illustrators painted war posters and donated their original art work as prizes to entice buyers in war bond drives. Some illustrators enlisted in the armed forces. Others used their talents in designing war media, from instructional booklets to film animation. Many became artist-war-correspondents, armed with pencil and paper in combat areas.

Members of the Society of Illustrators in New York City had among their hospital sketching group some jazz musicians. By day they would sketch, then stay on after dinner to play request numbers. Sometimes the hospital rocked with a jam session while a patient augmented the band with his own instrument.

At the end of the war, the illustrator strutted amidst a pageant of plenty. Advertising budgets had skyrocketed and magazines bulged with fiction, providing work for all who painted in the style of the innovators. Subtle changes became apparent. Unheralded, the fine arts painter, so sparingly used in editorial and advertising art, was emerging as an innovator. Although too avant garde to be widely marketable, he gave evidence of being the forerunner of a new approach.

His intense, turbulent expressions, his avoidance of photographic realism, his wilful lack of polished craftsmanship, imparted an unfinished look to his finished art. What appeared to be a rehearsal was the actual performance itself. Those functional little accessories that starred in other illustrations were absent in his works — the illustration being the star. The ferment of these drastic concepts and techniques developed as the major influence of today's illustrator.

Sports cars roared in from abroad; new country estates looked out on the suburban horizon. The illustrator partook of these luxuries and began to live the life he painted. The need to escape was already waning and, with it, escapist art. He had stretched the boundaries of editorial and advertising illustration; now came a call for new talent to explore the exposed areas.

John Gardner, in his book *Self-Renewal, The Individual and the Innovative Society*, published by Harper & Row, says:

> ". . . The revolution in modern art succeeded magnificently in shattering the rigidities of traditional art. It also fastened on the field of painting a mystique of rebellion and innovation which has hung around its neck like an albatross ever since."

Today, the march of time brings an echo to our ears as the pros cry out at the new venturesome art:
"Greasy fingerpainting!" "Too bizarre!" "Gimmicky!"

LYMAN MATTHEW ANDERSON (1907-) got his big break when some spot illustrations he'd made for an insurance company advertisement were accepted for exhibition in the New York Art Directors Club's annual show. Unknown to the acceptance jury, the original paintings were very large and when hung dominated the whole show. The pictures attracted much favorable attention and launched Lyman on the national scene as an illustrator.

Anderson had prepared himself well for the opportunity when it came. Born in Chicago, Illinois, he was a graduate of the Art Institute there, attended the Grand Central School of Art in New York City. Among his teachers were Pruett Carter, Walter Biggs, Harvey Dunn, Naum Los and Wayman Adams. In his early art work he did a great deal of illustration for pulp magazines, also a syndicated comic strip for King Features.

During his career, his clients have included such advertisers as Pepsi-Cola, Vitalis, New York Life Insurance Company, and Pan American; magazines such as *Woman's Home Companion, The Saturday Evening Post, Cosmopolitan,* and *American.* He has been a long-time member of the Society of Illustrators and is an honorary life-member of the Joint Ethics Committee of the Artists' Guild.

Lyman is currently teaching at the Famous Artists Schools in Westport, Connecticut.

Illustration for *Woman's Home Companion,* 1940.

COURTNEY
ALLEN

COURTNEY ALLEN (1896-) sold his first drawing to his home town newspaper, in Norfolk, Virginia at the age of 11. Thus encouraged, he decided early on an art career; later studied at the National Academy, the Corcoran School of Art in Washington, D. C., and with Charles W. Hawthorne in Provincetown, Massachusetts. His study was interrupted by 15 months spent in the American Army during World War I, 12 months in France, 8 of them at the front in the Camouflage Section.

Since then Allen has divided his time between illustrating for books and magazines, painting for exhibitions and, from 1946-50, teaching at the Huguenot School of Art in New Rochelle, New York.

During World War II, he was a regular participant in sketching trips with other members of the New Rochelle Art Association to Halloran Hospital on Staten Island, making portrait drawings of convalescent servicemen.

He has long been an active member of the New Rochelle Art Association, where he has won the Gold Medal for oil painting; also exhibited and won other awards at the Hudson Valley Art Association, Norfolk Museum of Arts and Sciences, National Academy, Allied Artists in New York, Chrysler Art Museum of Provincetown, and the Provincetown Historical Museum.

Collier's magazine story illustration for "The Boy Who had a Hero," by Albert Richard Wetjen, 1936.

Harry Anderson

HARRY ANDERSON (1906-   ) became a water colorist because of an allergy to oil paint. However, he employs tube opaque water colors, or tempera, whose properties most resemble the qualities of oils. With them he has retained the malleability of oil and added the spontaneity of the water medium.

Anderson (no relation to Lyman Anderson) was born in Chicago, attended the University of Illinois, graduated from Syracuse University in 1930. He has had studios successively in New York, Chicago, Washington, D. C., and is at present in Ridgefield, Connecticut.

His illustrations have appeared in most of the major magazines, and he exhibits regularly. A member of the American Water Color Society, he won the Grumbacher Purchase Prize in the 1956 Exhibition.

Anderson's homage to Winslow Homer, painted for the John Hancock Mutual Life Insurance Company.

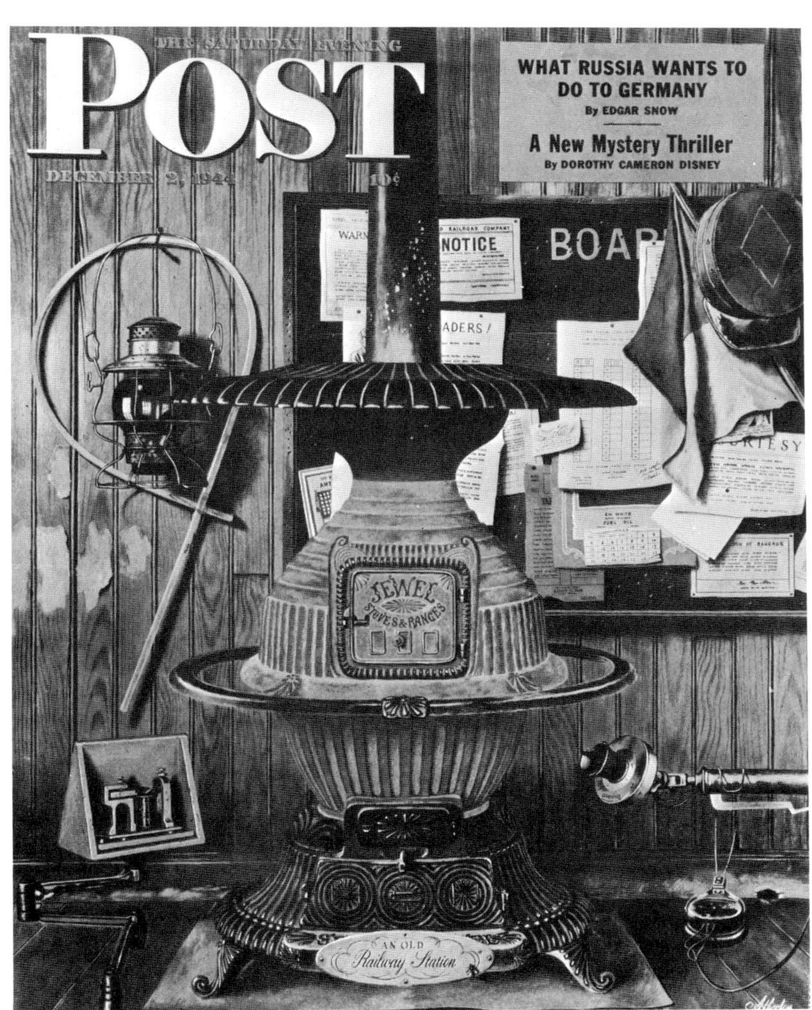

For JOHN ATHERTON (1900-1952) there was no line drawn between "fine" and "commercial" art. He painted pictures for advertisers, magazine covers, and galleries alike, all characterized by his strong sense of design, color, and good taste.

Atherton was born in Brainerd, Minnesota, studied at the College of the Pacific, and the California School of Fine Arts in San Francisco. He first worked in a number of West Coast art studios learning the basics of his craft. When he won a $500 first prize award in the annual exhibit of the Bohemian Club in 1929, it financed his move to New York.

There he began to do illustrations for advertisers, including General Motors, Container Corporation of America, and Shell Oil, and covers for *Fortune, Holiday,* and *The Saturday Evening Post.*

His first one-man show was held in Manhattan in 1936; in the "Artists for Victory" show in 1943, his painting, "The Black Horse" won the $3000 fourth prize from among 14,000 entries. It now hangs in The Metropolitan Museum of Art in New York. His work is also represented at the Whitney Museum, Museum of Modern Art, Chicago Art Institute, Pennsylvania Academy of Art, The Albright Art Gallery in Buffalo, and the Wadsworth Atheneum galleries in Hartford. He also was a member of the founding faculty of the Famous Artists Schools in Westport, Connecticut.

Atherton's great avocation was fishing. He tied flies of original design expertly, was a member of the Anglers' Club and author of a book *The Fly and the Fish.* His death occurred while he was on a salmon-fishing trip in New Brunswick, Canada.

The Saturday Evening Post cover illustration of an old railroad station interior of the Rutland Railroad at Shaftsbury, Vermont.

Baumgartner

WARREN BAUMGARTNER, N. A. (1894-1963) was born in Oakville, Missouri; the accompanying illustration is a painting of a fishing trip taken in the nearby Ozarks. The painting was commissioned by *True* magazine as the first of a series in which contributing illustrators were asked to take an ideal vacation and do a picture-story about it. For his holiday, Warren chose to go back home where he recorded his love of fishing, a passion since boyhood.

In the intervening years he had studied at the Art Institute of Chicago under Wellington J. Reynolds, at the Grand Central School with Pruett Carter and with Walter Biggs.

A very fine water colorist, Baumgartner painted pictures for both magazine illustrations and exhibitions, winning numerous awards in both fields.

He was a member of the Society of Illustrators, American Water Color Society, National Academy of Design, and the Salmagundi Club of New York.

Reproduced from *True* magazine, "Ozark Float Trip," 1947.

Lonie Bee

LONIE BEE (1902-   ) was born in Santa Rosa, California, and has remained there as one of the "West Coast artists."

After training at the University of California and the California School of Fine Arts and Crafts, he appeared on the national scene with his spirited illustrations for the magazines, *Collier's, American, Cosmopolitan, Woman's Home Companion, Woman's Day, Good Housekeeping,* and *The Saturday Evening Post.* For all of these, he painted numerous covers. Over the years, he has also painted designs for twenty-four-sheet posters, winning many awards and citations in this field.

Bee has exhibited at the Society of Illustrators in New York, The Bohemian Club, and San Francisco Museum of Art in California.

Water-color illustration for Faith Baldwin's serial in *Cosmopolitan* magazine, 1945.

Walter M Baumhofer

For years WALTER M. BAUMHOFER (1904-) painted cover designs for the pulps such as *Adventure* magazine. A bold, dramatic approach has characterized his work ever since.

A versatile performer, Baumhofer has illustrated for publications as diverse as the *Ladies' Home Journal, Outdoor Life, Cosmopolitan, True, Woman's Day,* and *Sports Afield.*

Baumhofer studied at Pratt Institute in Brooklyn, New York, and has been a long-time member of the Society of Illustrators.

Illustration for "The Lion," by Jack O'Connor, *Outdoor Life* magazine, February, 1964.

ROBERT BENNEY

In his work , ROBERT BENNEY (1904-) ably combines the roles of painter and reporter. During World War II, he was a war correspondent under the Office of the Surgeon General with assignments, successively, for the Navy and the Army in combat areas.

After the war, Benney began to specialize in producing art work for industry and agriculture, accepting commissions to record the operations of some of the nation's largest companies, including the American Sugar Refining Company, Standard Oil of New Jersey, American Tobacco, Chrysler Corporation, Shell Oil, Western Electric, General Foods, and numerous others. Many of these pictures have been used in annual reports, calendars, and advertising illustrations.

Benney was born in New York, studied at the Cooper Union Art School, Art Students League, National Academy, and Grand Central School of Art. Among his teachers were George Bridgman, Walter Biggs, Harvey Dunn, and Dean Cornwell. He himself has taught at the New York School of Visual Arts and at Pratt Institute in Brooklyn.

His work has won many awards and is represented in several collections and museums. He has also been an active member of the Society of Illustrators, serving on committees for education, exhibitions, and scholarships.

One of a series of documentary paintings and drawings for a "Visual Essay on the Sugar Industry," entitled "Harvesting Sugar Cane," (30 by 50 inches) for the American Sugar Refining Company.

GEOFFREY BIGGS

GEOFFREY BIGGS (1908-) was born in London, England, but went through high school in America and studied at the Grand Central School of Art. Among his teachers were Arthur Woelfle, Arshile Gorky, and Harvey Dunn.

Biggs' work, which is highly detailed and realistic, was first published in *Collier's,* where it attracted wide attention, and was soon followed by commissions from most of the other periodicals including *The Saturday Evening Post, True, Liberty, Woman's Home Companion, Coronet, Pic,* and *Good Housekeeping,* as well as from many major and minor advertising agencies in New York.

In addition, Biggs has found time to exhibit at the Society of Illustrators and the Midtown Galleries in New York.

War-time illustration for *The Saturday Evening Post* story, "Heaven is a Foxhole," by Richard Sale.

A

B

Gilbert Bundy

GILBERT BUNDY (1911-1955) was born in Centralia, Illinois, the son of an oil company scout. He was brought up in a succession of oil boom towns in Oklahoma. He eventually finished high school in Winfield, Kansas, and went to work for a Kansas City engraving company.

In 1929 Bundy headed for a career in New York and began to do cartoons for the old *Life* and *Judge* magazines.

In the early 'thirties he became associated with the fledgling *Esquire* magazine. His deftly drawn, risqué humor had much to do with the success of that magazine, which was also a valuable showcase for Bundy, and led to his spectacular popularity as an illustrator for most of the major magazines and many advertisers. These included campaigns for Cluett Peabody, Munsingwear and Sanka Coffee.

Bundy's pictures looked spontaneous but were the result of much careful research and study. He emulated the classic Chinese method of drawing from memory once he had made many preliminary studies from the model.

During World War II, Bundy covered the Pacific War Theatre as a combat artist for King Features. He went through a series of harrowing actions including Tarawa, Iwo Jima, and Okinawa; was the sole survivor of a direct hit on an Amtrak and spent a day and night in the water before being rescued.

Although he resumed his career in illustration after the war, Bundy never recovered from the severe shock of his experiences and took his own life in 1955.

A. Story illustration for *American* magazine.
B. *The Saturday Evening Post* illustration for "Good-Time Girl," by Lester Atwell.

John Clymer

JOHN CLYMER (1907-) was born in Ellensburg, Washington. His art education was acquired at the Vancouver School of Fine Art in Vancouver and the Ontario College of Art in Port Hope, Canada, as well as at the Wilmington Society of Fine Arts in Delaware and the Grand Central School of Art in New York. With this background, his loyalties have ever since been divided between the United States and Canada.

Clymer's first illustrations were made for Canadian publications, followed by editorial assignments for most of the American magazines; numerous advertising campaigns; and an extensive series of paintings of historic episodes in the United States Marine Corps, for the Marine Corps.

His paintings have been exhibited widely in both countries as well, with the North West Artists in Seattle, The Ontario Society of Artists, The Royal Canadian Academy in Toronto, Canada, The National Academy in New York, Salmagundi Club, Society of Animal Artists, and Hudson Valley Artists. Clymer is an artist member of the Grand Central Galleries.

Cover illustration for *The Saturday Evening Post.*

A

Courtesy of Famous Artists Schools. B

C

Stevan Dohanos

STEVAN DOHANOS (1907-) painted a series of pictures of fire plugs which reveals much about him as an artist. First, it is typical of him to have seen a picture possibility in such a commonplace subject. However, as a searching realist, he was not content merely to record the appearance of the hydrants but had to know all about how they worked, too. In the course of his investigation, he talked with town officials and hydraulic engineers, examined and made many sketches of various types of hydrants in other towns as well.

Dohanos studied nights at the Cleveland School of Art long enough to get a job as an apprentice letterer and, gradually, developed a solid studio background. A hard worker, he simultaneously did painting and engravings for national exhibitions.

In 1936 he painted an assignment for the Treasury Art Project in the Virgin Islands and, later, various mural commissions for federal buildings in Elkins, West Virginia, West Palm Beach, Florida, and Charlotte Amalie, Virgin Islands. His pictures are in the collections of the Cleveland Museum of Art, Whitney Museum, Pennsylvania Academy of Art, Avery Memorial of Hartford, New Britain Museum of American Art and of several private owners.

His illustrations have appeared in almost all of the major magazines; for several years he painted covers for *The Saturday Evening Post*. Twice a victim of tuberculosis himself, Dohanos has contributed Christmas seal designs to the National Tuberculosis Association and made many posters and designs for national and local charitable purposes. One of the latest of six commemorative stamps he has designed for the U.S. Post Office is on the theme, "Crusade against Cancer."

He is a member of the National Society of Mural Painters, Artists and Writers Club, Dutch Treat Club, a founding faculty member of the Famous Artists Schools, and served as president of the Society of Illustrators from 1961-63.

A. "Polynesian Navigation" painted for Travelers Insurance Company advertisement. It received the "Award for Distinctive Merit" at the Art Directors Club exhibit in New York, 1938.
B. "Two Fire Hydrants," 1948.
C. Typical Dohanos *Saturday Evening Post* cover.

D. Illustration for *The Saturday Evening Post* story, "Assignment in Brittany."

E. Poster for the President's Committee on Employment of the Handicapped, 1965.

A. "The Salesman," colored-ink advertising illustration.

Courtesy of John Hancock Mutual Life Insurance Company.

ALBERT DORNE

ALBERT DORNE (1904-1965), who was born and grew up on the lower East side of New York, had to leave school in the eighth grade to go to work. In 1963 he fittingly received the Horatio Alger Award for Achievement from the American Schools and Colleges Association, Inc.

In the intervening years, Dorne, through a combination of natural ability and strong drive, progressed successively from being an unpaid assistant to a commercial artist to one of New York's most successful advertising artists, still in his early twenties. He went on to become a leading editorial illustrator, was elected president of the New York Society of Illustrators (1947-48), and in 1948 became the founder-director of the Famous Artists Schools in Westport, Connecticut.

These remarkably successful correspondence schools sprang originally from Dorne's interest in helping aspiring artists who continually came to him for advice. In 1947, with a group of leading fellow-illustrators, he formed the Famous Artists Schools, which have expanded to include the Famous Writers School and the Famous Photographers School.

Among his achievements, Dorne ranked high his being co-founder of the Code of Ethics and Fair Practices of the Profession of Commercial Art and Illustration. In 1953 he was awarded the first Gold Medal for a "distinguished career" by the New York Art Directors Club. Adelphi College conferred on him an honorary Doctor of Fine Arts degree in 1958.

B

C

B., C. These illustrations for *Collier's* are a combination of line and colored inks. They clearly reveal Dorne's superb draughtsmanship — particularly of heads and hands — and his mastery of compositional organization. Note in the upper illustration how all of the major shapes serve to lead the viewer's eye to the fallen figure.

© 1944 by The Curtis Publishing Company.

A

© 1943 by The Curtis Publishing Company.

B

C

© 1945 by The Curtis Publishing Company.

JOHN FALTER

JOHN PHILIP FALTER (1910-) was born in Plattsmouth and reared in Falls City, Nebraska. He studied at the Kansas City Art Institute, at the Art Students League of New York on a scholarship, and at the Grand Central School of Art in New York. Among his teachers were Mahonri Young, George Wright, and Monte Crews.

Falter began his career in illustration early, starting with the pulps and, at 20, sold his first slick illustration to *Liberty* magazine. Talented and prolific, he soon added most of the other magazines, and many advertising agencies, to his roster of clients.

His most important pictures were painted for the covers of *The Saturday Evening Post*. Many of them were based on the experiences of his Nebraska boyhood, in small town or country settings. He also painted a notable series of street scenes in cities across the United States. These grew out of a chance visit of a *Post* art editor to Falter's studio; there a picture caught his eye, a painting of Gramercy Park which Falter had painted for pleasure.

John served in the Navy as a Chief Boatswain's Mate during World War II; later, was commissioned a Lieutenant on special art assignments.

Falter is a member of the Society of Illustrators, The Players, and the Philadelphia Sketch Club. Although he does not exhibit, his paintings are represented in several museums and private collections.

A. Painting of Gramercy Square in New York used for a *Saturday Evening Post* cover.
B. Falter's picture summarizes the anxiety of mothers all over America during World War II.
C. A nostalgic backward look at his school days.

Fred Freeman

From logging to layout work in a large department store, FRED FREEMAN (1906-   ) has accumulated a diversity of experience which has contributed greatly to his artistic development. He was a Naval Reserve Lieutenant Commander during World War II, skippered three different ships, taking part in actions at Guadalcanal, New Zealand, the Solomon Islands, Saipan, Guam, and the Aleutians. With this naval background, he was able to combine a technical knowledge with dramatic impact in his authoritative illustrations for *United States Submarine Operations in World War II*.

In his subsequent illustration career, Freeman has continued to combine this intricacy of documentary detail with strongly composed artistry. The burgeoning developments of space-age technology have been a special province for Freeman who has taken on many major illustration assignments for publications, such as *Collier's*, *The Saturday Evening Post*, and *Reader's Digest*.

Illustration for *United States Submarine Operations in World War II*, published by the United States Naval Institute, 1949.

JOHN F. GOULD (1906-   ) estimates that he did about twelve thousand adventure and detective story illustrations for pulp magazines before tackling *The Saturday Evening Post*. To prepare himself for the *Post*, he spent a year-and-a-half, picking a different story each week and re-doing the illustrations in his own way. A representative group of these, shown to the *Post's* art editor, won Gould his first commission.

Since then he has illustrated for *Redbook, Collier's, The Saturday Evening Post*, and numerous national advertising accounts.

Born in Worcester, Massachusetts, Gould studied at the Tiffany Foundation and was graduated from Pratt Institute where he then taught for 22 years. He has also taught at the Newark School of Fine and Industrial Art, as well as in classes at the Bethlehem Art Gallery near Newburgh, New York.

His expert water-color paintings are represented in many private collections.

World War II *Saturday Evening Post* illustration for "We Fought through to Murmansk," by Robert Carse.

© Cowles Communications, Inc.

A

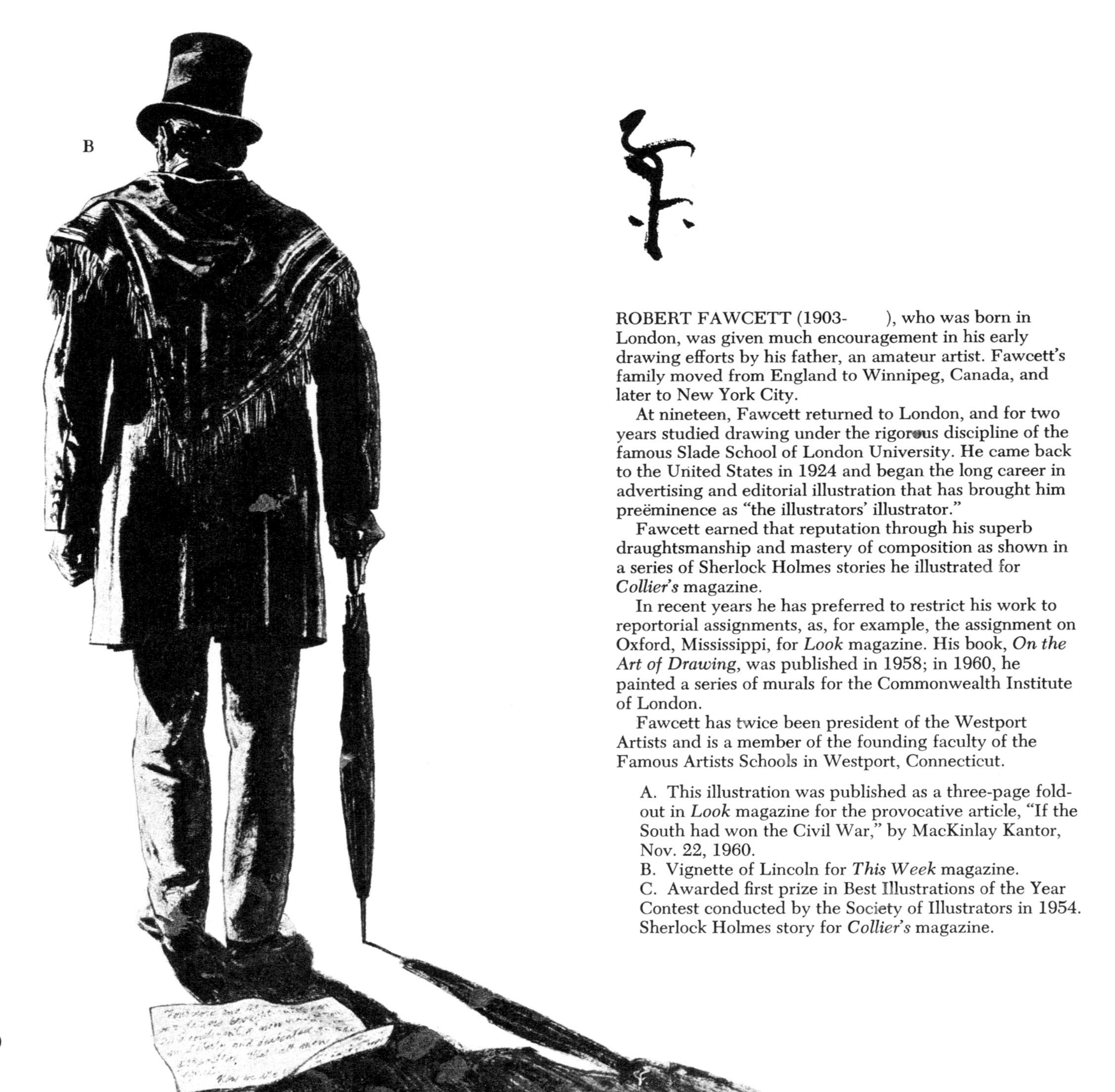

B

ROBERT FAWCETT (1903-), who was born in London, was given much encouragement in his early drawing efforts by his father, an amateur artist. Fawcett's family moved from England to Winnipeg, Canada, and later to New York City.

At nineteen, Fawcett returned to London, and for two years studied drawing under the rigorous discipline of the famous Slade School of London University. He came back to the United States in 1924 and began the long career in advertising and editorial illustration that has brought him preëminence as "the illustrators' illustrator."

Fawcett earned that reputation through his superb draughtsmanship and mastery of composition as shown in a series of Sherlock Holmes stories he illustrated for *Collier's* magazine.

In recent years he has preferred to restrict his work to reportorial assignments, as, for example, the assignment on Oxford, Mississippi, for *Look* magazine. His book, *On the Art of Drawing*, was published in 1958; in 1960, he painted a series of murals for the Commonwealth Institute of London.

Fawcett has twice been president of the Westport Artists and is a member of the founding faculty of the Famous Artists Schools in Westport, Connecticut.

A. This illustration was published as a three-page fold-out in *Look* magazine for the provocative article, "If the South had won the Civil War," by MacKinlay Kantor, Nov. 22, 1960.
B. Vignette of Lincoln for *This Week* magazine.
C. Awarded first prize in Best Illustrations of the Year Contest conducted by the Society of Illustrators in 1954. Sherlock Holmes story for *Collier's* magazine.

C

A

B

JOHN GANNAM

C

JOHN GANNAM, A.N.A. (1907-1965) was an intense, dedicated artist. He worked almost exclusively in water color and was a lifelong student of the effects of light and color. Oftentimes a particular problem would preoccupy him for months as he tried out innumerable variations. He kept on until satisfied, finally, that he understood such effects as sunlight and under-water rocks on the surface of a mountain stream or the glow of a fire in the sky, and its reflection on wet pavement as firemen fought a blaze.

Gannam worked at his paintings almost vertically, very freely, his brush loaded with water. He was after the broad, but exact effect, little concerned with details or with corrections which could be made later, if needed, with opaque.

John, who was born in Lebanon, grew up in Chicago but was forced to leave school to work, at 14, when his father died. He went through a succession of menial jobs until he eventually became a messenger boy in an engraving house. Here he first found a purpose for himself — to become an artist like the men who did the layouts, lettering, and drawings for engravings. Within a few years, by dint of close observation and a stiff schedule of self-education, he reached his goal, working for studios in Chicago and Detroit.

The next step was New York and, eventually, magazine illustration. He received his first manuscript from Henry Quinan of *Woman's Home Companion*, followed soon thereafter by work from most of the other magazines. Gannam always sought fresh, unstereotyped viewpoints which, with his excellent taste, kept him in constant demand by advertisers as well as publishers. His illustrations for campaigns of Pacific Mills, Ipana, and St. Marys Blankets are particularly memorable.

Gannam also exhibited his water colors, was an associate of the National Academy of Design, member of the American Artists' Professional League, the American Water Color Society, the Society of Illustrators, and had been recently appointed to the faculty and board of directors of the Danbury Academy of Arts.

A. Advertising illustration for St. Marys Blankets, 1953.
B. Burial scene for *Collier's* story, "The Smoky Years," 1935.
C. Illustration for *Collier's*, 1938.

Water-color illustration for *Fortune* magazine of "Vacations in Winter: Cat Cay," 1939.

HARDIE GRAMATKY —

As a boy, HARDIE GRAMATKY, N.A. (1907-   ) wanted to be a comic strip artist. He realized that ambition early, "ghosting" the Ella Cinders comic soon after completing his studies at Stanford University and the Chouinard Art Institute in Los Angeles. This preparation led to a job in Walt Disney's studio where, for six years, he worked his way up and finally became head animator.

In 1936, Gramatky came to New York to free-lance; some of his first assignments were reportorial paintings for *Fortune* magazine. He has since specialized in the water-color medium, and his illustrations for fiction, articles, and advertising have appeared in virtually all the magazines.

As a result of painting tugboats, he became interested in doing a children's book. His story, *Little Toot,* has been a perennial best seller ever since, was made into an animated film by Disney, is part of the CARE-UNESCO book program, and has been rated by the Library of Congress as one of the great children's books of all time. Since then he has written and illustrated many other books well known in the children's book field.

Gramatky has also painted and exhibited all over the world, has won thirty top water-color awards, including the Chicago International in 1942, the National Academy in 1952, and the American Water Color Society in 1962. His paintings are in the permanent collections of the Brooklyn Museum, Springfield Museum of Art, Toledo Museum, and many private collections.

HAMILTON GREENE

HAMILTON GREENE (1904-   ) has produced a great quantity of competent illustration, beginning with the pulp magazines, later for men's magazines – *Argosy, True, Cavalier, Elks* and for Dell publications.

Greene was appointed an overseas artist-correspondent for *The American Legion* magazine in 1944-45 and made many authentic, eyewitness drawings of fighting in the European theatre. While with a Ninth Army Patrol near Geilenkirchen, Germany, he was wounded in the stomach and lungs by sniper fire. According to an excerpt from a letter by the director of the Public Relations Division, Supreme Headquarters, A.E.F., "Mr. Green was conspicuously forward in every operation in which he participated and was well known to the personnel of the units he accompanied because of his place in the forward assault where he sought opportunity to watch the reactions of the American soldiers in the attack . . ." In 1951 Greene again served, as a war-correspondent in Korea, for *Blue Book* magazine.

Since that time he has specialized in the children's book field illustrating textbooks, fiction, and reading-aid programs.

It is an interesting footnote that his wife, June Kemble Greene, is the granddaughter of the eminent illustrator, E. W. Kemble. (See decade 1900-1910.)

Illustration for *Blue Book* magazine, "Dagwood Red Charlie-One" October, 1948.

grohe

GLEN GROHE (1912-1956) was born in Chicago and worked his way through the Art Institute and the American Academy of Art there. He obtained his first job with the Swan Studio in Chicago and in 1937 went to New York, joining the staff of an advertising magazine and later the Charles E. Cooper Studio.

He attracted the attention of magazine art editors through the originality and strong design of his advertising illustrations which he carried over into his work for periodicals, including *The Saturday Evening Post, This Week, Cosmopolitan,* and *Good Housekeeping* magazines.

Among Grohe's many advertising clients were the Dow Chemical Company, Conoco, and the Travelers Insurance Company. During World War II, he served as a consultant in the Graphics Division of the O.E.M. and did posters for the O.W.I.

Grohe was also interested in still and motion picture photography. He made a documentary film for the San Mateo County Recreational Department and had nearly finished a very imaginative film on the art work of patients in a mental institution at the time of his death.

Illustration for "The Murderer," a *Saturday Evening Post* story.

John Groth

JOHN GROTH (1908-   ), as a hopeful young artist, was advised by an artist friend to make a hundred drawings a day. John took the advice literally and kept up the practice for years. This driving pace trained him as an artist and shaped his free, impressionistic style of drawing.

Impressed by the vigor of his work, *Esquire* magazine hired him as its first art director. He promptly assigned himself on travel junkets to draw and paint for the magazine in Mexico, Russia, France, England, and Germany.

During World War II, as an artist-correspondent for the *Chicago Sun,* he was present at the liberation of Paris and the surrender of Berlin. He became a friend of Ernest Hemingway in France and out of this association came his assignment to illustrate Hemingway's *Men without Women;* Hemingway also wrote the preface for Groth's own book of war drawings and experiences, *Studio: Europe*. Groth later covered the Korean War, wrote and illustrated another book, *Studio: Asia.*

In the years between wars Groth continued to travel, has carried out assignments for *Look, Fortune, Sports Illustrated, Town and Country,* and has illustrated several classics including *War and Peace,* and *Grapes of Wrath.*

Groth teaches at the Art Students League and the National Academy of Design; he also paints and exhibits. His pictures are in several collections including The Museum of Modern Art, Library of Congress, and National Gallery of Art.

Sketch for *Studio: Europe*, of the link-up of the American Ninth Army and Russian First Ukrainian Army at Appollendorf, Germany, April 30, 1945.

GUSTAVSON

LEALAND R. GUSTAVSON (1899-1966) was born in the Swedish community of Moline, Illinois. He studied nights for several years at the Chicago Art Institute while working in printing houses, advertising agencies, and art services. He later resumed night classes studying under Walter Biggs and Harvey Dunn after moving East.

Although he illustrated for *The Saturday Evening Post, Collier's, McCall's,* and many other periodicals, Gustavson was one of the mainstays of *Blue Book* magazine for many years and in his illustrations for the blood and thunder stories managed to "kill a staggering number of people in all the diabolical ways an author can dream up . . ."

Along with his interest in art, he was an ardent sportsman. For several years he played tournament badminton throughout the East, holding a national championship title and several New England titles. He was just as interested in golf — as a player and in illustrating the fine points of the game for books and magazine articles.

He exhibited widely and won many awards, taught at the Chicago Art Institute and Ray Commercial Art School in Chicago, was a member of the Salmagundi Club, the American Water Color Society, and the Academic Artists Association.

Illustration for one of the David Lamson stories in *The Saturday Evening Post.*

R G Harris

ROBERT GEORGE HARRIS (1911-   ), from boyhood in Kansas City, Missouri, always knew he wanted to be an artist. After study with Monte Crews at the Kansas City Art Institute, he went East via motorcycle, attended classes at the Grand Central School of Art with Harvey Dunn, and the Art Students League under George Bridgman.

His first published art work was for Street and Smith's Western story magazines. He also did a considerable amount of pulp illustration before eventually graduating to the slicks.

Bob became noted for his highly finished and sympathetic renderings of children and young love, which made him a natural choice for art editors of the women's magazines — the *Ladies' Home Journal, Good Housekeeping,* and *McCall's.*

At present he is living in Arizona whence his many portrait painting commissions keep him traveling much of the time.

Illustration for the *Ladies' Home Journal.*

Hughes—

GEORGE HUGHES (1907-   ) conveys a feeling of realism and authenticity in his work by careful selection, and by emphasis on the essential characteristics of his subject matter.

Hughes is a native New Yorker and studied in New York at the Art Students League and at the National Academy of Design. Some of his early work included fashion drawing. And there was a stint as a special designer in the automobile field in Detroit.

For many years Hughes was one of the most prolific painters of *Saturday Evening Post* covers; in addition, he has done many editorial illustrations for the *Post* and other publications, including *McCall's, Woman's Day, American, Reader's Digest,* and *Cosmopolitan* magazines.

Illustration for one of a series of O'Malley stories by William MacHarg for *The Saturday Evening Post.*

Great good humor was the most characteristic trait of EARL OLIVER HURST (1895-1958), as an individual and in his illustration.

Hurst's illustrations look very facile and as though dashed off, in keeping with their spirit of fun. However, they are very soundly based on thorough preliminary preparation. In fact, for some time it was his practice to do every illustration twice to see how much more freedom and excitement he could add to the first rendition.

Hurst was born in Buffalo, New York, and attended the Albright Art School in Buffalo, the Cleveland School of Art, John Huntington School of Art; studied under Pruett Carter at the Grand Central School of Art, and Boardman Robinson at the Art Students League in New York.

He exhibited often and his work received many awards. He wrote and illustrated several juvenile books and was a contributing editor of *American Artist* magazine conducting a regular monthly column, "The Hurst Page," with information and interviews pertaining to commercial art and illustration.

Although Hurst illustrated for many publications, he was most closely identified with *Collier's* magazine for which he did this illustration in 1941.

KUHN

ROBERT F. KUHN (1920-   ) is more interested in drawing and painting animals than any other subject and always has been. As a boy he sketched animals continuously, later frequented zoos to draw them from life whenever possible.

In his youth, Bob's idol and mentor was Paul Bransom who offered him a great deal of personal encouragement and criticism. They still continue to be good friends.

Bob was born in Buffalo, New York, and studied at Pratt Institute in Brooklyn. Among the guest lecturers who influenced him there were Harold Von Schmidt and Paul Brown.

To further his study of animals under their natural conditions, Kuhn has traveled extensively in the wilderness areas of Newfoundland, Western Canada, Alaska and other parts of the United States, with several months in Africa, in both open country and the game preserves.

His first illustrations appeared in *Field and Stream.* He now works for most of the men's magazines, such as *True, Outdoor Life, Argosy,* and for the *Reader's Digest.* He has also illustrated numerous books, painted for calendars and advertisements.

Kuhn's authoritative knowledge of animals in action is vividly demonstrated in this dramatic illustration for *Argosy* magazine.

R.E. LOUGHEED

ROBERT E. LOUGHEED (1910-   ) never consciously decided to become an animal artist — it just happened naturally. He was born on a farm in Ontario, Canada, and from childhood on his subjects were animals, all kinds of animals, but particularly horses.

His first art training came through a correspondence course in commercial design which he worked at assiduously during the long Canadian winters. With this start, he got a job in the art department of an engraving and printing firm in Toronto; later he worked for the *Toronto Star Weekly* doing news illustrations.

From there, Lougheed headed for New York, supported himself by doing cover paintings for the pulp magazines and studied at the Art Students League under Frank Vincent DuMond.

Lougheed now divides his time between illustrating for publishers of *True, The National Geographic, Reader's Digest*; Brown & Bigelow, advertising; and painting for exhibitions and galleries. He regularly spends time painting animals in their natural habitats, traveling north of the Arctic Circle, throughout Canada, Alaska, and other parts of the United States.

Lougheed is a member of the Animal Artists Society, the Salmagundi Club, and the Hudson Valley Art Association.

"The Chestnut Rosinback," painted from sketches of the Ringling Brothers Circus. Reproduced in *American Artist* magazine, February, 1958.

A

Tom Lovell

TOM LOVELL (1909-) is an intense, serious artist who drives himself to the point of perfection he seeks in his documentary approach to illustration; no detail of research is too small to be verified. His settings are painted with a conviction based on many years of experience in painting from nature.

Tom was born in New York City and was graduated with a B.F.A. from Syracuse University where he studied with Hibbard V. B. Kline. While still in college, he did his first illustrations for the pulp magazines and continued on in this field to develop his technical facility.

With this solid apprenticeship, Lovell was a fully developed artist when he appeared in the major national magazines, and has since worked for nearly all of them.

During World War II, Lovell served as a staff sergeant in the U.S. Marine Corps Reserve. Many of his paintings of Corps history are now in the permanent collection of the Marine Corps.

He is a member of the American Water Color Society, the Society of Illustrators, having won a Gold Medal in their 1964 annual exhibition, and is also past president of the Westport Artists in Connecticut.

A. Illustration for "The E. A. Johnson Murders," which appeared in *True* magazine, April, 1957.
B. "Conquest of the Holy City," article by Franc Shor.

B

A

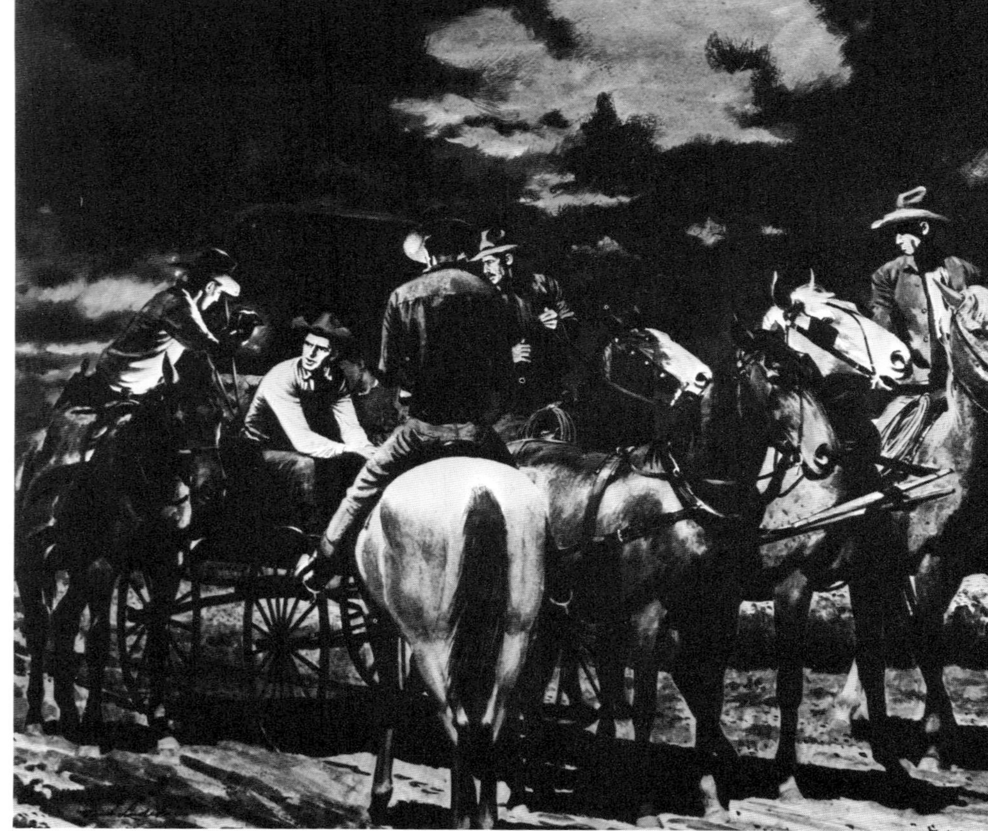

B

Fred Ludekens

FRED LUDEKENS (1900-) was born in Huoneme and is a third generation Californian. He grew up in Victoria, British Columbia, and during those years made several trips to Alaska.

His only art training was a night class under Otis Shepard at the University of California Extension.

Ludekens worked for the Foster and Kleiser outdoor advertising agency in San Francisco, then free-lanced for a time, and later became art director for the San Francisco office of Lord and Thomas. This gave him an insight into advertising art from the business point of view which helped him eventually to become one of the best advertising illustrators in the country.

A commission to illustrate a book about his boyhood country, *Ghost Town*, led *The Saturday Evening Post* to assign him a Western serial story. The success of these pictures thus launched his second career as an editorial illustrator; he has since pursued both, later adding another top position as co-creative director of Foote, Cone and Belding. He is at present Chairman of the Board of Directors of the Famous Artists Schools.

A. Illustration for *True* magazine.
B. *Saturday Evening Post* serial story illustration.
C. Illustration for "Battle Party," by William Chamberlain, *The Saturday Evening Post*.

C

The illustrations of PERRY PETERSON (1908-1958) were done with special flair and apparent spontaneity. Peterson took pride in creating this effect and worked hard in the preparatory stages to achieve it. Years of training in art studios gave him a complete technical command of the water-color medium which he used with strong three-dimensional effect.

Peterson was born in Minneapolis, Minnesota, and his first art education was through the Federal Schools' correspondence course, followed by brief attendance in the evening at the Chicago Art Institute. His early art jobs included catalog illustration for Montgomery Ward in Chicago, automobile renderings in Detroit, and advertising drawings for the Byron Musser Studio in New York.

After his first illustrations for *Liberty* magazine, published in 1942, he soon received assignments for stories in *Good Housekeeping, Woman's Home Companion, Collier's, The Saturday Evening Post,* and others, until his untimely death from burns received in an accidental fire in his New York studio.

Illustration for "Cauldron's Folly," in *The Saturday Evening Post.*

JOHN PIKE, N.A. (1911-   ) has been a lifelong student of the water-color medium despite some diversion along the way at such varied jobs as theatre designing, jewelry making, and as director of advertising for a Jamaican rum company.

Born in Winthrop, Massachusetts, Pike studied in Provincetown with Charles Hawthorne and Richard Miller. He next spent five years in Jamaica, W.I., before returning to this country where his one-man shows and illustration for magazines have made a full-time art career possible. He has illustrated not only for many magazines but also for advertising accounts, and has exhibited widely.

In addition, Pike has served in the Combat Art section, Corps of Engineers, heading a unit to record the United States occupation of Korea; also made paintings for the United States Air Force Historical Foundation in France, Germany, Greenland, South America, Formosa, and Japan.

Pike's work is represented in many collections, public and private; he has won numerous prizes, including the "Water Color U.S.A." Award, and the National Academy Hallgarten Prize. He is currently a member of the American Water Color Society, the Philadelphia Water Color Club, the Salmagundi Club, Woodstock Art Association, Grand Central Art Galleries, the Society of Illustrators, and the National Academy of Design.

Crash survivors in Equadorian jungle awaiting aid by helicopter of the United States Air Rescue Service.

A

The work of ALFRED CHARLES PARKER (1906-   ) is so varied and inventive that it is difficult in this space to choose pictures that represent him fully or summarize his career.

Since his arrival in New York from St. Louis in the mid-'thirties, Parker's illustrations have excited and beguiled public and publishers alike. As his popularity grew, so did the number of his imitators, and the Al Parker approach became the dominant one in the magazines. What set Al's work apart from his imitators, however, was not only his impeccable taste, but the originality of his thinking. Other artists were always one step behind him.

Each of Parker's pictures is unique in composition and color. He has used all of the media, and combinations of them, from children's crayons to polymer. His versatility is such that he once illustrated a whole issue of *Cosmopolitan* magazine by himself using a different name and style for each story.

In 1939 Parker did a mother-daughter cover for the *Ladies' Home Journal* which was immensely successful, creating the demand for a long series that followed and setting a whole new style for mother-daughter fashions.

A jazz buff, Parker had played saxophone in a band on a Mississippi river boat, and participated in many combination jam sessions and sketching trips to service hospitals during World War II.

Over the years he has won more than 25 gold medals and awards of excellence in Art Directors Club and Society of Illustrators shows. He is a past president of the Westport Artists and was elected to the Illustrators Hall of Fame in 1965.

Parker now lives in Carmel, California. He divides his time between Carmel and the East, where his duties as one of the founding faculty of the Famous Artists Schools in Westport, Connecticut require his presence. He uses New York City as a base for magazine assignments that may take him anywhere. One of his recent commissions was a series of paintings of the Grand Prix auto race of Europe for *Sports Illustrated*.

B

WANTED: SOMEONE INNOCENT

BY MARGERY ALLINGHAM

Part one of a two-part story

ILLUSTRATED BY AL PARKER

I didn't blame my uncle. I don't think anyone could have done that. I said as much to my landlady, the vast Mrs. Austin, one night when she sat on my bed squashing my feet in a wide gesture of intimacy in the horrible little room at the top of her house in Pimlico.

Mrs. Austin was a Cockney and kind and emotional, as they are, those stalwart old women whom no one suspected of gallantry until they suddenly produced it like a flag, and she had been saying with unintentional brutality that it was a shame I wasn't one thing or the other, neither the young lady of wealth I'd been trained to be, nor the go-getting milliner's apprentice I was doing my best to become. Thirty-five bob a week was not her idea of a living wage, she said, and I could not have agreed with her more; seven dollars, Sally would have called it. I put Sally out of my mind hastily. It didn't help to think of her when there was only Mrs. Austin to talk to.

The old woman shook her head at me, her festoon of chins sweeping the unfashionable choker of marble-size pearls she (Continued on page 136)

C

D

A. Color illustration painted from life in gouache for *Ladies' Home Journal*.
B. Among Parker's innovations were the candid camera closeup and the marriage of text and illustration in layout. Doublespread for *Good Housekeeping*, 1946.
C. Parker did over 30 covers based on the mother-daughter theme for the *Ladies' Home Journal* beginning in 1939.
D. Here is Parker's illustration for a suspense story in which a man plans to murder his wife. The horizon line was tilted to create a feeling of falling through the railing and the motor boat adds height to the balcony. The viewer's eye travels from the man's head, along the railing to its damaged part where the boat stops it momentarily, then on through the elongated shadow of the railing, and back to the man.

Reprinted with permission of The Limited Editions Club.

Henry C. Pitz

HENRY CLARENCE PITZ, A.N.A. (1895-) has been an outstanding performer in several fields, including illustrating for magazines and books, teaching and lecturing, writing on art subjects, painting and exhibiting.

His talents appeared early; while still in high school in Philadelphia he won a scholarship to study at the Philadelphia Museum School of Art and from there went on to the Spring Garden Institute. Among his teachers were Walter Everett and Maurice Bower.

Although Pitz has experimented with, and worked in, almost every medium, he has a special affinity for line drawing and book illustration. He has illustrated more than 160 books as well as for a whole range of magazines from *The Saturday Evening Post* to *St. Nicholas.*

Among his many popular art books are: *Pen, Brush and Ink, The Practice of Illustration, Drawing Trees, Ink Drawing Techniques,* and *Illustrating Children's Books.*

Pitz has exhibited nationally and internationally, winning awards too numerous to list here. His work is represented in many public collections, including the Library of Congress in Washington, D.C., and the Philadelphia Museum of Art.

Pitz has also served as director of the illustration course, Philadelphia Museum College of Art, Visiting Lecturer and Instructor, and Associate Editor of *American Artist* magazine.

Illustration for *Froissart's Chronicles,* 1961.

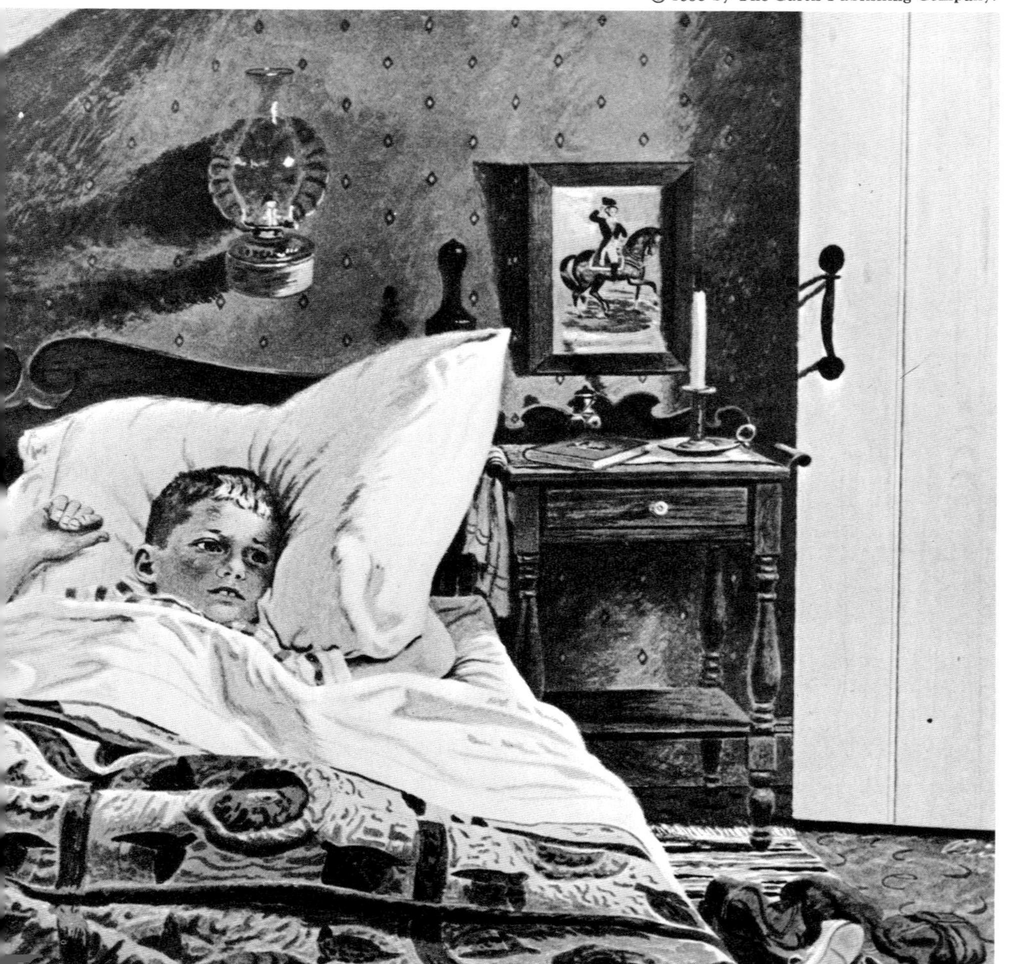

Prins

BEN KIMBERLY PRINS (1904-) was born in Leiden, Holland, but was brought to the United States at the age of one year. Reared in Brooklyn, he was a graduate of Pratt Institute and also studied at the Art Students League and the Grand Central School of Art. His teachers included Arthur Guptill, Ernest Watson, George Bridgman, and Dean Cornwell.

He began his career as an art director at Batten, Barton, Durstine & Osborn Inc., then at the Dorland International Agency, and at Lennen & Mitchell. By 1939, he was free-lancing and his drawings for an *Illustrated History of the Railroad* won him a Gold Medal at the Art Directors Club show in 1940.

Prins soon began to do magazine illustration for publications such as *Collier's, Woman's Home Companion, Pictorial Review,* and *The Saturday Evening Post* for which he also painted a number of covers.

Prins is a member of the Society of Illustrators, The Art Directors Club of New York, and the Wilton Historical Society.

Illustration for *The Saturday Evening Post* story, "Unwanted," by Kingsley Tufts.

Ray Prohaska

RAY PROHASKA (1901-) was born in Mulo, Yugoslavia, and came to America at the age of eight. He studied at the California School of Fine Arts in San Francisco, and followed this with several years of commercial work on the West Coast and in Chicago.

He came to New York in 1929 and obtained his first illustration manuscripts from *Delineator* and *Woman's Home Companion*. Prohaska's contemporary style and careful characterizations soon won him a long list of other magazines as clients, and many advertising commissions as well.

Along with his illustration, he has also painted for exhibition and won several prizes, including the Hallmark Award 1949, Audubon Medal 1954, John Marin Memorial Award 1962, M. Grumbacher First Prize 1958, and Society of Illustrators' Gold Medal 1963.

Prohaska served as president of the Society of Illustrators in 1959-60, taught at the Art Students League in 1961 and is currently Artist in Residence at Washington and Lee University in Lexington, Virginia. He has just recently completed a large mural depicting the communications media for the Department of Journalism and Communications at the University.

Illustration for the story, "Lily Hunter and the U.S.A.," by Viña Delmar.

PAUL RABUT

PAUL RABUT (1914-) immerses himself so thoroughly in research for his illustrations that he becomes an authority on the subject matter of his assignments. This has led to his long-time interest in United States history, in logging, in Northwest Indian culture and artifacts, as well as other primitive art: Oceanic, pre-Columbian, and especially African wood-carvings and masks. He is a consultant for collectors and galleries on the subject of primitive art and has one of the finest private collections in the country.

Rabut attended the College of the City of New York, the Art School of the National Academy of Design, the Grand Central Art School, and the Art Students League; his teachers included Jules Gottlieb, Harvey Dunn, Ivan Olinsky, and Lewis Daniel.

His first break came when one of his early story illustrations for *American Girl* magazine won the Art Directors Club Medal in their annual exhibition in 1942. This led directly to commissions from *The Saturday Evening Post* and other major magazines. Since then he has won several additional Art Directors Club awards for both editorial and advertising illustrations, and his work was selected for the State Department advertising-art traveling exhibition to Europe and South America in 1952. He has exhibited widely and is represented in the permanent collection of the U.S. Medical Museum, Washington, D.C.

The White Pass & Yukon Railroad, painted for the General Electric Company calendar, 1959.

Walter Richards

WALTER D. RICHARDS (1907-   ) worked in black and white for many years as an advertising artist; his illustrations are characterized by a mastery of values whether in monochrome or full color.

Richards was born in Penfield, Ohio, and was graduated from the Cleveland School of Art. He first worked in the famous Sundblom studio in Chicago, later for the Tranquillini studio in Cleveland where he met and worked with Stevan Dohanos. Next, Richards moved to New York where he joined the Charles E. Cooper studio and then free-lanced as an illustrator for most of the magazines and many national advertising accounts.

Through the years he has continued to experiment and to paint for national and international shows in water color and print-making. He is an active member of the American Water Color Society, Society of Illustrators, Connecticut Water Color Society, Westport Artists, and the Fairfield Water Color Group. His work has won many awards including four consecutive first prizes in lithograph at the Cleveland Museum of Art 1935-38.

"How Music entered George Gershwin's Life," an advertising illustration for the Magnavox Company, 1945.

Nicholas F. Riley

NICHOLAS F. RILEY (1900-1944) taught many hundreds of students of illustration (including the writer) in his years as a teacher at Pratt Institute. His thorough grasp of fundamentals and his gentle courtesy in presenting them won the respect of his classes and conveyed to many a lasting sense of idealism for the art of painting and illustration.

Riley was born in Brooklyn and was graduated from Pratt Institute. This was followed by two years of study with M. Scott in Paris. One of his portrait paintings was selected and hung in the Paris Grand Salon in 1925.

He began his teaching career at Pratt in 1927, soon after his return to America, and continued there to the time of his death. In the meantime, he also contributed many illustrations to *The Saturday Evening Post, Woman's Home Companion, Good Housekeeping, Redbook,* and other magazines.

He was a member of the Salmagundi Club, the Lotus Club, and the Society of Illustrators.

Illustration for a *Saturday Evening Post* story, "A Man's Mother," by Gladys Hasty Carroll.

Courtesy of the Capehart Corporation.

A

Robert Riggs

ROBERT RIGGS, N.A. (1896-) is a painter and lithographer of monumental compositions, yet achieves his effects through meticulous means. In lithography, he works from black to white, picking out detail with a scraper blade. For color he uses dry tempera mixed with mastic varnish and alcohol, a medium that dries immediately and allows him to paint over successive layers if necessary.

Riggs was born in Decatur, Illinois, and studied for two years at James Milliken University in Illinois. He followed this with a year of study at the Art Students League in New York, terminated by two years in the Army during World War I. Following the armistice, he stayed for several months to study at the Académie Julian in Paris.

After his return to the United States, Riggs spent several years sketching for the N. W. Ayer & Son advertising agency, and produced many excellent advertising illustrations. Over the years, he has been a consistent prizewinner in the annual Art Directors Club shows.

His simultaneous efforts in fine arts contributed to his success in both fields. His favorite lithographic subjects have been the circus and prize fighting; many of his prints are in museum collections including the Brooklyn Museum, Library of Congress, and the Dallas Museum of Fine Arts.

Riggs has collected a great many primitive artifacts during extended trips to Europe, North Africa, India, and Thailand. A part of his studio and living quarters, therefore, constitutes his personal museum.

A. "The Coronation Scene," from Moussorgsky's "Boris Godounov." Painting for the Capehart Collection.

B. Lithograph of the Baer-Carnera Fight used as an illustration in *This Week* magazine for the story, "The Baer and the Tortoise," by Eddie Eagan.

B

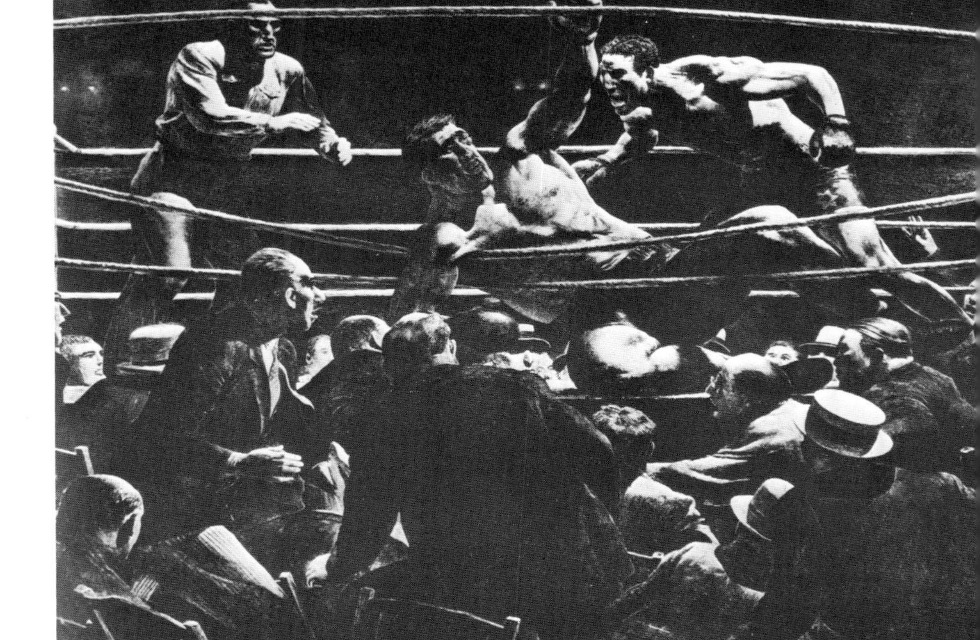

Courtesy of the Rehn Gallery.

FRANK REILLY

FRANK JOSEPH REILLY, A.N.A. (1906-   ) is a great teacher. In addition to the qualities which have made him an outstanding illustrator, Reilly has a scientist's sense of order and analytical acumen combined with a missionary's enthusiasm for his subject. Reilly was Bridgman's successor at the Art Students League in New York and, for over 29 years, his classes were the largest there. He has recently founded his own school, the Frank Reilly School of Art in New York City.

Frank received his own instruction at the League under George Bridgman and Frank Vincent DuMond. He later worked as Dean Cornwell's assistant on several mural projects, and it was Dean who influenced him most, both as artist and teacher.

Reilly has illustrated for many editorial and advertising assignments. Outstanding were those for Pennsylvania Railroad, and Continental Distilling Corporation. He also designed a 63-foot mosaic mural for the Bronx High School of Science; he exhibits, lectures, and writes an art column.

He is an associate member of the National Academy of Design, painter-member of the Art Commission of New York City, member of American Artists' Professional League, Allied Artists, Century Association, National Society of Mural Painters, Salmagundi Club, Artists' and Writers' Guild, Art Students League, and the Society of Illustrators.

Committee examining recast Liberty Bell, Pass and Stow's Foundry, Philadelphia, 1753. Painted as an advertising illustration for the Continental Distilling Corporation, Philadelphia, Pennsylvania.

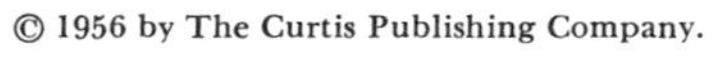

DICK SARGENT

RICHARD SARGENT (1911-   ) has done many cover paintings for *The Saturday Evening Post.* As seen here, they are characterized by their good humor and insight into human frailties. He also has illustrated for *Fortune, Woman's Day, American, Photoplay,* and *Collier's* magazines.

Sargent, who was born in Moline, Illinois, received his art education at the Corcoran School of Art, and Phillips Memorial Gallery in Washington, D. C. He also worked with Ben Shahn.

His pictures have been exhibited in many parts of the United States, including New York City, Washington, D. C., and San Francisco, California. He is a member of the Society of Illustrators in New York, and currently is living in Spain.

A timeless theme presented by Sargent in contemporary terms for this colorful *Saturday Evening Post* cover.

Edward Shenton

EDWARD SHENTON (1895-) specializes in black-and-white illustration and manages to exploit a great variety of value and textures from the line medium. His drawings, although quite realistic, are also stylized and decorative as shown here.

Shenton was born in Pottstown, Pa., studied at the Pennsylvania Museum School of Industrial Art, and the Pennsylvania Academy of the Fine Arts, where his teachers included Thornton Oakley, George Harding, and Henry McCarter. He won the Lee Prize in 1922, and the Cresson Traveling Scholarships in 1923-24 which enabled him to do further study in Paris.

Although Shenton has illustrated for *The Saturday Evening Post, Collier's,* and *Reader's Digest,* his line technique is ideally suited for books, and he has illustrated for many book publishers including Scribner's, Doubleday, Random House, Harcourt Brace, and W. W. Norton.

In addition, Shenton has had an active career in editing and writing. One of his earliest jobs was as an editor for the Penn Publishing Company, and he has also served as a part-time editor for Macrae Smith. His short stories have appeared in *The Saturday Evening Post, Collier's, Scribner's,* and *Cosmopolitan,* and he has written and illustrated several books. His wife, Barbara Webster, also has written a number of books about Pennsylvania country life, which he has illustrated charmingly.

His mural projects include a wall of the Chester County Court House in West Chester, Pennsylvania, and two large facing panels in the Chapel of the War Memorial Cemetery at Saint-James in Brittany, France.

In addition to all of these assignments, Shenton also taught classes at the Moore College of Art in Philadelphia and at present teaches at the Pennsylvania Academy of the Fine Arts.

From Longfellow's *Hiawatha,* Best in Children's Books, published by Doubleday and Company, 1960.

Schwinn

BARBARA E. SCHWINN, (1907-), later Mrs. F. Bertram Jordon, wanted to be a fashion designer from the time she was twelve, when she first cut out and made her own dresses. To prepare for this she studied at the Parsons School of Design in New York and at its branch in Paris.

Her first work after graduation was making accessory and fashion drawings for department stores; in a short time she was able to obtain top assignments from Lord & Taylor, Macy's, and Best & Co. This was followed by a period of drawing for continuity strips and, later, cover designs and magazine illustrations for such publications as *Collier's, Cosmopolitan, American, The Saturday Evening Post,* and the *Ladies' Home Journal.* Many of her illustrations have also appeared in European periodicals.

She has recently turned to portraiture, with an international clientele, including Queen Sirikit of Thailand, Princess Grace of Monaco, Deborah Kerr, Conrad Hilton, and Maurice Pate, Director of UNICEF. She has just completed a painting of Princess Margaret of Britain, who had not previously posed for an American artist.

Illustration for the story, "Come Back to Sorrento," *Collier's* magazine, January 12, 1952.

A

Amos Sewell

B

AMOS SEWELL (1901-   ) has special empathy for children and also particularly enjoys doing homespun, rural subjects. These special gifts were ideally combined in the illustrations he made for a series of stories about Babe, Little Joe, Big Joe, and Uncle Pete by R. Ross Annett that ran for over 20 years in *The Saturday Evening Post*.

Sewell was born in San Francisco and studied nights at the California School of Fine Arts, working days in a bank. After some years of this he decided to try his luck as an illustrator in the East. To get there, he shipped out as a working hand on a lumber boat going by way of the Panama Canal.

In New York he studied at the Art Students League and at the Grand Central School of Art. Among his teachers were Guy Pène DuBois, Julian Levi, and Harvey Dunn. At the same time he began to do black-and-white, dry-brush illustrations for the pulp magazines.

His first major manuscript was illustrated for the *Country Gentleman* in 1937, next came the *The Saturday Evening Post*, for which he subsequently painted many covers. This led to commissions from the other national magazines. Sewell has also illustrated for many major advertisers, and his work has won awards from the Art Directors Clubs of New York and Cleveland, been exhibited at the Society of Illustrators and in traveling exhibits both here and abroad.

A. Illustration for *The Saturday Evening Post*.
B. Vignette in charcoal for *Post* illustration.
C. *Saturday Evening Post* story, "The Wedding Gift."

C

A

Noel Sickles

NOEL SICKLES (1911-   ) is a master in the use of line. His brush work is direct and spare, each stroke reduced to the most expressive minimum. Although he uses color very effectively, it is usually subordinate to the drawing — often applied in thin washes over the basic black-and-white brush rendering.

Sickles' approach grew logically from his early career as a newspaper artist and cartoonist. He established a whole new style of cartooning in his adventure strip, "Scorchy Smith," by indicating full light and shade in his black-and-white drawings.

Seeking to develop further as an illustrator, Sickles abandoned the strip and began to accept advertising and editorial commissions. Among these was a notable series of World War II drawings for *Life* magazine. These resulted in his being placed under contract by both the War and Navy Departments in Washington to do similar illustrations for instruction in the Armed Services, much of his work highly confidential.

After the war, Sickles resumed his free-lance illustration career with special emphasis on his interest in American historical subjects. He has since made many outstanding illustrations for *The Saturday Evening Post, Life, This Week* and the *Reader's Digest* condensed books.

A. "Saloon, Taxco, Texas, late 1870's." This line drawing combined with a small amount of charcoal and Liquitex is one of a personal series of drawings and paintings, typical of Sickles' present work.
B. One of Sickles' expressive illustrations from the *Life* magazine publication of Hemingway's *The Old Man and the Sea.* The strength and dignity of the drawings in line and halftone are a perfect complement to the spirit of the manuscript.

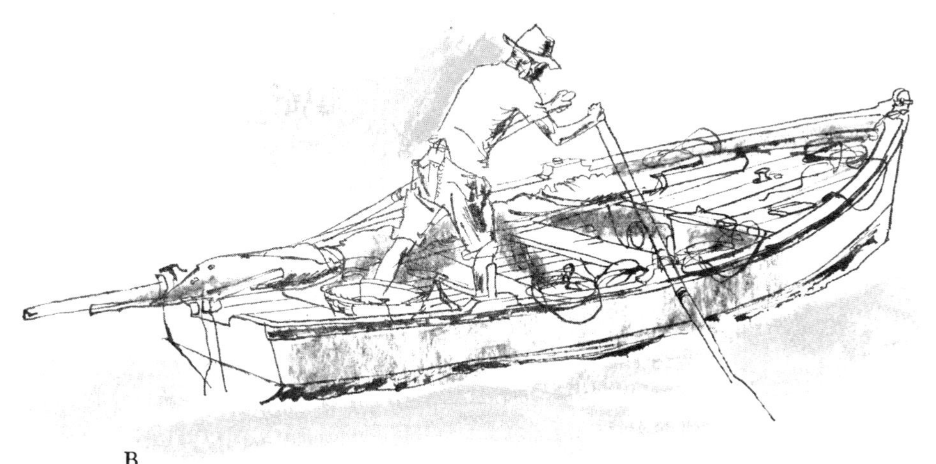

B

A

Courtesy of the John Hancock Mutual Life Insurance Company

Stahl

BENJAMIN ALBERT STAHL (1910-) has been influenced in his development by many artists. Early idols of his were Paul Bransom, Frank Hoffman, and Roy Spreter. Later, he found inspiration in the works of Degas, Renoir, and El Greco. For a youngster with no formal training beyond a wasted year of art in high school, this study of the artists he admired was the best possible way to learn how to paint.

As a boy, Stahl was encouraged to become an artist by his grandmother who took him to visit the Chicago Art Institute and the Marshall Field Art Galleries. At 17 he got a job as an errand boy and apprentice in an art studio and within five years had landed a job as an illustrator with one of the top studios in Chicago.

In 1937, *The Saturday Evening Post* editors saw one of his advertising paintings of a seascape and invited him to illustrate a sea story. From then on he has painted illustrations for nearly all of the magazines and for many national advertising campaigns.

Stahl's recent activities have included a series of illustrations for the Bible; a book he has written and illustrated, *Blackbeard's Ghost*, published by Houghton Mifflin, and an ambitious project for a Museum of the Cross to be built in Sarasota, Florida. He has designed the building, and is painting the large mural Stations of the Cross around which the Museum will be built. All this is in addition to his regular illustration and portrait painting.

Stahl has taught at the Chicago Academy of Fine Arts and at the American Academy of Art in Chicago. He also is one of the founding faculty members of the Famous Artists Schools in Westport, Connecticut.

A. Here Stahl has dramatically established the scale of the small figures against the dark bulk of the whale, the opposing directions of the antagonists emphasized by the contrasting value of the white foam.
B. The influence of Degas is evident in Stahl's impressionist approach to this illustration for the *Woman's Home Companion*. 1947.

Stahl

A

B

A. Renegade whites supplying Comanches with rifles for the story, "Big Hunt," by James Warner Bellah, *The Saturday Evening Post*.
B. "Lash of Fear," another *Post* story by James Warner Bellah.
C. All of the drama of man against the might of the sea is vividly summarized in this illustration for *True* magazine, 1953.
D. Here Von Schmidt has depicted the relationship of a newly-arrived, inexperienced officer with battle-hardened troops for the story, "Replacement," in *The Saturday Evening Post*.
E. The artist's intimate knowledge of animals has made it possible to convincingly delineate an action that could never be posed. For *American* magazine.

C

D

E

HAROLD VON SCHMIDT

HAROLD VON SCHMIDT (1893-). grew up in the West a generation after Remington and Russell but has felt a close kinship with them and the old West throughout his painting career. A native Californian, Von Schmidt was orphaned at five and reared by his grandfather who had been a Forty-niner. His grandfather's stories, together with his own experiences as a construction worker, lumberjack, and cowhand gave him an authentic insight into the earlier era.

He studied at the San Francisco Art Institute and the California College of Arts and Crafts, also with Worth Ryder and Maynard Dixon. His first art work was as an art director for Foster & Kleiser, followed by illustrating for *Sunset* magazine.

In 1924 Von Schmidt came East to study further with Harvey Dunn. He acknowledges the tremendous effect that Dunn's teaching had on his career. It was Dunn who taught him to paint the epic rather than the incident. He has kept to this high standard in his illustrations of the West, the sea and other subjects ever since.

He has been an ardent athlete all his life, was a member of the American Olympic Rugby Football team at Antwerp, Belgium, in 1920. Feeling that an artist should also be active in civic affairs, he served as Selectman, Town of Westport, Connecticut, for eight years, on the Board of Finance, Police Commission, and Public Library Board.

During World War I, Von Schmidt did posters for the U.S. Navy; during World War II he was an invited artist-correspondent for the U.S. Air Force, European Theatre of Operations, and artist-correspondent for King Features Syndicate in the Pacific Theatre of Operations.

Twelve of his paintings depicting the westward trek and the Gold Rush of 1849 hang in the Governor's office in Sacramento, California; five Civil War paintings are in the permanent collection of the United States Military Academy at West Point, and many others are in private collections.

Von Schmidt is a life trustee of the Artists' Guild, New York, was president of the Society of Illustrators, 1938-41, member and officer of the American Indian Defense Association, president of the Westport Artists, 1950-51, and a founding member of the Famous Artists Schools in Westport, Connecticut.

Jon Whitcomb

JON WHITCOMB (1906-) has made his name synonymous with pictures of young love and glamorous, beautiful women. During World War II, a series of illustrations for advertisements he created on the theme, "Back Home for Keeps," became a pin-up fad for women deprived of their husbands or sweethearts.

Jon was born in Weatherford, Oklahoma, and reared in Manitowoc, Wisconsin. He attended Ohio Wesleyan University and was graduated from Ohio State where he did pictures for the school publications and worked during the summer painting posters for a theatre in Cleveland.

This was excellent training ground, and Jon, although he had majored in English with an ambition to write, switched to art classes. After graduation he was able to obtain work in a series of studios doing travel and theatre posters, as well as general advertising illustrations.

In 1934, he moved on to New York to combine studio work with free-lance illustration. His first manuscripts were illustrated for *Collier's,* followed by *Good Housekeeping,* and then the others in succession as Whitcomb's pretty girls began to attract enthusiastic readership.

His career was interrupted by World War II when he was commissioned a Lieutenant, j.g. in the Navy. His assignments varied from mine-sweeping duty off the East coast, to the Public Relations Department in Washington, to the Pacific as a combat artist with the invasions of Tinian, Saipan, and Peleliu. After hospitalization for tropical infections, he was discharged in 1945 and resumed his art career.

Whitcomb's writing ability became useful when he began to do a monthly series of sketches and articles for *Cosmopolitan,* about motion picture stars, called "On Location with Jon Whitcomb." He has also written several short stories, two children's books about poodles, *Coco,* and *Pom Pom's Christmas,* and a book about feminine glamour, *All About Girls.*

A

Courtesy of Community Silverplate by Oneida Silversmiths.

He is a member of the founding faculty of the Famous Artists Schools and travels extensively to paint portraits and interview film celebrities.

A. One of the "Back Home for Keeps" advertisements, 1943.

B. Illustration for a love story by Adela Rogers St. Johns.

B

Reprinted by permission, *Good Housekeeping* magazine, © 1954 by the Hearst Corporation.

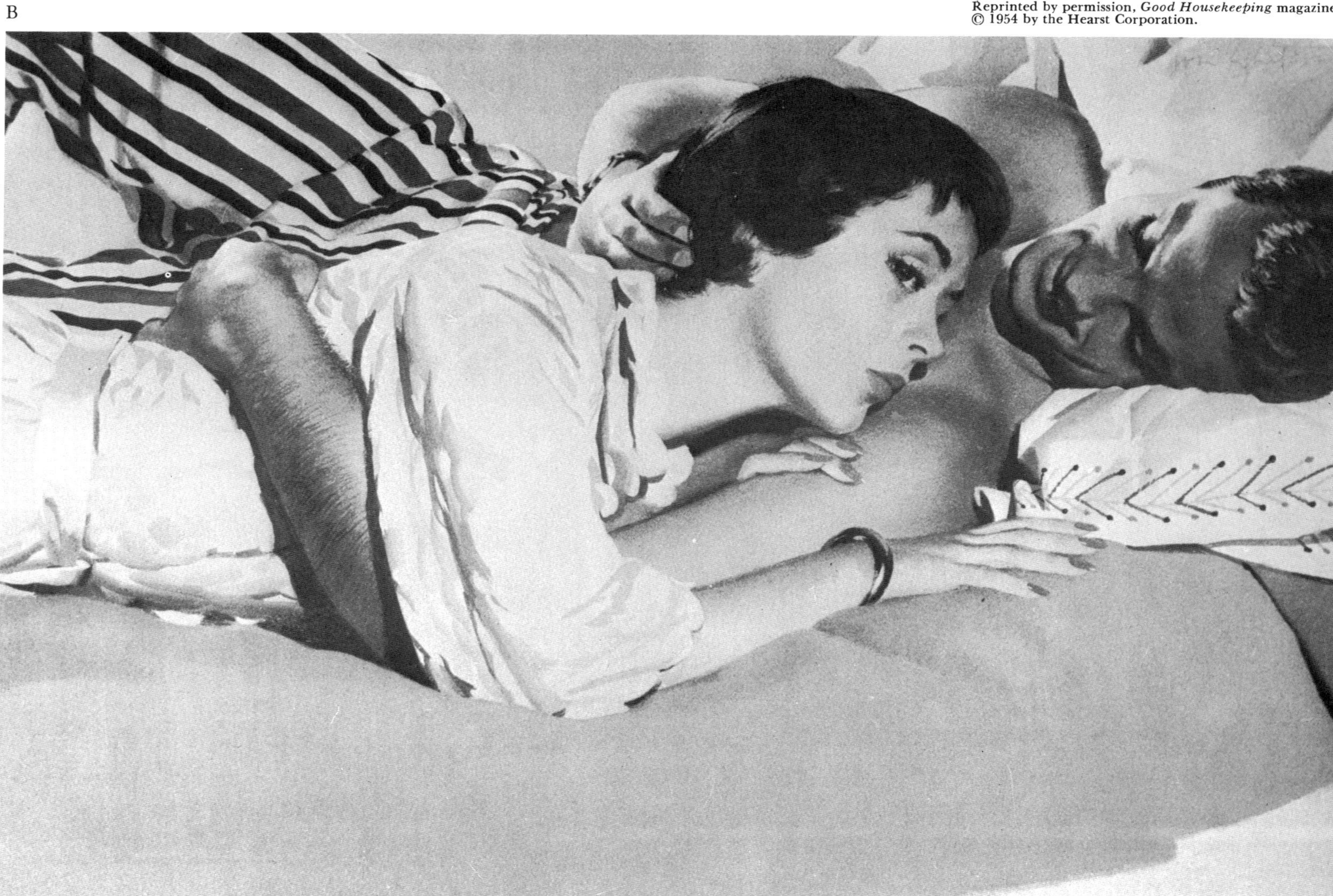

Varady

FREDRIC VARADY (1908-   ) was born in Budapest and attended the Royal Hungarian Academy of Art there. Upon graduation he began to do movie posters, worked on theatre set designs and made fashion drawings.

He left Hungary in 1927 and worked at a succession of art jobs from painting lampshades to murals in private houses in Istanbul. He did fashion drawing and suit designing in Paris and in Berlin, before coming to the United States to establish himself as a free-lance fashion artist.

Varady's dramatic flair for drawing and his meticulous rendering made a very favorable impression on magazine art editors, and he obtained his first manuscript to illustrate, from *American* magazine in 1939. This was soon followed by commissions from most of the major magazines including *Cosmopolitan, Good Housekeeping, McCall's, Collier's, Redbook, Today's Woman,* and *The Saturday Evening Post.*

Varady has now returned to fashion illustration exclusively and also exhibits his paintings when time permits.

Illustration for a *Saturday Evening Post* story.

LYND WARD

LYND WARD, A.N.A. (1905-   ) first came to prominence as an artist for his woodcut novel, *God's Man.* He eventually produced several others including *Mad Man's Drum, Song without Words,* and *Vertigo.* These books established Ward as an original talent; magazine and book publishers have kept him busy ever since.

Much of his work has been in wood engraving, but to keep his outlook fresh, he has experimented with lithography, pen or brush and ink, water colors, oils, casein, and other media.

Ward had prepared for his career thoroughly, with four years at Columbia University studying theory of design, art history, and teaching methods. This was followed by a year as a special student at the State Academy for Graphic Arts at Leipsig, Germany, where his instructors were Hans Mueller, Alois Kolp, and George Mathey.

He has illustrated many of the classics for the Limited Editions and Heritage Book Clubs; also collaborated with his author-wife, May McNeer, to produce some of his finest illustrations. A member of the Society of Illustrators and the Society of American Graphic Arts, he has won many awards including the Caldecott Medal, John Taylor Arms Memorial Prize, Library of Congress Award, and Limited Editions Club Silver Medal.

Illustration for *America's Abraham Lincoln,* by May McNeer, published by Houghton Mifflin Company, 1957.

Welch

JACK W. WELCH (1905-) is a tall Texan from Cleburne. He was educated at Temple University and took the W. L. Evans correspondence course in cartooning. This was enough to launch him as a newspaper artist; he worked for papers in Texas, California, Seattle, Chicago, Philadelphia, and New York.

The next logical step was as an advertising agency sketch man; he spent several years doing sketches and comprehensive drawings for advertising layouts. His sense of humor and feeling for action, freely rendered, made him a natural for doing children, and he began to do the "finishes" for advertisers, such as Keds, Jello, Pullman, and Traveler's Insurance.

These illustrations, in turn, brought his work to the attention of *The Saturday Evening Post* for which he did a number of memorable covers; then other magazines, including *Family Circle* and *Woman's Day*.

His work has brought Welch several awards in annual New York Art Directors Club shows and for outdoor advertising art.

Saturday Evening Post cover rendered in pastels.

MORTIMER WILSON (1906-) from Lincoln, Nebraska, has a rich, sumptuous style of painting, based in part on his training as a portraitist. His father, a composer, had wanted his son to follow a musical career, but both violin and piano were discarded when Mortimer showed a genuine interest in drawing and painting.

Wilson studied painting at the Art Students League in New York, continued studying on his own and painted a few portraits. He also became involved in summer theatre work as a director while teaching painting on the side.

The need for earning enough money to marry on, prodded him into trying story illustration. The combination of his dramatic experience with the painter's craft produced a fresh approach, and Wilson soon became a popular illustrator for *American* magazine, *The Saturday Evening Post*, and *Woman's Home Companion*, as well as for advertisers including Maxwell House Coffee and Woodbury Facial Soap.

Illustration for *American* magazine.

1950-1960

ILLUSTRATORS 1950-1960

Isa Barnett
James R. Bingham
Bruce Bomberger
Joseph Bowler
Ward Brackett
Austin Briggs
McCauley Conner
Bernard D'Andrea
Joe DeMers
Stanley W. Galli
Denver Gillen
Louis S. Glanzman
Albert Gold
Robert Tompkins Handville
Raymond F. Houlihan
Bill Johnson
Robert Jones
Morgan Kane
Robert Lavin
James Lewicki
David Stone Martin
Robert Theodore McCall
John R. McDermott
Franklin McMahon
Stanley Meltzoff
Al Muenchen
Paul Nonnast
Fred Otnes
Gustav Rehberger
Robert Riger
Ken Riley
Morton Roberts
Alex Ross
John Scott
William Arthur Smith
Tracy Sugarman
Robert A. Thom
Thornton Utz
M. Coburn Whitmore

The Decade: 1950-1960

by Austin Briggs

DRAWING BY BERNARD FUCHS

It was during the 'fifties that a healthy revolt against the slick, photograph-oriented illustration then in vogue really began to gather adherents. This revolution was accelerated by the demise of several national periodicals in a losing competition with television for presentation of fictional escapism. Other floundering publications sought salvation in acquiring a new image — anything different and strident enough to retain the attention of a wavering public.

These conditions produced an opportunity for the illustrator to be truly creative with a freedom from the restraints of the past never before experienced. Yet, despite the present ferment in both illustration and the so-called fine arts, there is hardly enough genius to go around. A neighbor of mine remarked, after glancing through the latest Illustrators Annual, "All the pictures appear to have been done by the same five or six people!"

In the meantime, the illustrators of the past have fallen into the grip of the same stultifying watchfulness that infects the fine art establishment. Each appearance of a novelty compels the established illustrator to take inventory of his resources and to decide whether it is to his advantage to embrace the novelty or to fight it — I am now quoting Harold Rosenberg from his book, *The Anxious Object*. He continues, speaking of the gallery painter — but it is the same for us — "Must the artist weigh the advisability of a new move against the likelihood that the style with which he is identified will continue to arouse interest? — Has the time come to unload and take on something new, and if so, whose judgment ought one to follow, one's own? or some current loud noise?"

It has been my contention that illustration has lived mainly on ideas from the avant garde, and to quote a speaker from the last Aspen Conference, "The calamity threatening us now is what happens when the avant garde has no formal thought to pass down to the professional level?"

Let's remind ourselves that last year's fresh idea is today's cliché. The field we love and live on is infected with thieves and peddlers. No new brush stroke can appear in any publication but some skillful craftsman in a studio can master it by the following noon. I am not opposed to these people because of their mastery of technique, but rather because they are not provoked to perform out of an observation of humanity . . . Really it's because they have observed and coveted the success of another. Should they ever look at the public, whom we must actually see in order to communicate, they would see nothing at all. A Japanese poet once wrote, "When you look in a mirror, you do not see your reflection: Your reflection sees you!"

Because our reading habits have changed so drastically, the printed picture carries a greater responsibility than ever before to function literally as copy . . . as text . . . I have been fortunate enough during a long career to invent and abandon a whole series of technical innovations, and these techniques have had much to do with the length of that career; but today we are awash in a veritable sea of Liquitex. Technique without the merest shadow of content is our "Stencilled Brillo Box." We must make our pictures easier to read and identify with than the written or spoken word. I am certainly not opposed to innovation. I do not suggest that we, like Christopher Isherwood, become cameras with the shutter left open, but we are goofing a great opportunity through a kind of simple inertia. Even the good, new artists are less interested in solving the problem than in "doing what they want."

The artist's traditional role is to lead, but we seem to have lost the necessary virility with which to do it. Everyone knows that we see things as we are, and not as they are, so why copy artists as fallible as ourselves? Let's stop feeling threatened by truly new ideas and have some of our own.

The past has always seemed a pendulum . . . what was in would surely go out, and what was out, in! But now, with the pendulum eager to swing in our direction . . . nobody swings!

Excerpt from a talk before the Minneapolis-St. Paul Association of Professional Artists, 1965.

Austin Briggs

ISA BARNETT (1924-   ) was born in Carbondale, Pennsylvania. He studied at the Philadelphia Museum School of Industrial Art and the Barnes Foundation. Among his teachers were Henry Pitz, Robert Riggs and, later Robert Fawcett, who gave him special instruction.

His art career was postponed by World War II — he was a much-decorated United States paratrooper — but by 1946 he had sold his first illustration to *Argosy* magazine. This was soon followed by assignments from *American Weekly, Life, True, The Saturday Evening Post, Cosmopolitan, Outdoor Life, American Heritage, This Week,* and many others.

Barnett has exhibited at the Art Alliance in Philadelphia, won Gold Medals in Cleveland and at Philadelphia Art Directors Shows.

He has taught at the Philadelphia Museum School, the Moore Institute, and at present, between illustration assignments, teaches at the Philadelphia College of Art.

Illustration for an article about the Remington Rolling Block Gun, *American Weekly,* 1960.

Bingham

JAMES R. BINGHAM (1917-   ) won the New York Art Directors Club medal for magazine editorial art in 1945 for this dramatically beautiful landscape. This was fitting recognition for an illustrator who has produced a long series of strongly composed pictures in many national magazines.

Bingham was born in Pittsburgh, Pennsylvania, and studied at the Carnegie Institute of Technology. Aside from his World War II stint animating Army Air Force films, and his appointment as a Naval officer attached to the Office of Research and Invention, he feels that his life has been singularly uneventful. This is in direct contrast to the usual subject matter of his illustrations, for he has long been associated with Erle Stanley Gardner's Perry Mason serials and other mystery stories in *The Saturday Evening Post.*

In addition to editorial work, Bingham has done much advertising illustration for clients such as Philadelphia Whiskey, Gulf Oil Corporation, Air Transport Association, and Caterpillar Tractor Co.

Illustration for "The Pool," by Dana Burnet for *The Saturday Evening Post.*

Bowler

JOSEPH BOWLER (1928-) knew early that he wanted to be an illustrator and accomplished it by making his first sale to *Redbook* magazine at the age of 22. He has since become one of the top performers, and his romantic illustrations appear regularly in *McCall's, Good Housekeeping, Redbook, Ladies' Home Journal,* and other publications.

Born in Forest Hills, New York, Bowler studied at the Art Students League under Frank Reilly, Robert Hale, and Howard Trafton. In 1948 he joined the staff of the Charles E. Cooper Studio, noted for developing talented young artists, and from there launched his illustration career.

Among his other activities, he has made recruiting posters for the Air Force and is represented in the permanent collection of the Air Force Academy in Colorado Springs. He has also appeared as guest lecturer at the Parsons School of Design in New York.

His work has won many awards in various annual exhibitions of the New York Art Directors Club and Society of Illustrators.

Bowler uses subtle values and careful control of color to emphasize the reflection of the young actress for the story "Image of a Starlet," by George Bradshaw in *The Saturday Evening Post.*

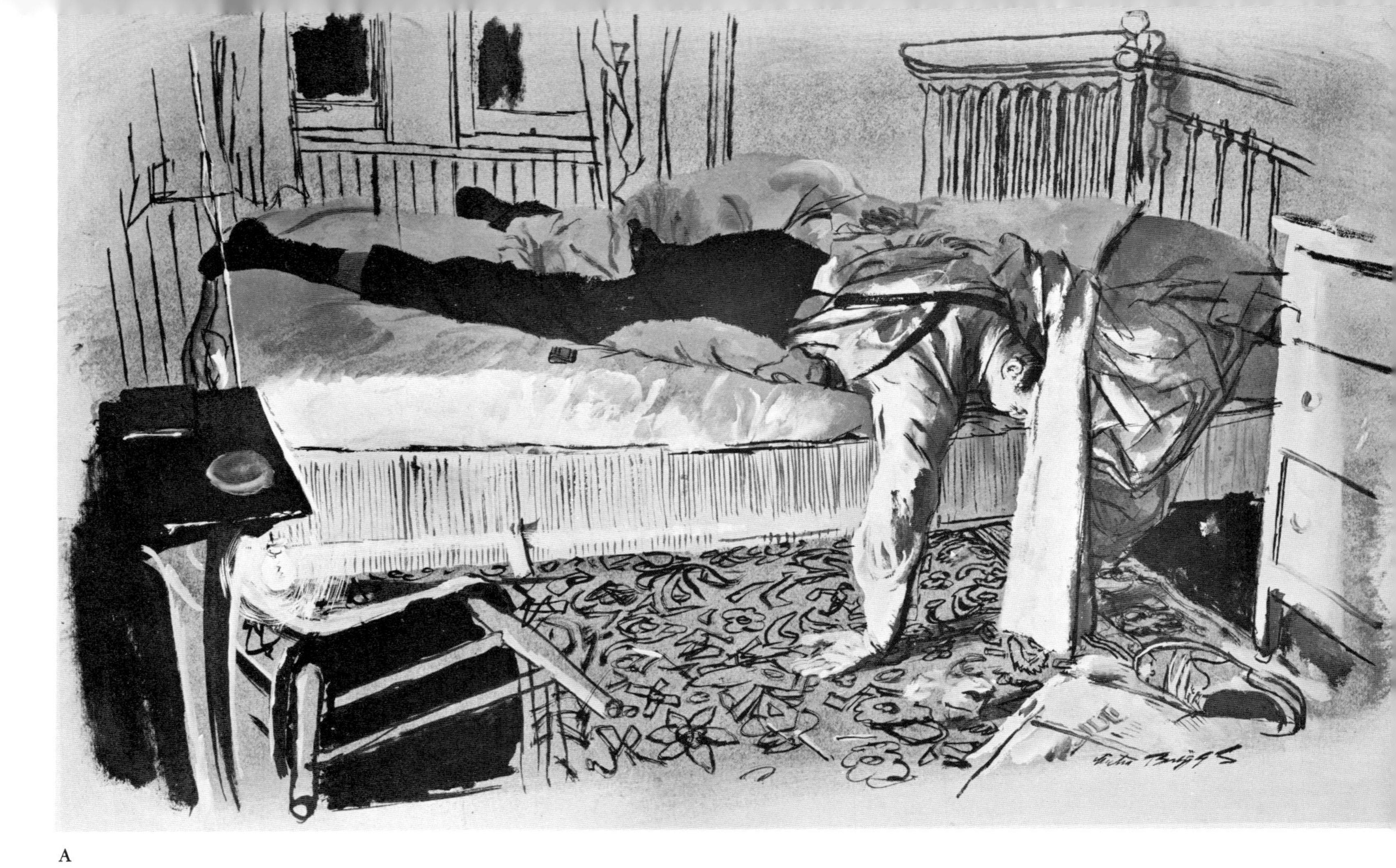

A

B

Reproduced with permission of *TV Guide* magazine.

A. Illustration originally in red, gray, and black for *Cosmopolitan* magazine.
B. This drawing is one of an advertising series for T V Guide. To get more strength in the reproductions, Briggs separated the drawing, made in line, from the tonal wash which was painted as an overlay. The engraver made a "combination" plate from the line and halftone negatives.
C. Another facet of Briggs' versatility is shown in his ability to depict the Madison Avenue advertising executive (for *TV Guide*) or the rural Southerner, with equal insight and authority, as in this painting for *Look* magazine, "Okefenokee Swamp."

Austin Briggs

AUSTIN BRIGGS (1909-) did some of his early illustrations for *Blue Book* magazine on the textured surface of white window shade cloth. It was his answer to obtaining a halftone effect for a magazine restricted to line reproductions.

Such resourcefulness and experimental enterprise has characterized Briggs' entire career. Once he has mastered a particular medium or method of working, he is never long satisfied with either. In the process, he has left his many imitators behind and, for over 30 years, has kept his work fresh and contemporary.

Briggs was born in a private railway car on a siding near Humboldt, Minnesota. His father was an electrical engineer employed in installing telegraphic equipment, and his family traveled along. Austin grew up in Detroit, Michigan, and was awarded a scholarship to the Wicker Art School. After a brief stay there, followed by a semester at the City College of Detroit, he had an opportunity to become assistant to an automobile illustrator, doing figures to set off the automobile.

Ambitious to do story illustration, he made some drawings for the *Dearborn Independent*. With these as samples, he tackled New York where he obtained work from *Collier's*, *McClure's*, and *Pictorial Review*. He also continued to study and enrolled in classes at the Art Students League under George Bridgman and Jack Duncan.

This auspicious beginning was blighted by the Depression as the magazines retrenched. Briggs, who had not yet developed his own individual style, was expendable. For the next several years, he did a variety of art work, from movie posters to ghosting the drawings for the comic strip, "Flash Gordon." He also began to do pulp illustration for Don Kennicott of *Blue Book* magazine. *Blue Book* became a new training ground; the care that Briggs lavished on these assignments began to bring out in him a more individual point of view. He attracted the attention of *Redbook*, then *Cosmopolitan*, *The Saturday Evening Post*, and others. From that period on, Briggs has been a prolific illustrator who continues to innovate and to grow as an artist.

C

Bruce Bomberger

BRUCE BOMBERGER (1918-) is a native Californian who, except for a year in New York, has made his career there as one of the "West Coast Artists." He has had a varied background of experience, from art service, to Lord & Thomas, to free-lancing, to a partnership in an art service, and finally back to free-lancing again.

Bomberger, who is a past-president of the San Francisco Society of Illustrators, has done a wide variety of advertising illustration in addition to editorial drawings and paintings for *True, The Saturday Evening Post, Cosmopolitan, Good Housekeeping, This Week,* and other publications.

In this dry-brush illustration for *The Saturday Evening Post,* Bomberger dramatically uses the flashlight to create a strong pattern of light and shadow and to heighten the feeling of mystery and tragedy.

Ward Brackett

WARD BRACKETT (1914-   ) is a sound painter who developed his abilities through many years as a studio artist. He was born in Milwaukee, Wisconsin, and studied at the Layton School of Art there. At the age of 20 he was fortunate enough to be taken on at the Stevens, Sundblom and Stultz studio in Chicago. From there he went to the Grauman Studios in 1938 and to the Charles E. Cooper Studio in New York in 1940.

During World War II, Brackett was attached to the Quartermaster School where his duties involved doing a large volume of visual aids and training posters.

Since the war he has free-lanced for the Crowell-Collier magazines, *McCall's*, *Good Housekeeping*, *Parents'*, *Redbook*, *Reader's Digest*, *Cosmopolitan*, and others, represented by Barry Stevens and later by James Perkins.

In 1953 he traveled with a USO troupe to Japan and Korea, doing portrait sketches of Army and Marine personnel in hospitals and rest centers, as well as artillery emplacements. In 1964 he toured the United States Air Force bases in Spain, with other illustrators, to make reportorial drawings and paintings. This work is represented in the Air Force Academy art collection.

Illustration for Andrina Iverson's story, "The Way of a Man."

Reprinted by permission *Good Housekeeping* magazine, © 1960 by the Hearst Corporation.

Conner

MC CAULEY CONNER (1913-   ) sold his first covers to *The Saturday Evening Post* while still an art student. He studied at the Philadelphia Museum School with Henry Pitz and at the Grand Central School of Art in New York under Harvey Dunn.

Service in the Navy interrupted his career for several years, after which he joined with Bill Neeley to form an art agency, Neeley Associates.

Conner has also had an active free-lance career as an illustrator for the *Post*, *McCall's*, *Cosmopolitan*, *Redbook*, *Woman's Day*, *Argosy*, *Woman's Home Companion*, *Ladies' Home Journal*, and other magazines.

Conner is a member of the New York Society of Illustrators, has exhibited at the Palm Beach Galleries, and the Country Art Gallery in Westbury, Long Island. His work won the Philadelphia Art Directors Award in 1959.

Observe how Conner has used the change from a linear drawing to a tonal painting to emphasize his center of interest in this illustration for *Collier's* magazine.

D'Andrea

BERNARD D'ANDREA (1923-   ) has experimented successfully with many different media and approaches for his editorial illustration, as suggested by the requirements of each story. He also has had an active career as a painter, affiliated with the Alan Stone Galleries in New York City.

D'Andrea was born in Buffalo, New York, and studied at Pratt Institute in Brooklyn. Later he studied at the Brooklyn Museum Art School with Reuben Tam. His first work, as an advertising artist, was interrupted by service in the Army during World War II. He made his first sale to *The Saturday Evening Post* after the war and now is an active illustrator for most of the magazines.

His wife, Lorraine Fox, is an accomplished painter and illustrator in her own right; her work is included in this book. They recently have had a husband-and-wife exhibit of paintings and drawings in the Hall of Art at Nassau Community College in Garden City, New York.

Illustration for *Cosmopolitan* magazine and reproduced in *Illustrators '59*.

Joe De Mers

JOE DE MERS (1910-   ) successfully depicts the American girls of today, not as stereotypes, but as a diverse array of dazzling females — sweet, predatory, or sophisticated. To dress them, he enlists the fashion expertise of his wife, Janice, for styles that will not become dated in the six months between painting and publication. His compositions are distinguished by their rich color and effective mood.

De Mers was born in San Diego, California, and attended the Chouinard Art School in Los Angeles. Among his teachers were Pruett Carter, Lawrence Murphy, and later, Reuben Tam, at the Brooklyn Museum Art School. De Mers spent about ten years as a production illustrator and designer for motion pictures, mostly for Warner Brothers Studios.

His first illustration assignment was for *Fortune* magazine in 1937, followed by assignments from *Esquire*, and then from most of the other major magazines in the United States and Europe. He is one of several illustrators who have found a steady market for second rights to pictures for publishers in England and on the Continent.

De Mers has exhibited at the New York Museum of Modern Art, Corcoran Museum of Art, the Los Angeles County Museum, various Art Directors Club shows, and at the Society of Illustrators in New York. He taught at the Chouinard Art School from 1934-37 and currently teaches at the Parsons School of Design in New York.

Note the bold use of informal balance in this colorful illustration for *The Saturday Evening Post*.

Stan Galli

STANLEY W. GALLI (1912-   ) spent seven of his formative years between high school and art school doing many odd jobs. The Depression was on, and he worked successively as a roustabout and ranch hand near Reno, Nevada, an apprentice in a Reno bakery, a longshoreman in San Francisco and, as a member of the Teamsters' Union, went through all the violence of a coastal strike.

Galli finally saved enough to enroll at the California School of Fine Arts in San Francisco (now the San Francisco Institute of Art). Hired out of art school by a San Francisco art service, he became a partner in the firm just before World War II. He was then called into special service by the Navy Department to work at structuring educational programs and materials. After the war, he returned to his art service partnership but found the business aspects of this too demanding and decided to return to drawing and painting as a free-lance illustrator.

He has since been called upon to depict a wide variety of subjects in his illustrations for both advertising and editorial assignments. As he says, "I am grateful now that my difficult pre-art school experiences were so diverse. They helped me to know many people, their work, and their ways. This all helps in conceiving the common denominators of communication."

"The Moonflower Vine," illustration for *McCall's*, 1963.

DENVER GILLEN (1914-   ) was born in Vancouver, British Columbia, Canada, the son of a sea captain.

Gillen had no intention of becoming an artist until, at 17, a protracted illness kept him in a hospital bed for several months. As therapy, the doctor, who was an amateur artist, interested his patient in drawing. When Denver was well again, he obtained a beginner's job in the art department of the Hudson's Bay Company. He also studied with Frederick Varley during this time and began to go on outdoor painting expeditions.

Later he progressed from studios in Toronto and Chicago (including a stint for Montgomery Ward's art department making catalog drawings) to a variety of free-lance assignments on every possible subject. In the process, he was evolving his own personal style, strongly linear, and began to obtain manuscripts to illustrate from *Collier's*, *True*, *Outdoor Life*, and many other magazines including a long stint at the *Reader's Digest*.

In addition to magazine and advertising assignments, Gillen has continued to do independent paintings, exhibiting at the Toronto Museum, the Chicago Art Institute, the Society of Illustrators in New York, and the Oehlschlaeger Gallery in Chicago. He has also completed a series of mural paintings for the Missouri Pacific Railroad.

Illustration for "The Blizzard That Tested the Great Plains," by Bill Hosokawa, *Real* magazine, August, 1957. Reprinted, condensed, in the *Reader's Digest*.

In this day of specialization, ALBERT GOLD (1916-   ), is a rarity — the complete artist. He is a realist, but does not try to see photographically; a painter-reporter for the printed page as well as for exhibition walls; a social commentator in his choice of subject, and a gifted and articulate teacher.

Gold was born in Philadelphia and attended the Philadelphia Museum College of Art, studying under Earl Horter and Henry Pitz.

During World War II, he was assigned to *Yank* magazine and spent three years as an artist-correspondent in Europe. The rigorous training of that on-the-spot selection and drawing has shaped his work since.

Much of his postwar commissioned work for publications, such as *Ford Times*, *Argosy*, *What's New* (Abbott Laboratories), *Lincoln-Mercury Times*, *Holiday*, *The Lamp*, *Bulletin* magazine, and others, has been of a reportorial nature.

Gold has also exhibited regularly in the major shows, has won two Tiffany Foundation grants, the Prix de Rome (1942), the Sesnan Gold Medal from the Pennsylvania Academy of the Fine Arts, and numerous other awards.

During this period, from 1946 to the present, he has also found time to teach at the Philadelphia Museum College of Art, is Associate Director of the Graphics Department there.

"Pre-game Taping," for article, "An Afternoon with the Eagles," *Sunday Bulletin* magazine, Philadelphia. © 1962, Bulletin Company.

LOUIS S. GLANZMAN (1922-   ) had no formal art training but, from childhood on, a strong urge to draw impelled him to train himself. He accomplished this largely through study of the George Bridgman anatomy textbooks, *Art Instruction* magazine, (predecessor of *American Artist*), an out-dated set of an art correspondence course, and the on-the-job training of drawing for comic books.

The Army gave Glanzman his first acquaintance with art on a professional level when he was attached to the *Air Force* magazine art department in New York. There he was able to fill in many of the gaps in his art background and by the time of his discharge was ready for a career as a free-lance illustrator.

True magazine bought his first pictures in 1948. He has continued to contribute to *True*, and also to most of the other magazines, ranging in subject matter from *Life* magazine to *Seventeen*. He also illustrates for many book publishers.

Glanzman is a jazz afficionado who enjoys arranging jam sessions for recordings and writes reviews for record companies, but otherwise his hobby is painting.

"The Throwing of the Bones," an illustration for *Collier's* magazine in which Glanzman skillfully creates the eerie mood of a magic ritual through the superimposed linear drawing of African masks and carvings.

ROBERT TOMPKINS HANDVILLE (1924-) paints both for exhibition and for editorial publication. His illustrations appear in a wide variety of magazines including *Sports Illustrated, The Saturday Evening Post, Reader's Digest, Boy's Life, True, Woman's Day, National Geographic* and *Argosy.*

At the same time, Handville has exhibited throughout the country and has won many awards. Among them are the Ranger Fund Purchase Prize 1960, Audubon Artists Anonymous Prize 1960, Arthur Butler Award 1961-62 for American Water Color, and the C.F.S. Award, American Water Color Society Annual Exhibition, 1964.

Born in Paterson, New Jersey, he studied at Pratt Institute and the Brooklyn Museum Art School under Reuben Tam. He is a member of the New York Society of Illustrators and the American Water Color Society. Handville has also taught at the Newark School of Fine and Industrial Arts and the Parsons School of Design in New York City.

"Ronnie Bull of the Chicago Bears." Cover illustration for *Sports Illustrated.*

Robert Handville for *Sports Illustrated,* © 1963 Time, Inc.

RAYMOND F. HOULIHAN (1923-) started out by doing cartoons for his home town newspaper in Worcester, Massachusetts. This short career as a cartoonist was interrupted by World War II.

Houlihan was assigned as a combat soldier to an armored division in Europe. There during his spare time, he helped to start a battalion newspaper. Gradually his duties were shifted to allow him time for special map-making projects and to make sketchbook drawings of terrain and inhabitants. He believes that this training was extremely valuable in his development.

After the War he returned to the *Worcester Telegram* but found himself increasingly interested in becoming an illustrator. Through the G. I. Bill, he was able to go to the Art Students League in New York where he attended classes under Reginald Marsh, John Groth, and Jon Corbino.

Soon afterward he began to obtain work from *Blue Book, Pic, Coronet,* and then from many other magazines and book publishers. His pictures are all distinctly linear in nature — even in halftone — and lend themselves ideally to the historical subject matter he enjoys. Some of his most distinguished work has been in black and white for *American Heritage.*

Courtesy *American Heritage.*

Frontispiece for American Heritage Book selection, "Sitting on a Gusher," by Hildegarde Dolson, 1959.

BILL JOHNSON (1929-) paints adventure and dramatic action subjects.

Following World War II, there was a spectacular growth in magazines oriented to men, and Johnson's work has appeared in most of them, including *True, Argosy, Outdoor Life, Saga,* and *Cavalier.*

Another almost parallel growth has been the paperback book with illustrated covers, selling millions of copies. This, too, has been a natural field for Johnson who has painted cover designs for many of the major publishers, including Bantam, Gold Medal, Crest, and Avon Books.

Bill, who was born in Seattle, Washington, attended the Cornish and Burnley Art Schools in Seattle. He was awarded a full scholarship to the Chicago Art Institute and also studied at the Chicago Academy of Fine Arts.

His work has been exhibited at the Northwest Painters in Seattle, the Westport Artists in Connecticut, and the Society of Illustrators in New York.

Illustration for *True* magazine, "The Man Who Started the War," August, 1963.

Morgan Kane

MORGAN KANE (1916-   ) has adopted a very effective practice which has contributed much to his growth as an illustrator. Between assignments, he spends his time trying out new approaches for hypothetical stories. Art directors have been so impressed by these samples that, in several instances, they have bought the picture to hold for an appropriate story. In the case of the illustration reproduced here, *McCall's* had a story written especially to fit it.

Kane was born in Wilmington, Delaware, and won a scholarship to the Cleveland Art Institute. This was followed by three-and-a-half years in the Air Force during World War II. After the war, he got a job doing advertising illustrations in Chicago and obtained his first story manuscript for *Extension* magazine. Eventually, he has illustrated for nearly all of the major periodicals.

Morgan is also an expert photographer, a member of the Artists' Guild of Chicago, Westport Artists, and Society of Illustrators in New York.

The story, "The One-Faced Girl," appeared with this Kane illustration in *McCall's* magazine, February, 1961.

McCall

ROBERT THEODORE McCALL (1919-   ) is well qualified to do aviation and aerospace illustration; during World War II, he was an Army Air Corps bombardier instructor. Since the war, he has traveled around the world with special trips to Europe, Africa, the Far East, Japan, India, and the Middle East, as a guest of the United States Air Force for various documentary painting projects and contributions to the U.S.A.F. art collection in Washington, D. C., and Colorado Springs, Colorado.

McCall is from Columbus, Ohio. He studied at the Columbus Fine Arts School and the Art Institute of Chicago. Following his military service, he worked as an illustrator with Bielefeld Studios in Chicago, for three years, and then joined the Charles E. Cooper studio in New York. In addition to his aviation subjects, he has done a wide range of advertising, industrial, and general editorial illustrations which have appeared in most of the magazines.

He is a member of the Aviation Writers Association and the Society of Illustrators in New York.

Painting for United States Air Force poster, 1963.

ROBERT JONES (1926-   ) became an illustrator by way of cartooning. Born in Los Angeles, he was doing animation drawings for Warner Brothers while he was still in high school.

After high school, Jones became a gunner and aviation radio operator in the Navy. He next attended the University of Southern California for two years, followed by another two-and-a-half years at the Art Center School in Los Angeles.

He was still interested in humorus illustration when he joined the Charles E. Cooper studio in New York, and his early fiction assignments in *The Saturday Evening Post* were on whimsical subjects. He has gradually expanded his field, however, and now illustrates a wide variety of subject matter for many national publications.

Illustration for "The Girl Who Said No," by Mel Heimer, *McCall's* magazine, March, 1963.

Bob Lavin

ROBERT LAVIN (1919-) ably combines drama and fact in his paintings of industrial and mechanical subjects. This has made him a successful illustrator for such accounts as General Electric, National Steel, and United Engineers, as well as fictional subjects involving planes and ships for *The Saturday Evening Post, Reader's Digest, American Weekly, Argosy, Newsweek,* and others.

Lavin was born in New York City and obtained his B.A. at the College of the City of New York. He also studied at the National Academy of Art School under Ivan Olinsky.

He is an active painter and exhibitor, won second prize in the Long Island Annual Art Show in 1962, and is a member of the Society of Illustrators, and the American Water Color Society.

Lavin was recently appointed Professor of Art at the College of the City of New York where he has been teaching since 1957.

Illustration for "Triumph of the Boon," by C. S. Forester, in *The Saturday Evening Post.*

© 1962 by The Curtis Publishing Company.

LEWICKI

JAMES LEWICKI (1917-) is a scholar as well as an artist; many of his painting projects have arisen from ideas suggested by research. He is probably best known for his several major series for *Life* magazine including "The Folklore of America," a five-part series consisting of 66 paintings, later expanded to a book, *The Life Treasury of American Folklore;* the "Pageant of Life," on evolution, "The Origin of Christmas," "Christmas Legends," and others. His paintings are all distinguished by their originality of concept, their authenticity, and their color.

Lewicki was born in Buffalo, New York, and majored in art in the Buffalo Technical High School. He attended the Albright Art School there, won a scholarship to the Detroit Society of Arts and Crafts School, graduated from Pratt Institute in 1939, and also studied at New York University.

His first assignment while still at Pratt was a book, *New York from Village to Metropolis,* published in 1939. From that time on Lewicki has had commissions from nearly every magazine and from many book publishers.

He has also exhibited widely, won many awards, traveled extensively on research, served as Chairman, Fine Arts Committee of the Long Island Arts Center, taught design at the Evening School of Pratt Institute from 1946-52. He is at present Professor of Art and Chairman of the Visual Arts Department at C. W. Post College, Long Island, New York.

"Johnny Appleseed," from the American Folklore series, painted with egg-oil on a gesso panel.

James Lewicki for *Life* magazine © 1960 Time, Inc.

David Stone Martin

DAVID STONE MARTIN (1913-) feels that too many young artists insist on working in an atmosphere removed from society. Consistent with his own philosophy, he has always been an active social participant while maintaining his own highest artistic standards.

With no formal art training beyond high school in Chicago, Martin began his career as a graphic designer. He has designed publications and is an expert calligrapher. Among his major projects were designs and murals for the "Century of Progress" Chicago World's Fair, and he has served variously as a supervisor of a Federal Arts project for the Elgin State Hospital in Illinois, art director of T. V. A. for six years and, as assistant to Ben Shahn, doing murals. He was artist-correspondent for Abbot Laboratories and for *Life* magazine during World War II. He also worked for the O.S.S. and was an art director in the Office of War Information in 1942-43. Since the war he has followed a free-lance career, participating in many advertising illustration projects for clients such as the Disc Company of America and C.B.S. Television.

Martin uses a calligraphic line that has been widely imitated. No one else, however, has matched his ability in presenting the essence and mood of his subject in that very personal way.

His advertising and editorial illustrations have received a great many citations and awards, and examples of his work are included in numerous Art Directors Annuals.

He has also found time to teach — at the Brooklyn Museum School of Art in 1948-49, and at the Workshop School of Advertising and Editorial Art in New York in 1950.

Advertising illustration for television program, "The Secret Life of Danny Kaye," on behalf of the United Nations International Children's Emergency Fund. C.B.S. Television, 1957.

McMahon

FRANKLIN McMAHON (1921-) is a Chicagoan by birth and education. He attended the Art Institute, the Harrison Commercial Art Institute, and the Institute of Design there. Among his many teachers were: Francis Chapin, Paul Weighardt, E. W. Ball, Emerson Woeffler, and Richard Fillopowski.

A B-17 navigator during World War II, McMahon was shot down over Mannheim, Germany, and spent the last three months of the war in German P.O.W. camps.

After the war, he re-established his studio in Chicago and began to do free-lance illustration for advertising, magazines, and books. In addition, he has pursued an active career in painting and has won many awards.

McMahon is essentially a reportorial artist with an especially strong sense of line. He also has an innate feel for composition — he can begin a drawing at a given point without prior planning, or blocking in, and carry it through to a finish. This gives his work a look of on-the-spot authenticity which a more finished rendering based on photographic information would not provide. He does, in fact, work directly from his subjects whenever possible, and his assignments have taken him to many parts of the world for most of the leading publications. In recognition of McMahon's many talents, the Artists' Guild of New York chose him as "Artist of the Year" in 1963.

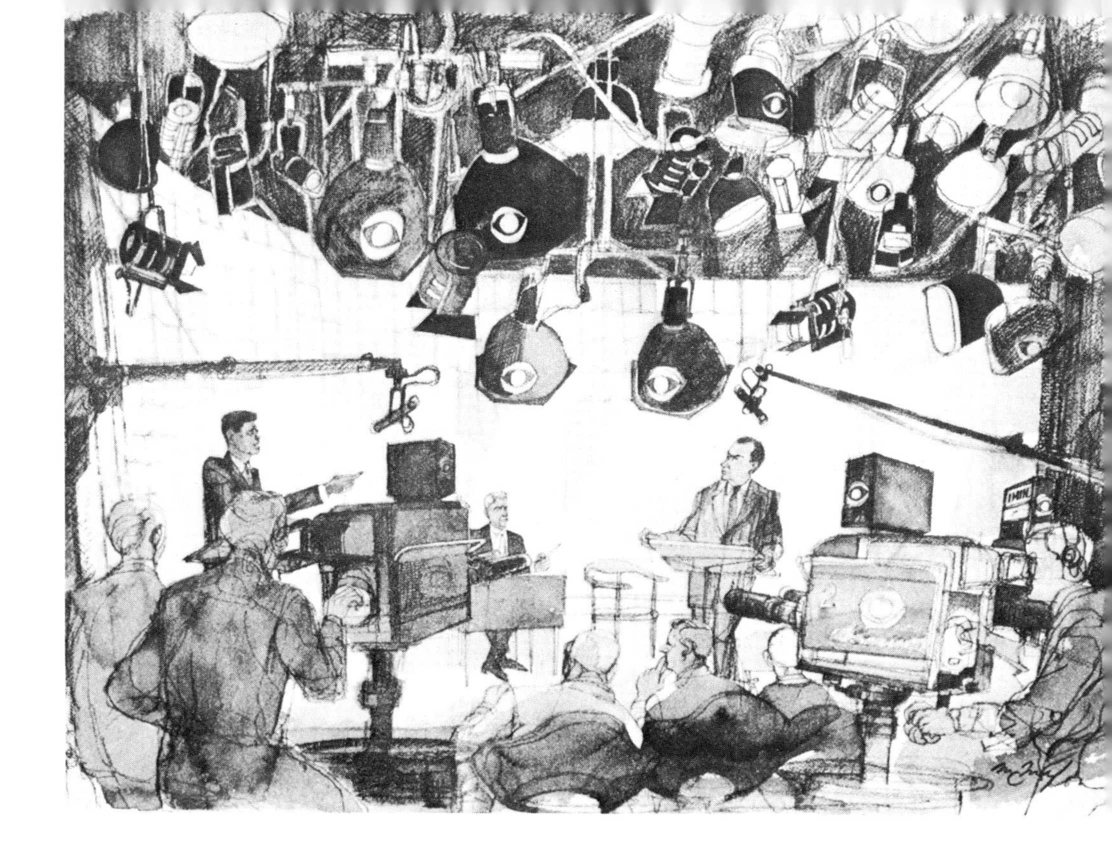

The Kennedy-Nixon Debates. Illustration for "Inside Kennedy's Election," by James A. Michener in *Look* magazine, May 9, 1961.

McD

A few years ago, with a group of his illustrator friends, JOHN R. McDERMOTT (1919-) made a home movie, "Dawn Patrol," as a parody on all World War I movies. The project became so interesting that John decided to use the motion picture camera as a serious art medium and with his friends as volunteer actors produced a memorable documentary film on the Civil War, "Pickett's Charge," which was shown twice in 1957 by C.B.S. Television. In 1964 he received a Ford Foundation Grant for further film experimentation, and has made a film of the Marines at the Battle of Belleau Wood in 1918, again with his group of amateur actors.

McDermott was born in Pueblo, Colorado. After finishing high school in Hollywood, he went to work for the Disney Studios as an animator. This ended at the outbreak of World War II, and McDermott became a marine in the Pacific Theatre. During part of this time, he served as a combat artist and made drawings for the Corps' records of actions in the Solomons, Guadalcanal, Guam, and Okinawa.

At the end of the war some of these drawings were seen by *Blue Book*, and this began McDermott's illustration career, establishing him as expert in military subjects and depiction of action.

Illustration for "Cause without a Rebel," by John Keats, for *Venture* magazine, August, 1964.

SM

STANLEY MELTZOFF (1917-   ) taught history of art at the College of the City of New York for several years and, subsequently, felt compelled to measure his own painting efforts against those of the great masters — a frustrating experience when his technical ability was short of his critical knowledge. However, he has since developed a brilliant facility, and his interpretation of 20th-century science and industry are worthy of comparison with the great still life and landscape artists of the past.

Meltzoff who was born in New York City, had attended the Art Students League, the National Academy of Design, and the College of the City of New York, earning a B.S. and M.A. in History of Fine Arts. His prewar teaching was interrupted by four years in the service during World War II while he was art editor with *Stars and Stripes* overseas. He resumed teaching after the war, with limited classes, which enabled him to continue his own painting.

One of his first painting opportunities was a commission for a cover for *Scientific American* magazine. This proved to be an ideal assignment requiring Meltzoff's particular blend of realistic symbolism and knowledge of science and art. He has since done more than 40 of these covers, as well as many industrial and advertising paintings, for such clients as Rohm and Haas, Socony-Mobil, Anaconda, and illustrations for *The Saturday Evening Post, True, Life,* and others.

"Skeleton in the Sky," painting for the United Engineers advertisement in *Fortune* magazine, 1958.

Al Muenchen

AL MUENCHEN (1917-   ) painted this picture of the aftermath of a dramatic Air Force C-130 plane landing during a "whiteout" at McMurdo's Williams Field in Antarctica. Blinded by a blizzard, the plane was guided down by G.C.A. into soft snow. After the storm, the Seabees welded together a special sled which was dragged to the plane and managed to tow it undamaged back to its runway.

Muenchen's painting was done in connection with his trip to Antarctica for the Air Force to record the life and work of personnel based there. It is part of the Air Force permanent Art Collection.

Al was born in Cincinnati, Ohio, and attended the Chicago Art Institute and Carnegie Institute of Technology, Pittsburgh, Pennsylvania. He first worked for Pittsburgh Studios in 1937 and did a considerable amount of advertising illustration prior to his fiction assignments. He now divides his time between advertising and editorial illustration for most of the major magazines.

He has been an active member of the Society of Illustrators, serving on the exhibition committee in 1962, and was recently appointed to the Joint Ethics Committee for the Graphic Arts.

Antarctica painting for U.S.A.F. Documentary Art Program.

© 1948 by The Curtis Publishing Company.

nonnast

PAUL NONNAST (1918-   ) chose an artist's career because of a heart condition in his youth, but he has been working at it strenuously ever since.

He was born in Carlisle, Pennsylvania, and was graduated from the Philadelphia Museum School of Art in 1940. Nonnast worked first for the McCandlish Lithograph Corporation and the *Philadelphia Record.* Since 1942, he has done free-lance advertising illustration for many national accounts including Armco, Bell Telephone, Chevrolet, Masonite, Dole Pineapple, and United Air Lines.

The Saturday Evening Post gave him his first illustration assignment in 1947; he has since contributed regularly to the *Post, Cosmopolitan, Field and Stream, Argosy, Reader's Digest* and others.

Nonnast has won two Gold Medals in Philadelphia Art Directors shows and served as head of the Advertising and Illustration department of the Moore Institute of Art in Philadelphia from 1943 to 1946.

A serious photographer as well, he has traveled widely in the United States, Canada, and Europe, and sold many Kodachromes taken with his Rolleiflex and Leica M-3.

Illustration for story, "The Cowardice of Tom Royce," by Chad Oliver. Reproduced by permission of *The Saturday Evening Post.*

Fred Otnes

FRED OTNES (1925-   ) is a native of Junction City, Kansas, was educated at the American Academy and the Art Institute of Chicago.

His illustrations, distinguished by expert draughtsmanship, have appeared in a wide variety of magazines, including *Town and Country, True, The Saturday Evening Post, Argosy, Redbook,* and the *Reader's Digest.*

As a member of a group known as "Artists Associates," Otnes has also been active in the field of advertising illustration. Among his clients have been General Motors, Chevrolet, Ford, Chrysler, Dobbs Hats, Italian Lines, and Tennessee Gas Transmission Company.

His work has been exhibited extensively and has won awards in Chicago, New York, Detroit, Cleveland, and Minneapolis Art Directors shows.

Illustration for "Ride Against the Sioux," by William Chamberlain in *The Saturday Evening Post.*

© 1961 by The Curtis Publishing Company.

Rehberger

GUSTAV REHBERGER (1910-) was born in Riedlingsdorf, Austria, where even as a child, he showed remarkable talent. Soon after being brought to the United States, at the age of 13, he won a scholarship to study at the Art Institute of Chicago. Following this training, he achieved early success as a designer and illustrator.

After serving in the Air Force during World War II, Rehberger opened a studio in New York, where he has divided his time between making independent drawings and paintings, and illustrating for leading magazines, motion picture promotion and national advertising campaigns.

While solidly rooted in powerful form and structure, his art reaches freely into the creative and imaginative, finding expression in non-objective as well as representational painting. Rehberger exhibits nationally, teaches figure painting, drawing, and composition, and periodically gives painting demonstrations and lectures. He was recently honored by a one-man show at the Society of Illustrators.

Rehberger has painted many religious themes. This crucifixion was one of a series of four New Testament pictures for *Everywoman's* magazine in 1956-57; in oil over casein on a gesso ground.

Robert Riger for *Sports Illustrated*. © 1957 by *Time, Inc.*

ROBERT RIGER

ROBERT RIGER (1924-) is a student of sports who draws, paints, photographs, analyzes, and writes expertly about the outstanding performers.

Riger was born in New York City where he studied at the High School of Music and Art and at Pratt Institute. His early ambition was to become a teacher but he switched to advertising design while at Pratt. After graduation he worked as a layout artist for *The Saturday Evening Post*. This was followed by art and advertising agency work until he got the chance to combine his love of sports with drawing for the newly launched *Sports Illustrated* magazine.

He was one of the first illustrators to use a sequential series of action drawings in revealing the key to championship form in baseball, boxing, football, and other major sports. To research these, Riger had to become an expert photographer, taking endless shots, in order to analyze and select the significant details for his drawings.

More recently Riger has become associated with television coverage of outstanding sports events, combining drawing with personal commentary. His book, the *ABC Wide World of Sports,* featuring his drawings and photographs of some of these competitions, was published by the American Broadcasting Company in 1965. He has also recently published a book in collaboration with Branch Rickey, *The American Diamond.*

One of a series of drawings for Riger's article, "Mantle: Seven Views of a Genius," published in *Sports Illustrated.*

Ken Riley

The illustrations of KEN RILEY (1919-   ) are remarkable on many counts: strength of draughtsmanship, effective composition, the color and quality of the painting, and the portrayal of mood. Riley's pictures reveal that he is clearly a master of all these, particularly in his use of color. He is at home with almost every subject and period — some of his finest pictures were painted for the historical Captain Hornblower stories, by C. S. Forester, in *The Saturday Evening Post*. His work has appeared in most of the national publications from *Reader's Digest* to *Life* magazine and in a variety of media from line to full color.

Born in Missouri, Riley studied under Thomas Hart Benton at the Kansas City Art Institute. Then to New York, where he studied under Frank Vincent DuMond at the Art Students League, and under Harvey Dunn at the Grand Central School. In his approach, Riley has successfully amalgamated the viewpoints of teachers whose methods differed radically and has added to this his own personal direction.

Illustration in casein for "Violent City," by John and Ward Hawkins in *The Saturday Evening Post*.

Morton Roberts

MORTON ROBERTS (1927-1964) crowded a full career into his very short life but gave promise of much greater things to come. His command of technique was lush and full, and he applied it with equal facility to paintings for exhibition and publication in magazines. He was also a teacher of life drawing at Pratt Institute in Brooklyn.

Among his best-known pictures were those made for *Life* magazine, on Rasputin, in a history of Russia, and an outstanding series on the "Story of Jazz." He also illustrated for many other publications, including *Collier's*, *True*, *Reader's Digest*, *Redbook*, and Bantam Books.

Roberts was born in Worcester, Massachusetts, and was graduated from the Yale School of Fine Arts. Among his many prizes were the Edwin Austin Abbey Fellowship from the National Academy of Design, the American Water Color Society's Pratt Purchase Prize, and the First Altman Prize, also from the National Academy of Design.

"A Perfect Death," one of the series of paintings for *Life* magazine recording an historic era of the South and the origins of jazz as the Negro's contribution to American music.

Morton Roberts for *Life* magazine © 1958 Time, Inc.

John Scott

JOHN SCOTT (1907-) developed his strong, sound approach to illustration by the simple expedient of hard work.

He got his first art assignments from the Western pulp magazines. He estimates that, from 1930 until the outbreak of World War II, his drawings and cover paintings for such publishers as Street and Smith and Dell ran into thousands.

During the war, Scott was overseas as a staff artist on *Yank* magazine and, among his other assignments, visited hospital wards to sketch portraits of the wounded men.

After returning home, John began to work for the general magazines, such as *This Week*, *Woman's Day*, and the Canadian publications, *Chatelaine* and *Toronto Star*. He gradually gravitated to the men's magazines, however, including *True*, *Elks*, *Argosy*, and *Sports Afield*. He particularly enjoys the hunting and fishing assignments, which give him an opportunity to go on location in the wilderness to write and paint.

"Pike Fishing," an advertising illustration for Garcia Corporation, 1962. ⟶

ALEX ROSS (1909-) who was born in Dunfermline, Scotland, came to the United States at the age of three. With early ambitions to be an industrial designer, he studied nights for two years under Robert Lepper at the Carnegie Institute of Technology, Pittsburgh, Pennsylvania.

Otherwise self-taught, Ross got a job in the Rayart Studios in Pittsburgh. From there he progressed to Pitt Studios, and then to the Charles E. Cooper studio in New York. Two years later he sold his first cover design to *Good Housekeeping* magazine. This was followed by a total of 130 paintings over the next 12 years. In the meantime, he was doing editorial illustrations for most of the other national magazines, including *Collier's, The Saturday Evening Post, Ladies' Home Journal,* and *Cosmopolitan.* He has also illustrated several books, among them the recently published *Saints, Adventures in Courage,* for Doubleday and Company.

Ross, who paints many experimental pictures in water color and in mixed media, exhibits regularly and is a member of the American Water Color Society, the Society of Illustrators, and the Fairfield Water Color Group.

In 1953 he was awarded a Master of Arts honorary degree by Boston College.

"Alaska Alert." The Elmendorf Air Force Base in Anchorage, Alaska, painted by Ross as a member of the Society of Illustrators who collaborated with the Air Force documentation program. Now in the permanent United States Air Force Art Collection.

A

B

WILLIAM ARTHUR SMITH, N.A. (1918-) has made pictures for a broad spectrum of uses and in a great variety of media. To each picture, whether for exhibition or publication, he brings a distinctive and highly creative viewpoint.

Born in Toledo, Ohio, Smith studied at the University of Toledo, Grand Central Art School and Art Students League in New York, l'Académie des Beaux-Arts, and l'Académie de la Grande Chaumière in Paris, and with Theodore J. Keane in Toledo.

Smith's work is represented in many collections, including the Metropolitan Museum of Art and the Los Angeles Museum; he has exhibited in nearly every important museum in the United States. He has also had one-man exhibitions in more than 20 principal cities of Europe and Asia.

Among his many prizes are the Gold Medal of Honor, American Water Color Society; National Academy of Design (two prizes); Society of American Graphic Artists' Award for Lithography; Winslow Homer Memorial Prize, and the Society of Illustrators Gold Medal Award for Advertising Illustration.

He has taught at the Grand Central Art School, Pratt Institute in Brooklyn, lectured at many colleges in the United States and abroad. Past-president of the American Water Color Society, he is also a member of the executive committee of I.A.P.A., the International Association of Art (Painters, Sculptors and Graphic Artists), an affiliate of UNESCO.

A. Walt Whitman, one of an outstanding series of portraits of historical personages, painted for the John Hancock Mutual Life Insurance Company.
B. Illustration for *Redbook* magazine, December, 1960.

A. The Watchers, "Look at them white girls walkin' with them niggers."

Tracy Sugarman

TRACY SUGARMAN (1921-) initiated a personal assignment of reporting the student voter-registration efforts in Mississippi. Feeling strongly about the issues and wanting to make a contribution as an artist in a reportorial series of drawings, he enlisted sponsorship of the project by the Columbia Broadcasting System and the United States Information Agency.

These sensitive line and wash-drawings were made from on-the-spot observation, often under dangerous conditions, but honestly and without sensationalism. Tracy made over 100 drawings. Many of these, in addition to their original use in a documentary film for the C.B.S. "Eternal Light" program, and exhibition by the United States Information Agency, have also been used in *The Saturday Evening Post*, *New York Times Magazine*, and other magazines and newspapers.

Sugarman was born in Syracuse, New York, and was graduated from Syracuse University in 1943. He also studied at the Brooklyn Museum Art School with Reuben Tam.

His illustrations have appeared in *Fortune*, *Collier's*, *Esquire*, *Woman's Home Companion*, *American*, *Parents' Magazine*, *Boy's Life*, and *Gentlemen's Quarterly;* and he has illustrated books for Simon and Schuster, Doubleday, Random House, and Scott Foresman Company.

In addition to membership in the Society of Illustrators, he has been president of the Westport Artists, the Westport-Weston Association for the United Nations and active in other community activities.

Reproduced without captions in the *New York Times Magazine*, February 21, 1965.

B. Demonstration, "No singing – keep it silent. Don't answer, don't answer."

A

A. Drawing, Society of Illustrators bulletin, 1946.

B. Illustration for "Girl Overboard," in the *Ladies Home Journal.*

B

C

M. COBURN WHITMORE (1913-) has described his three primary interests as "racing cars, illustrating, and smart clothes on good-looking women." The racing cars are a hobby, but he is thoroughly professional in his illustrations of beautiful women. Probably no other illustrator has been so inventive over so long a time in doing variations on the theme of "boy meets girl."

Coby was born in Dayton, Ohio, and attended the Dayton Art Institute there. Next he went to Chicago as an apprentice in the studio of Haddon Sundblom and Edwin Henry, and attended the Chicago Art Institute nights. Following his apprenticeship, he worked for the Chicago *Herald Examiner* and the Charles Jensen studio in Cincinnati. Then he moved to New York, for a long association with the Charles E. Cooper Studio, and also began to get illustration assignments from the major magazines including *McCall's*, *Ladies' Home Journal*, *Redbook*, *Good Housekeeping*, *Cosmopolitan*, and *Woman's Day*. Many foreign publications have purchased the second rights to publish his pictures abroad.

Whitmore has exhibited at Art Directors shows in New York, Philadelphia, Chicago, and Westchester, winning many awards and citations.

C. Illustration for a *Saturday Evening Post* story by David Walker, "Looking the Other Way," March 31, 1962.

R O B E R T   T H O M

ROBERT A. THOM (1915-   ), in 1948 took on an assignment for a series of historical paintings for Parke, Davis & Company to illustrate the story of pharmacy. To make the 40 paintings constituted a monumental, ten-year effort in research and consultation in order to insure the necessary accuracy of concept and of detail.

This series was followed by another equally demanding one of 45 paintings to illustrate the history of medicine. These paintings were reproduced in magazine advertisements and later enlarged and distributed widely among druggists. The original paintings have been exhibited in every state of the Union, and most of Canada, and represent institutional art — and advertising — at its best. The two series have won numerous awards.

Thom was born in Grand Rapids, Michigan, and had brief art training at the Institute of Fine Arts in Columbus, Ohio, and under Robert Brackman at Noank, Connecticut. He opened his own studio in Detroit, Michigan, and did commercial illustration for General Motors, Dodge Division Chrysler Corporation; Bohm Aluminum, and others prior to his Parke, Davis commissions.

He taught at Michigan State University-Oakland in 1962-63 and is at present working on a *History of Michigan* for the Michigan Bell Telephone Company.

"Founding of the American Medical Association," one of the *History of Medicine* series.

Thornton Utz

THORNTON UTZ (1914-   ) likes to work out the poses of his figures with drawings — rapid, free sketches that clearly express the mood or mental attitude of his characters. Once this has been established, he then poses and photographs his models, as nearly as possible, in the predetermined positions. The photos furnish the factual details of folds and lighting which lend added authenticity to his original poses.

Utz has used this approach effectively for his humorous *Saturday Evening Post* covers as well as for more serious fiction illustrations for *Cosmopolitan*, *McCall's*, *Ladies' Home Journal*, *Redbook*, and *Good Housekeeping*.

Thornton has participated in the joint Society of Illustrators-Air Force Art Program and received a citation from Gen. Curtis LeMay, for documenting the airlift of Hungarian refugees. Utz also received the Governor Bryant of Florida Award for his Freedom Posters.

He was born in Memphis, Tennessee, and studied under Burton Callicott in Memphis. He also attended the American Academy of Art in Chicago, later taught at the Chicago Art Institute. Utz, who now lives in Sarasota, Florida, is a member of the Sarasota Art Association, the New York Society of Illustrators, and the Chicago Artists' Guild.

Cover design for *The Saturday Evening Post*.

1960's

ILLUSTRATORS 1960's

Robert K. Abbett
Thomas B. Allen
David Blossom
James Neil Boyle
Mia Carpenter
Joseph S. Cleary
Alan E. Cober
Ted C. CoConis
Guy Deel
Don DeMauro
Jack Dumas
Mark English
Lorraine Fox
Marvin Friedman
Bernard Fuchs
Bob Gill
Milton Glaser
John Gundlefinger
Philip Harrison Hayes
Russell Hoban
Mitchell Hooks
Victor Kalin
Henry Koehler
Sanford Kossin
Arthur Lidov
Frank C. McCarthey
John McClelland
Jerry W. McDaniel
Robert E. McGinnis
Frank Mullins
Robert Peak
George Edward Porter
Jack Potter
Richard M. Powers
Anthony Saris
Harvey Schmidt
Daniel Schwartz
Robert Shore
Ross Barron Storey
Herbert Tauss
Howard A. Terpning
Edward Vebell
Gilbert M. Walker
Robert Weaver
William H. Whittingham
Ben Wohlberg

The Decade: 1960's

by Bernard Fuchs

When I got out of art school there was a great aura of glamour surrounding the top illustrators. No more. There are very few illustrators today that all the kids know about. Nobody new has come up with a style and made it stick for ten years as once he might have.

The present-day illustrator is not like the one in those days — rich, glamorous, with a plush studio. No "characters" anymore; the image has changed. We're like the new, studious baseball pro who breaks into the big league. He's a businessman now, and goes about the occupation of playing baseball as a business — very serious about it. And the average ballplayer today is far better than his predecessor.

Present-day illustration, too, has changed, moved forward, since the so-called golden era of Illustration. Illustration will always have a long way to go, and while now there is less of it around to do, at least it's doing a better job, in my opinion.

Today editorial people look for the guy they know will do something he hasn't done before. You may not stand or fall on each job you do — a lot of people are nice and don't condemn you for a bad one. But if a job you do reverts to what you were doing two years ago then, I think, you're in real trouble.

The greatest thing that this whole business has done in the last ten years is to introduce variety, not only in the freedom of the illustrators and in the fresh ways that illustration can be done, but also in opening up new sources of assignments. Added to story and advertising illustration are the new reportorial projects like those initiated by *Fortune, Sports Illustrated, Esquire, Holiday*, and *Look*. Several magazines are experimenting with art in other ways. Even articles on food have been handsomely illustrated by still life paintings in *Redbook* and *McCall's*.

It's hard for the illustrator to compete with the photographer in the news magazines, although coverage of trials, or stories like the Bay of Pigs invasion, where no photographers were present, show what the illustrator *can* do.

Actually, it doesn't really matter whether an assignment is done by the artist or the camera. The point is, is the story illustrated right? Is there an idea in the illustration? There is no limit to the amount of freedom offered to the artist today. The only problem is the freedom within himself and how capable he is of doing this thing the way he feels it should be done. I think if you're honest about it, if you take an honest, detached approach to the solution of your problem, that will come nearer to solving it than the greatest technique. As Austin Briggs says: "Illustrators are so wrapped up in being new and different they lose sight of what they're supposed to be doing." I don't care how facile you are, if you can't apply this fluency to the problem you're working on, or if you apply it falsely, you haven't done the job.

If you are "with" your own times and can translate your ideas into valid, original pictures, then you can make your own contribution. The field has never been so fast-changing and unpredictable as in the 'sixties — or so demanding of the illustrator's mind as well as his brush.

B. Fuchs.

DRAWING BY AUSTIN BRIGGS

Art Abbett

ROBERT K. ABBETT (1926-   ) was born in Hammond, Indiana. He holds a B.S. from Purdue University and a B.A. from the University of Missouri. In addition, he studied nights at the Chicago Academy of Fine Art.

He started his professional career as a writer for a public relations agency in Chicago but, wanting to be an artist, became apprenticed to the Stevens-Gross Studio. He next transferred to the Bielefeld Studios, and from Chicago went to New York with the Alexander Chaite Studios.

Abbett had made his first magazine illustrations for *Extension* magazine in Chicago and began to take on more assignments in New York, gradually spending more time on his own projects. He now free-lances entirely for such magazines as *True, Argosy, Redbook, This Week, Reader's Digest, Sports Afield*, and publishers including Bantam Books, Dell, Signet, Fawcett, Ballantine, and Pyramid Books.

Robert taught the techniques of editorial illustration at the Silvermine Guild in Norwalk, Connecticut, from 1959-62. He is past president of the Westport Artists and a member of the Society of Illustrators in New York.

Illustration for *True* magazine, "The Gentleman was a Thief," by Neil Hickey, August, 1961.

Tom Allen

THOMAS B. ALLEN (1928-   ) invests in his work a serious yet poetic feeling that is a stimulating combination of old and new points of view. The pen-and-ink cross-hatching method Tom uses had its vogue before the turn of the century, yet in his hands it becomes a new method for exploring form and creating an atmospheric effect. A dampened paper surface is often used to blend the lines into tonal rather than linear rendering. In his paintings, too, Allen combines a feeling of old and new in his almost primitive style of dealing with contemporary subjects. As a result his pictures are set apart from the usual printed material and gain increased attention for his reportorial subject matter for such publishers as *Esquire, Sports Illustrated, McCall's, Life, Redbook, Playboy,* C.B.S., Signet Classics, and Harper & Row.

Allen was born in Nashville, Tennessee, spent two years at Vanderbilt University and obtained a B.F.A. after another four years at the Art Institute of Chicago. He exhibits regularly, is represented in New York by the D'Arcy Gallery and has won numerous awards, including the New York Art Directors Club Gold Medal and Society of Illustrators Gold Medal. He has taught at the School of Visual Arts in New York from 1958-64 and is now on leave.

Illustration for a story by Jack Kerouac, "Visions of Gerard," for *Show* magazine, July, 1963.

Boyle

JAMES NEIL BOYLE (1931-   ) is a native of Canada, born in Granum, Alberta. He first studied at the Banff School of Fine Arts in Alberta, then for three years at the Art Center School, and for two years at the Chouinard Art Institute in Los Angeles.

His professional career has been on the West Coast beginning, after graduation from Chouinard, with Tri-Arts Studio and then with an association of free-lance artists called Group West.

Boyle has illustrated for the *Reader's Digest, Saturday Evening Post, Cosmopolitan, Westways, This Week, Ladies' Home Journal*, and *Argosy* magazines. He has also designed many record album covers for Capitol, R.C.A., Imperial, and Dot records. He is currently teaching at the Art Center School of Los Angeles.

Boyle, who is past president of the Society of Illustrators of Los Angeles and member of the Art Directors Club of Los Angeles, exhibits regularly in their annual shows and those of the Society of Illustrators in New York.

Illustration for a William Saroyan story, "Boys and Girls Together," in *The Saturday Evening Post*.

Courtesy of *Safari* magazine.

This painting was made in designers' colors and a plastic medium, painted on a rough gesso surface, creating the unusual textural effects. It won the Gold Medal Award of Excellence in the Illustrators' '63 exhibition.

DAVID BLOSSOM (1927-) is the son of Earl Blossom. He learned about illustration by growing up and living with it in his father's studio. In addition, he studied for a year at the Yale School of Fine Arts and for two years of night school at the Art Students League under Reginald Marsh.

For the next 14 years he worked as an art director for the J. Walter Thompson advertising agency in New York.

With this thorough ground work, David decided in 1961 to become a free-lance illustrator. He started at the top by selling his first illustration to *The Saturday Evening Post* and has since added numerous other magazines and national advertisers, such as Pan-American Airlines and Pontiac Motor Division of General Motors.

MIA CARPENTER (1933-) has an excellent sense of composition and design which she combines with the subtle sensitivity that distinguishes her work.

Mia is a Californian, from Los Angeles, and obtained her B.A. from the Art Center School there.

Her first work was for *Seventeen* magazine in 1957, and she has since illustrated for *Redbook, Ladies' Home Journal, Good Housekeeping, McCall's, Parents'* magazines, and the *New York Times*. In addition, she has illustrated a book for Harper & Row.

Miss Carpenter's work has been exhibited at the annual shows of the New York Society of Illustrators where, in 1962, she won the Gold Medal for advertising art.

Illustration for Tanner of North Carolina, 1964.

JOSEPH S. CLEARY (1926-) is a West Coast painter, who finds distance no impediment to working for magazines in the East. These include *The Saturday Evening Post, Parents', Ladies' Home Journal,* and *Argosy*.

His exhibition activities are centered in the West, however, at the San Francisco Museum of Art, the M. H. De Young Memorial Museum of San Francisco, the Jack London Show, and California State Fair. He has won many awards, including several firsts.

Cleary was born in Long Beach, California, and studied at San Francisco State College, Mills College, and the California College of Arts and Crafts in Oakland. He is a member of the East Bay Art Association, the Bohemian Club of San Francisco, and taught at the California College of Arts and Crafts from 1955-57.

Illustration for a *Saturday Evening Post* story by MacDonald Harris, "The Koto Students."

Cober

ALAN E. COBER (1935-) was named "Artist of the Year" in 1965 by the Artists' Guild in recognition of his original sense of design and expressive use of line. Although Cober's work is largely linear, his is not in the traditional approach for line reproduction since, to suit his ends, he freely and effectively uses it with halftone or color.

Cober was born in New York City. He had begun the study of law at the University of Vermont before deciding to become an artist. After attending the New York School of Visual Arts and the Pratt Institute Graphic Center, he obtained his first art work as a fashion artist. With this as a background, and another two years attached to the art unit in the Special Warfare School at Fort Bragg, he was able to begin free-lancing for periodicals, books, and national advertising accounts.

Illustration for a *Redbook* story, "The Carefree Years," by Lee McGiffin, 1965.

T CoConis

The illustrations of TED C. CoCONIS (1927-) have been distinguished by their careful design and subtle good taste since they first appeared in *Redbook* magazine in 1961.

He has since also illustrated for *Good Housekeeping, Parents', Ladies' Home Journal, Woman's Day, Argosy,* and *Esquire*.

CoConis was born in Chicago, Illinois, and went to the American Academy of Art there. Prior to appearing in magazines, he was affiliated with the Alexander Chaite Studios in New York. In 1959 he taught at the San Francisco Academy of Art.

This illustration was reversed when it appeared but reads effectively either way. For an article in *Parents'* magazine by Margaret Mead, "They Learn from Living Things."

Don De Mauro

Although DON DE MAURO (1936-) has had but a brief career in illustration, his pictures for *The Saturday Evening Post, Cosmopolitan, Good Housekeeping,* and *Boy's Life* have all been distinguished by a fine sense of design and color.

Don is from Mount Vernon, New York, and studied at the Chouinard Art Institute in Los Angeles. He now lives in Vermont and is actively pursuing a fine arts painting career.

Illustration for "A Voice in the Willows," by Hobart Skidmore in *The Saturday Evening Post*.

GUY DEEL (1933-) contributed a fresh outlook to his series of illustrations for Douglas DC-8 advertising, his stylized linear technique contrasting conspicuously with surrounding pages of photographic illustration.

These attracted the attention of magazine art editors and won him assignments from *Redbook, True, The Saturday Evening Post, Good Housekeeping, This Week, Westways, Reader's Digest,* and *Esquire* for which he now works regularly.

Deel was born in Tuxedo, Texas, attended the Chouinard Art Institute and was graduated from the Art Center School in Los Angeles. Among his teachers were Pruett Carter, Reynold Brown, and Jack Potter. He has been teaching at the Art Center School himself since 1962.

His work has been exhibited in Art Directors and Illustrators shows in both Los Angeles and New York and he has won numerous awards.

Illustration for Graham Greene story, "Dream of a Strange Land," which appeared in *The Saturday Evening Post.*

Courtesy of the Weyerhaeuser Company.

JACK DUMAS (1916-) was born in Seattle, Washington, where he attended the Cornish School of Allied Arts and the Seattle Academy of Art, studying under Ernest Norling.

After his first work for the *Los Angeles Examiner* editorial art department, Dumas joined a commercial art service with Ren Wicks. This was followed by a five-year Army stint, beginning in 1941, with a topographical engineering battalion. After the war he moved to San Francisco and the helpful influence of Maurice Logan, Willard Cox, Stan Galli, and Fred Ludekens..

An enthusiast of the outdoors and wildlife, he now lives on Bainbridge Island, Washington. This distance, however, has not been a barrier to his illustrating for such publications in the East as *Sports Afield, The Saturday Evening Post, Argosy,* and Bantam Books. He has also illustrated for West Coast advertisers, notably the Weyerhaeuser Company of Tacoma, Washington.

MARK ENGLISH (1933-) minimizes the modeling in his paintings with subtle changes in color and value while emphasizing the overall pattern of shapes. His drawing is very sensitive, and he is particularly effective in picturing children.

English was born in Hubbard, Texas. He attended the University of Texas as well as the Art Center School in Los Angeles where he studied with John LaGatta and Joe Henninger.

After considerable studio and advertising experience with the automobile industry, he got his first fiction illustration assignment from *The Saturday Evening Post.* Since then he has also contributed to several other publications, including *Redbook, Parents', Ladies' Home Journal,* and *Good Housekeeping.*

His work has been exhibited widely and has won awards from the New York Society of Illustrators and the Art Directors Clubs of Pittsburgh and Detroit.

Illustration for "The Recitation Prize," by Jean T. Freedman, *Redbook,* 1964.

B

Bernard Fuchs for *Sports Illustrated* © 1961 Time, Inc.

BERNARD FUCHS (1932-   ) was named "Artist of the Year" in 1962 by the Artists' Guild of New York, signalizing his position at the top of the illustrator's profession at the youthful age of 30. His pictures for *McCall's, Redbook, Sports Illustrated, Cosmopolitan,* and other magazines are probably more admired — and imitated — than those of any other current illustrator.

Fuchs does not consider himself a painter, but has done official portraits of both Presidents Kennedy and Johnson. He met President Kennedy just before the Cuban crisis and has subsequently painted several pictures of the late President, two of which are now owned by Mrs. Kennedy.

Bernard was born in O'Fallon, Illinois, and attended the Washington University Art School in St. Louis. For five years after graduation, he worked for Detroit advertising art studios. He then moved East to Westport, Connecticut, and began to do editorial magazine illustration.

He has had one man shows for the Westport Artists and the Society of Illustrators and has participated in many group shows, including the United States Information Agency Graphics Exhibition in Russia.

A. "Portrait of the Artist," by Eileen Jensen, illustrated for *McCall's* magazine, July, 1964.
B. Illustration for *Sports Illustrated,* September, 1961.
C. Illustration for Part One, "Kennedy," by Theodore C. Sorensen, *Look* magazine, 1965.

C

lorraine fox

LORRAINE FOX (1825-   ), who is Mrs. Bernard D'Andrea, also has been active as an illustrator. Born in Brooklyn, she studied at Pratt Institute and the Brooklyn Museum Art School under Reuben Tam.

Her first illustrations were for *Better Homes and Gardens* in 1947 and have since appeared in many other publications, including *Woman's Day, Seventeen, Good Housekeeping, Cosmopolitan, Ladies' Home Journal, Redbook,* and *McCall's.*

She has exhibited her work at the Society of Illustrators annual shows, New York and Philadelphia Art Directors Club exhibits, the Brooklyn Museum, New York City Center Gallery, and Silvermine Guild New England exhibits, winning several Gold Medals and other awards. Lorraine is currently teaching at the Parsons School of Design in New York and has recently been appointed to the faculty of the Famous Artists Schools in Westport, Connecticut.

Illustration for *Ingenue* magazine, 1963.

FRIEDMAN

MARVIN FRIEDMAN (1930-   ) exhibits a thorough knowledge of drawing in rendering the most complex subject matter with a direct reportorial manner. His color is vibrant and exciting, his control of values impressive.

Friedman was born in Chester, Pennsylvania, and his sound training was acquired at the Philadelphia Museum School of Art where he studied under Henry C. Pitz and Ben Eisenstat.

His first published work was for small religious publications; he is now illustrating for *Good Housekeeping, Cosmopolitan, Ladies' Home Journal, Playboy, Changing Times, This Week, Cavalier, Redbook,* the *Ford Times, Better Homes & Gardens,* and *Family Weekly.*

Illustration for Noel Coward story, "Mrs. Capper's Birthday," in the *Ladies' Home Journal.*

gill

BOB GILL (1931-   ) is a free-lance designer and illustrator. In spite of his youth, Gill has had considerable influence on graphic design in current illustration, by his own example and through his teaching at the School of Visual Arts in New York, and at Pratt Institute in Brooklyn. Together with John Lewis, he has recently summarized his credo in a book, *Illustration: Aspects and Directions.* Another book of his, written with Alan Fletcher and Colin Forbes, is *Design: Visual Comparisons* (both Reinhold, 1964). In collaboration with Alastair Reid, Gill also has written and illustrated a number of children's books.

Gill studied at the Philadelphia Museum of Art and at the Pennsylvania Academy of the Fine Arts. His work has been exhibited at The Museum of Modern Art as well as at the New York Art Directors Club annual shows, American Institute of Graphic Arts, Package Designers Council, and Type Directors Club.

At present he is a partner in the design and architectural office of Crosby/Fletcher/Forbes/Gill of London, England.

Advertising illustration for Merck, Sharp & Dohme.

MILTON GLASER (1929-   ) is a native of New York where he attended the High School of Music and Art, and Cooper Union Art School. Following graduation, he received a Fulbright scholarship which allowed him to study etching in Italy under Giorgio Morandi. Later, Glaser spent another period in Italy for a concentrated eight months' study of lithography.

In 1954 Glaser was a founder, and is still a member of, the Push Pin Studios formed with several of his Cooper Union classmates. Glaser's work is characterized by directness, simplicity, and originality. He uses any medium or style suggested by the problem — from primitive to avant garde — in his designs for book jackets, record album covers, advertisements, and direct mail pieces, as well as for magazine illustrations. His work has won numerous awards from Art Directors Clubs, American Institute of Graphic Arts, Society of Illustrators, and Type Directors Club.

Glaser currently is teaching part time at the New York School of Visual Arts.

Illustration for the story, "No Love for the Lonely," by Joan Williams in *The Saturday Evening Post.*

This illustration by JOHN GUNDELFINGER (1937-   ) won an Award of Excellence in the Illustrators '63 exhibition. Although done from photos, it is deliberately non-photographic. Several studies were made to get the feeling of the subject, followed by a finished pencil drawing. Thin washes of umber oil pigment were next painted over the drawing for the tonal areas and finally accents of grays and whites were added in tempera.

John was born in Saint-Dié, France, and studied at the School of Visual Arts in New York under Jack Potter and Phil Hays. He began free-lancing immediately after finishing school and sold his first illustration to *Redbook* in 1959. Since then he has added to his list of clients. *The Saturday Evening Post, Ladies' Home Journal, Good Housekeeping, Reader's Digest, Seventeen,* and *McCall's,* and has won several awards for his pictures, including a Gold Medal in the 1962 exhibition of the Society of Illustrators.

Since 1962 Gundelfinger has also been teaching drawing at the School of Visual Arts in New York City.

Illustration for booklet on *Liberia,* by Bankers Trust Company, 1963.

Philip Hays

In his work, PHILIP HARRISON HAYS (1932-) makes a deliberate break with the traditional evolution of illustration. Yet in this, he also borrows heavily from earlier eras. As with the current fashion trend in the revival of short skirts and the look of the 'twenties, so he has been drawn to the old look combined with a contemporary point of view. The result is both novel and provocative and has won for him a total of 29 awards from the Society of Illustrators, National Society of Art Directors, Art Directors Club of New York, and the American Institute of Graphic Arts, including one Silver and two Gold Medals.

His work is represented in the Graphics collection of The Metropolitan Museum of Art and currently in the United States State Department Exhibition of "Graphic Arts in America" on tour in Europe including the U.S.S.R.

Hays was born in Sherman, Texas, and grew up in Shreveport, Louisiana. He attended the Kansas City Art Institute, the Ringling School of Art in Sarasota, Florida, and the Art Center School in Los Angeles. He has taught illustration at the School of Visual Arts in New York City since 1956 and headed the Department of Illustration since 1961.

Illustration for *Cosmopolitan* magazine story by Margaret Cousins, "Paris Opening," October, 1958.

HOBAN

RUSSELL HOBAN (1925-) has a probing, exploring approach to painting which makes his work complex and exciting. His paintings express his own many-sided talents, and he has pursued his artistic career despite the distractions of success in other directions.

Prior to World War II, in which Hoban served in the United States Infantry in Italy, he briefly attended Temple University and the Philadelphia Museum School. After the war he resumed school under the G. I. Bill but soon gravitated to New York and a varied series of jobs, including silk screen designing, production work for small magazines, art direction for *Printer's Ink,* story board sketching, animation drawing. He was assistant director in television production at Batten, Barton, Durstine & Osborn Inc., for five years, did television advertising, and also made a documentary film.

Feeling that he was drifting away from his real interest, however, Hoban decided to concentrate on free-lance painting. As a start, he began to draw and paint the boxers, managers, and other characters of Stillman's Gym in New York. This led to his first commission to illustrate a *Sports Illustrated* article on Stillman's, and he has since done many boxing themes and other sports events for them.

These pictures led to commissions from *True, Time, Fortune, Redbook,* and numerous advertising agencies for all kinds of subjects. He has also written and illustrated several children's books of his own in addition to writing those for his wife, Lillian Hoban, to illustrate. They currently have 14 titles in print. In between, he has taught at the Famous Artists Schools in Westport, Connecticut, and the School of Visual Arts in New York City.

"Johannson vs. Patterson," painted in casein, for *Sports Illustrated.*

Mitchell Hooks

The career of MITCHELL HOOKS (1923-   ), like that of many other artists of the post-World War II era, has been involved to a great extent with paintings for paperback book covers. His interpretations have a strong poster quality, in keeping with the need to hold their own on display with other competing titles on the bookstands, but also have a subtlety and sensitivity that attracts a closer and longer look.

In addition to his book designs for Avon, Bantam, Dell, Popular Library, and Fawcett publications, Hooks has illustrated for *Cosmopolitan, The Saturday Evening Post, Ladies' Home Journal, Redbook, McCall's, Woman's Day,* and other magazines.

Mitchell was born in Detroit, Michigan, and obtained his art education at the Cass Technical High School there. Later he studied further with James Billmeyer in New York. After the war, and occupation duty as a Second Lieutenant in Germany, he returned to New York to begin his free-lance illustration career.

This striking painting was considerably cropped, into an oval shape, when it appeared as a cover design for *The Novice*, by Giovanni Arpino, published by Bantam Books.

Victor Kalin

VICTOR KALIN's (1919-   ) versatility is such that it is difficult to identify his style. Unlike many artists who develop a strong, easily identifiable technique, he is so interested in experimentation that his work looks constantly new.

In the field of illustrating for paperback books, this is an ideal qualification, for the whole industry is so competitive that the drive is always to look as contemporary as possible.

Kalin was born in Belleville, Kansas, and was graduated with a B.F.A. from the University of Kansas. He also taught classes in painting and drawing there in 1941-42. During World War II he made maps, did art work for training manuals, three-dimensional assembly drawings, and also served as a field correspondent for *Yank* magazine.

His first illustrations were done for the *American Weekly*, and although he does other magazine and advertising illustration, as well as record album covers, the majority of his pictures are painted for paperback covers.

Here Kalin has made effective use of the soldier's head as a "negative" to illustrate the cover for *Panzer Ghost Division* by Thomas Goethals.

Published by Avon Books.

HENRY KOEHLER (1927-   ), who was born in Louisville, Kentucky, has been interested in art from early childhood. He was graduated from Yale with a B.A. choosing ". . . to get myself a liberal education rather than an art school one on the assumption that my interest in art would prompt me to seek the learning of it on my own volition, whereas I would not be so apt to educate myself in other directions. . . ." However, at Yale he did work as an assistant to Carl Rollins, then head of the Yale University Press, and was also art director of the *Year Book*, of the *Yale Record*, and the *Yale Literary Magazine*. This, plus summers in Louisville doing package design with Terrell Dickey, prepared him for a studio job in New York with Charles E. Cooper, as a designer and later as an illustrator.

Eventually Koehler began to take on free-lance assignments and now works full time for such magazines as *Town and Country*, *Sports Illustrated*, *Vogue*, *Esquire*, *Reader's Digest*, *Family Circle*, *Good Housekeeping*, and *Ladies' Home Journal*.

Koehler has also participated in the joint Illustrators-Air Force project and produced a memorable series of drawings of the airlift of Hungarian refugees in December, 1956.

SANFORD KOSSIN (1926-   ) strikingly demonstrated in his powerful series of pictures for *Life* magazine's re-creation of the Bay of Pigs invasion, the role the illustrator can play in summarizing the total effect of war action in a way that the camera cannot. Each of his pictures highlights a major phase of the tragedy from the initial landing to final overwhelming defeat.

Kossin, who was born in Los Angeles, studied there for four years at the Jepson Art Institute under Rico Lebrun and Herbert Jepson.

His first work after coming East in 1953 was for science fiction magazines. He also illustrated children's magazines before graduating to *Life*, *Good Housekeeping*, *Parents'*, *Redbook*, and other national publications. In addition, he does some advertising and paperback book assignments.

Kossin is a member of the Society of Illustrators; his work has been represented in annual exhibitions there and at New York Art Directors Club shows.

Opening illustration for *Life* magazine article, "We Who Tried," May 10, 1963. Tusche on gesso ground.

Sanford Kossin for *Life* magazine © 1963 Time, Inc.

Arthur Lidov

ARTHUR LIDOV (1917-   ) holds an A.B. in Sociology from the University of Chicago but is self-taught in art. He has a strong conviction that the only valid art form of the twentieth century is illustration.

This conviction is also his own challenge which he has capably met, in commissions for a wide variety of magazines, including *Fortune, Collier's, The Saturday Evening Post, Redbook, Good Housekeeping, American, Cosmopolitan, American Mercury, The Sign, Life, Sports Illustrated, Field and Stream, Parents'*, and *True*.

Lidov's paintings have been exhibited at The Museum of Modern Art, the Art Institute of Chicago, the National Gallery in Washington, D. C., and others, as well as in Art Directors Club exhibits in New York, Chicago, Detroit, Milwaukee, and the American Institute of Graphic Arts, winning numerous awards.

Lidov's creative approach is exemplified here by one of his series of paintings interpreting *Life* magazine's articles on "The Human Body."

Arthur Lidov for *Life* magazine, © 1962 Time, Inc.

McCarthy

FRANK C. McCARTHY (1924-   ) does strong, dramatic, masculine illustration with very effective use of white areas and vignetting. He is a master technician and strong colorist whose pictures are always exciting to look at.

McCarthy is a New Yorker who studied at Pratt Institute and at the Art Students League under George Bridgman and Reginald Marsh. He developed his talent early and was in his mid-twenties when he began to obtain illustrating commissions from *American* magazine and *Collier's*. These were soon followed by *Redbook, Argosy, True, Outdoor Life,* and others, as well as a great many paperback covers for Bantam Books, Signet, Dell, Avon, and Popular Library. In addition, he has done illustration for Ballantine, Goodyear, Warner Brothers, Columbia Pictures, United Artists, Twentieth-Century Fox, and other advertisers.

He has exhibited at annual shows of the New York Society of Illustrators and won several awards.

Illustration for story by Budd Schulberg, "Murder on the Water Front," *Collier's*, 1954.

John McClelland

JOHN McCLELLAND (1919-) was born in Stone Mountain, Georgia, and attended the Alabama Polytechnic Institute, the Grand Central School of Art, and the Art Career School of New York City. He also studied with Jerry Farnsworth.

John is especially successful in painting children and was commissioned to paint a portrait of Mrs. John F. Kennedy with her children, for *Good Housekeeping* magazine. He is affiliated with Portraits, Incorporated, and paints as much for exhibition as for publication. His work has won several first prizes and other awards at shows in New York, Boston, New Haven, Hartford, Atlanta, and at regional exhibits.

McClelland first illustrated for *Collier's* magazine in 1947 and has now worked for most of the national publishers, including *Woman's Day, Good Housekeeping, McCall's, Redbook, American, This Week, American Weekly,* and the *Ladies' Home Journal.*

He taught at the Silvermine Guild of Artists in Norwalk, Connecticut, for several years, and also teaches a private class in painting at the New Canaan, Connecticut, Historical Society.

Christmas catalog cover painting for Miles Kimball Company, 1964.

Jerry McDaniel

JERRY W. McDANIEL (1935-) in his work relies mostly on line which he uses with a sophisticated, light touch. Combined with line is an equally good sense of pattern employed for emphasis and visual excitement. This has won him several citations of merit in the annual exhibitions of the New York Society of Illustrators. He has also exhibited in Ohio, Maine, Berlin, London, and Paris.

McDaniel was born in Vinton County, Ohio, and studied at both the Columbus College of Art and Design, in Ohio, and the New School for Social Research in New York City. Among his teachers were Joseph Canzani and Angelo Savelli.

He was only 22 when he did his first illustrations for *Redbook* magazine in 1957 and has since added *Ingenue, Good Housekeeping, American Girl, Men's Wear, Seventeen,* and other publications as clients.

Active in the work of the Society of Illustrators, McDaniel has been House Chairman and served on several special committees.

Drawing, institutional promotion for Lester Rossin Creative Group Inc. Published in *Illustrators '63.*

ROBERT E. McGINNIS (1926-   ) is a fine draughtsman and painter, particularly of women — good or bad — for paperback covers. The predatory female, shown here, appeared in print only four-and-a-half inches high, painted with the dash and style of a lifesize drawing-room portrait. This approach has kept McGinnis one of the busiest and most prolific painters for cover designs. He has worked for virtually all the paperback publishers. In addition, he has illustrated for the *Ladies' Home Journal, The Saturday Evening Post, True, Woman's Home Companion, Good Housekeeping, Saga, Argosy,* and other magazines. He also did the titles for the Hollywood movie, "Hallelujah Trail."

A hard worker, McGinnis was recently commissioned by *Good Housekeeping* magazine to do an illustration but, intrigued by the picture possibilities of the story, he completed four paintings. The editors, in turn, were so impressed by the pictures that they printed all four.

Robert was born in Cincinnati, Ohio, and studied both at Ohio State University and the Central Academy of Commercial Art in Cincinnati.

Cover painting for *The Corpse that Never Was,* by Brett Halliday.

Courtesy of Dell Publishing Co.

© 1963 by The Curtis Publishing Company.

FRANK MULLINS (1924-   ) uses an impressionist's brush and color with very carefully controlled values to paint muted but highly effective illustrations. In this Central Park skating scene, he used yellow-greens, red-violets, and blues in high key against the grayed-white surface of the ice to create a charming and festive atmosphere.

He varies his color to suit the mood, from boxing or golfing assignments for *Sports Illustrated* to fiction settings for *The Saturday Evening Post* or *Redbook.* His range of subjects is also diverse — he has illustrated for *American Heritage, The Book of Knowledge,* J. P. Lippincott Co., and a series of several paintings and drawings reporting on oceanography as experienced aboard the "Chain" out of the Woods Hole Oceanographic Institution for *Chemical and Engineering News.*

Frank is also an active member of the Society of Illustrators in New York and has exhibited in their annual shows.

Cover painting for *The Saturday Evening Post.*

George Porter

GEORGE EDWARD PORTER (1916-) was born in Perry, Florida. He studied at the Ringling School of Art in Sarasota and the Phoenix Art Institute in New York under a distinguished group of teachers, including Lucille Blanche, Thomas Fogarty, Sr., Franklin Booth, Lauros Phoenix, and Reuben Tam.

During the war years of 1944-45, he did historical and combat art for the Fifth Air Force in the Far East and for the Navy. Under the auspices of Dr. Charles Mayo, and the American Red Cross, he had a one-man show in the hospital at NADZAB, a base in New Guinea.

Since the war, Porter has done both advertising and editorial illustrations appearing in *Good Housekeeping, McCall's, Redbook, The Saturday Evening Post, Woman's Day, Parents'*, and the *Ladies' Home Journal.*

Porter is a member of the Society of Illustrators and has served as chairman of the exhibition committee for editorial art. He also exhibits at their annual shows as well as at those of the Art Directors Clubs of New York and Baltimore.

Illustration for "After the Kids have Gone," by Steve McNeil, in *The Saturday Evening Post.*

Potter

JACK POTTER (1927-) prefers black and white to color, and his favorite line is black wax crayon or charcoal. He also insists that his drawing be only from life — that drawing from photographs is criminal! Although this point of view no longer has many protagonists, there is no question that Potter is an excellent draughtsman who does not need to work from photographs and that his drawings are all the better for it. Certainly he has had a strong influence on current illustration, both as a practitioner and as a teacher. He taught for three years at the Art Center School in Los Angeles, and more recently at the School for Visual Arts in New York.

Potter is a Californian. He studied in Los Angeles at both the Art Center School and the Jepson School under Rico Lebrun. He also feels a kinship with Vuillard, Toulouse-Lautrec, and the post-Impressionists.

His work has appeared in national magazines, such as *Cosmopolitan, McCall's, Ladies' Home Journal, Woman's Home Companion*, and for many national advertisers, including Coca-Cola, Northeast Airlines, and Fuller Fabrics.

In this impressionistic Paris sidewalk café scene, Potter displays his strong sense of outline and pattern.

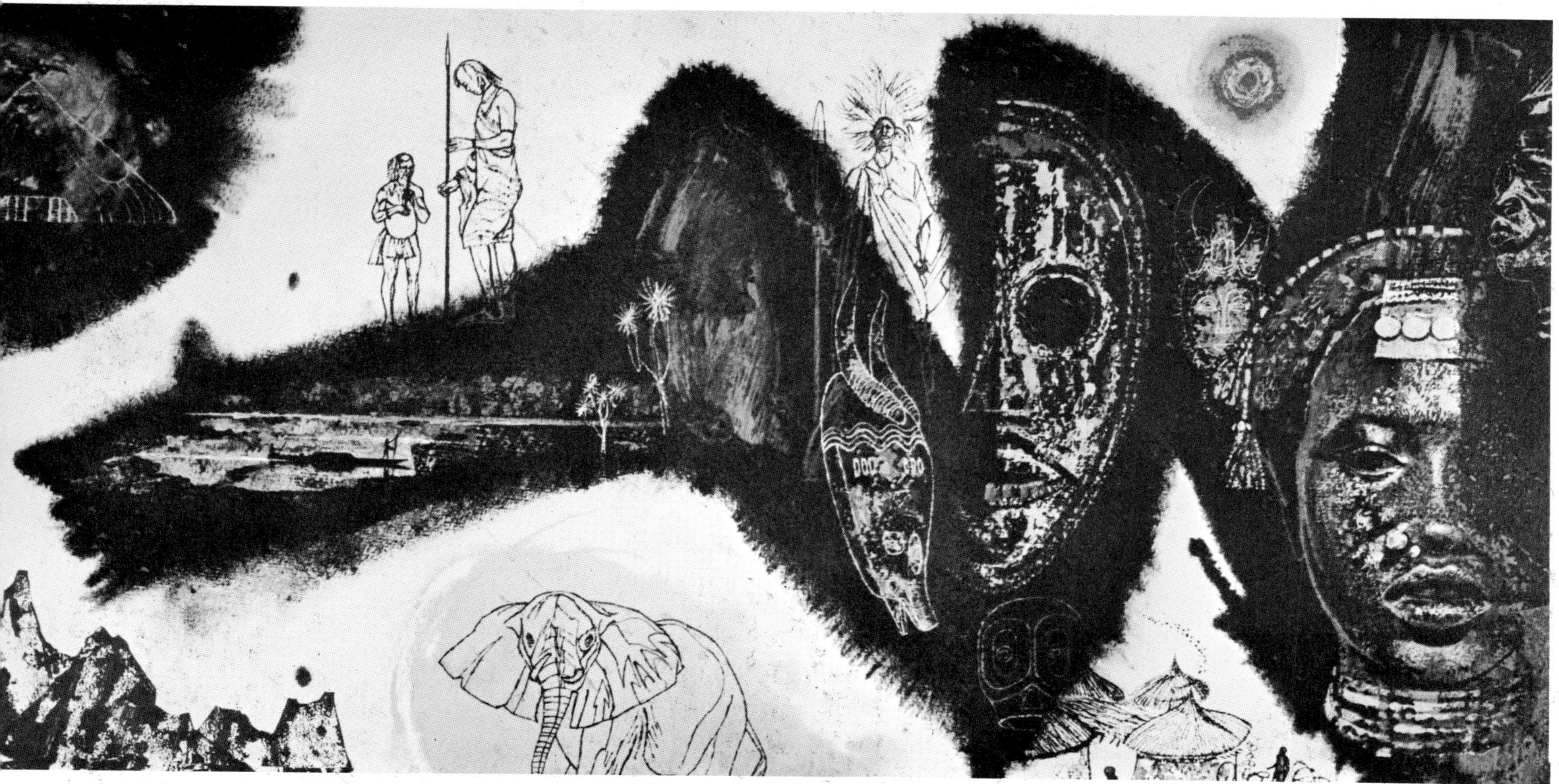

Powers

There is nothing orthodox about the work of RICHARD M. POWERS (1921-), whether for publication or for exhibition. He cuts through directly to the picture-idea using the means as sparingly as possible. His work belongs to no one school, and he varies his approach to fit his subject.

As an illustrator, Powers has done a number of children's books, cover designs for many of the classics of poetry and literature for Dell Publications, and a series on "Major Cultures of the World" for World Publishing Company. He has also illustrated for *Esquire, The Saturday Evening Post, Redbook, Life,* and *Natural History* magazines.

He is associated with the Rehn Gallery in New York and has had several one-man shows. He was included in a New Talent Exhibition at The Museum of Modern Art in 1952 and has also exhibited at The Metropolitan Museum of Art, the Corcoran Gallery in Washington, D. C., the National Academy of Design, and the Whitney Museum.

Powers was born in Chicago and studied at Loyola University, the Chicago Art Institute, and the University of Illinois. Later he worked with Julian Levi at the New School for Social Research in New York, and studied with Jay Connaway in Maine and Vermont.

Jacket design for *The Peoples of Africa,* by Colin Turnbull for the World Publishing Company, 1962.

Saris

ANTHONY SARIS (1924-) researches his pictorial subjects thoroughly before planning any layouts or compositions, preferring to keep completely receptive to any new ideas suggested in the course of his inquiry. Similarly he does not make preliminary drawings but, having worked out the problems in his mind, makes his finished renderings while there is still a creative challenge to be met, rather than redo an approved sketch. This method produces some occasional failures which must be redone, but Saris works rapidly — usually in pen and ink with tone or color added — so that the time factor is not unduly important. He spends much more time in research and planning than in the rendering itself.

Saris was born in Joliet, Illinois, but moved to New York City while a boy, attended Pratt Institute, the Brooklyn Museum Art School, and the New School for Social Research. He himself has taught at Pratt Institute since 1956.

He has illustrated for most of the major publications and many national advertisers including pharmaceuticals, and his work has won numerous awards in exhibitions for New York and Washington Art Directors Club shows, New York Society of Illustrators, Outdoor Advertising Show, and the American Institute of Graphic Arts.

"Fear is a Phantom," illustration for Tennessee Gas Transmission Company advertisement, 1962.

A

Robert Peak for *Sports Illustrated* © 1963 Time, Inc.

B

A really skilled performer makes his artistry appear easy, and for this reason the paintings and drawings of ROBERT PEAK (1928-) look deceptively simple. To those who have followed his work, it is apparent that the process of simplification has gradually evolved over a period of years as a result of his deliberate effort to subordinate detail to idea. This emphasis on idea requires a lot of preliminary thought and experimentation but, once determined, the actual rendering may require only a few hours. Peak keeps his outlook fresh by rejecting conventional solutions, always looks for a new aspect of a subject or pose and, for this reason, prefers to work from life whenever possible.

Bob was born in Colorado and brought up in Kansas. Although he liked to draw, he first studied geology at the University of Wichita. With time out for Army service, and his interest in art revived, he followed this up with two-and-a-half years at the Los Angeles Art Center School.

Moving East to become an illustrator, he found the first few years very difficult and groped to develop his own point of view. It was after he stopped looking at the work of other illustrators and concentrated his efforts on strengthening his own direction that he began to attract the attention of the major publishers and advertisers.

His work has since regularly appeared in the annual Art Directors Clubs shows and Society of Illustrators exhibitions where he has won many awards. He was named "Artist of the Year" by the Artists' Guild of New York in 1961.

C

Courtesy of Trans World Airlines.

D

Courtesy of the F. & M. Schaeffer Brewing Company.

A. One of a series of paintings made for an article on professional football.
B. Illustration as it appeared in *Cosmopolitan* magazine, February, 1964.
C. Advertising design for T.W.A., 1963.
D. Portrait drawing of James Cagney for W.C.B.S.-T.V. Award Theatre.

Harvey Schmidt

HARVEY SCHMIDT (1929-   ), fresh from the University of Texas, with a personal and unusual portfolio, landed his first art job in New York for the graphics design department of N.B.C. Television. There he had the opportunity to design and execute the title illustrations for national network shows. Schmidt learned to eliminate any superfluous details that would interfere with communicating his ideas. This strength and directness has characterized his work for free-lance magazine and advertising assignments since.

Schmidt was born in Dallas and spent his boyhood between drawing and teaching himself to play the piano by ear. At the University of Texas he continued to follow both art and music, and wrote a musical in collaboration with lyricist Tom Jones while still in school. The two have again successfully collaborated in "The Fantasticks," the off-Broadway hit revue, now in its sixth year in New York.

His first Broadway musical score was for the David Merrick hit, "110 in the Shade"; he is now working on two new Broadway scores. Schmidt recently completed a short art film with Tom Jones, called "A Texas Romance 1909," for which he composed the music in addition to doing a section of paintings along with Robert Weaver, Elaine Morfogen, and Robert Benton.

Although this division of talents tends to limit his output in art, he has continued to do picture reportorial assignments for clients, such as *Fortune* magazine, Abbott Laboratories' *What's New, The Lamp* — a Standard Oil of New Jersey publication, *Sports Illustrated*, and others, winning numerous top awards and medals from the Society of Illustrators and Art Directors Clubs' annual exhibitions.

This illustration of the Syracuse Regatta won the Society of Illustrators' Gold Medal in the Illustrators '64 exhibition.

Robert Shore

ROBERT SHORE (1924-   ) has a painter's interest in texture, color, and abstract design. His subjects are presented strongly with a minimum of detail and have great impact on the printed page.

Born in New York City, Shore studied at the Cranbrook Academy of Art in Detroit, Michigan, and at the Art Students League of New York. He was awarded a Fulbright Fellowship in painting in 1952. His work has been exhibited at the Detroit Institute of Fine Arts, the Smithsonian Institution and the National Gallery in Washington, D. C., and at Cornell University.

Shore has illustrated for a long list of magazines, including *Seventeen, Redbook, Pageant, The Reporter, Park East, Esquire, Show Business Illustrated, Woman's Day;* for book publishers, such as Macmillan Company, Rinehart & Company; for advertisers, E. R. Squibb & Sons, National Broadcasting Company.

He has also been an instructor at the Henry Street Settlement, Cooper Union, and at present teaches at the School of Visual Arts in New York City.

Illustration for *Redbook* magazine article, "Not Like Other Children," by Bernard Asbell.

DANIEL SCHWARTZ (1929-) started out to be a painter and had several one-man shows at the Davis Gallery in New York City before doing his first illustrations for *Sports Illustrated* in 1958.

Schwartz is a native New Yorker and was graduated from the High School of Music and Art. His B.F.A. was earned at the Rhode Island School of Design, and he also studied with Yasuo Kuniyoshi at the Art Students League in New York. Schwartz was awarded the Louis Comfort Tiffany Fellowship in Painting in 1956 and 1963, a Gold Medal for Editorial Art at the Society of Illustrators exhibition in 1961.

Continuing to combine his painting for the gallery and for publication, he has had additional one-man shows in Cincinnati, San Francisco, and New York. His illustrations have appeared in many of the major magazines, including *Esquire, Life, Redbook, Playboy, McCall's,* and *Fortune.*

Illustration, first published in *Esquire* magazine, depicts the crash of racing driver Stirling Moss for the "Over-Reachers," by Gay Talese, December, 1963.

ROSS BARRON STOREY (1940-) although still at the beginning of his career, has already had considerable experience and displays a thoroughly professional facility.

Born in Dallas, Texas, he studied the Famous Artists Course and attended the Art Center School in Los Angeles. Storey's first illustrations for publications were for the Sunday magazine of the New York *Journal American,* followed by *This Week* magazine, *Woman's Day, Children's Digest, Reader's Digest, Co-Ed,* and for various paperback publishers including Avon, Fawcett, and Pocket Books.

He has also done numerous advertising illustration assignments and received awards for his work from Art Directors Clubs in Los Angeles, Denver, and Dallas.

"V-E Day 1945," illustration for *This Week* magazine, 1965.

HERBERT TAUSS (1929-) paints his subjects with the greatest economy of means — no extraneous detail intrudes on his picture concept. This approach requires complete technical competence to carry it off, as he does here, in this bold rendering for a story in *McCall's* magazine.

Tauss is a New Yorker who received his only art training at the High School of Industrial Arts in New York.

His first illustrations were made in 1949 for *Pageant* magazine. He has grown steadily in his work for other publications which include *American Weekly, Argosy, The Saturday Evening Post, Magazine Management, Redbook, Parents'*, and *McCall's* magazines.

He has received numerous citations for his work from the Art Directors Club of New York, the Society of Illustrators, and *ca*, the journal of commercial art and design.

This illustration accompanied the George Sumner Albee story, "Some Like Them Strong," in *McCall's*, 1962.

HOWARD A. TERPNING (1927-) made use, in this picture, of the natural shapes of the ship's construction as directional pointers to the honeymoon couple. The man's dark jacket set against the picture's high-key background brings out powerful value contrasts which served further to emphasize the couple. With the man's head turned, the viewer is thus subtly led to the face of the girl as the center of interest. This illustration when reproduced in *McCall's* was cropped considerably at the top to allow for a one-and-a-half-page spread but still retained all of its compositional strength. In addition to *McCall's*, Terpning has also illustrated for *Good Housekeeping, Reader's Digest, Field & Stream, Redbook, True*, and *Cosmopolitan*.

Terpning was born in Oak Park, Illinois, and studied in Chicago at the American Academy of Art and the Chicago Academy of Fine Arts. After service in the Marines in World War II, he went to New York to do advertising, editorial, and motion picture illustration. Among others, he did posters for the films, "Cleopatra," and "The Sound of Music."

He is a member of the Society of Illustrators in New York, and Westport Artists in Connecticut.

Illustration for "The Beauty," by Mel Heimer, *McCall's* magazine, June, 1963.

B

A

GILBERT M. WALKER (1927-) has occasionally used other media, but he is essentially a pen-and-ink artist. And, although he attended the Art Students League for brief study with Reginald Marsh and with Robert Beverly Hale, he is otherwise self-taught. He has been a prolific sketcher since childhood and was doing professional advertising agency art work while still in high school.

The Army has shaped Walker's career largely, assigning him to various art projects on the West Coast. With the advent of the Korean War, he was recalled to service at the Pentagon, as an army artist, in the offices of the Chief of Staff and Chief of Information. After discharge he stayed on in Washington to do illustrations for many publications, such as *Nation's Business, U.S. News and World Report, Changing Times, Combat Forces Journal*; later moved to New York where he has continued to free-lance for other publishers, including *American Heritage, Harper's* magazine, and Doubleday. This work is largely reportorial, and he has done several additional *Sketch Books* on World War II; the Korean War; U.S. Air Force; the Castro Movement; Johns Hopkins Mental Hospital; and histories of the United States Army, the American Red Cross, and the U.S. Marine Corps.

Walker's work has won him Gold Medals and distinctive Merit awards in Washington, D.C., and in New York, as well as several book awards. He also taught art at the College of the City of New York from 1957-61.

"The American Fighting Man: from Minute Man to G.I." Pen drawings for "Wide World 60," N.B.C. Television booklet, 1960.

EDWARD T. VEBELL (1921-) brings the same intensity to his art work as to his other major interest — fencing. He has represented the United States on two Olympic fencing teams and on one World Championship team; is still ranked as one of the top épée men in the country.

Vebell is one of the top illustrators, too, a pro who can take on a difficult assignment, on virtually any subject, and do it quickly and competently. An expert photographer, he directs and takes his own reference pictures of models and settings, has a large collection of costumes and props, such as guns, swords, and helmets. Because of his background he does many illustrations of war and military subjects, as well as sports.

He grew up in Chicago and very early began to attend art classes, first at the Professional Art School, and The Harrison Art School, under E. W. Ball; later with scholarships, at the American Academy of Art and the Commercial Art Institute. After a short while with the Nugent-Graham Art Studios, he was inducted into the Army. Vebell spent the war years on the staff of *Stars and Stripes* in Europe, served as illustrator-reporter in France and Italy, including the taking of Monte Cassino. Following the war, he spent an additional two years in Paris as a free-lance illustrator for French publications.

In 1947 Vebell returned to the United States and to free-lance for American publications which, by now include most of the major magazines such as *Life, True, Reader's Digest, Outdoor Life,* and *Sports Illustrated.*

He is an active member of the New York Fencers Club as well as the Westport Artists and Society of Illustrators.

A. Sketch of Field Marshall Goering at the Nuremburg War Trials which Vebell covered for *Stars and Stripes.* Done with field glasses from pressbox with a fountain pen, brush, and saliva.

B. This illustration for *True* magazine has the same feeling of immediacy as Vebell's reportorial drawing technique.

A

B

C

RWeaver

ROBERT WEAVER (1924-   ) has a strong conviction that the role of the illustrator should be a decidely active one. He believes that the artist should make his contribution at the thinking stage as well as in painting the picture itself, whether it's for an advertising client or an editorial assignment. He has helped to create a climate for this point of view by the many creative pictures he has painted under this obligation to himself for *Fortune, Life, Look, Sports Illustrated, Cosmopolitan, McCall's, True, Seventeen, Town and Country*, and *Esquire*.

Born in Pittsburgh, he studied at Carnegie Institute of Technology, the Art Students League in New York, and the Accademia Delle Belle Arti in Venice.

Weaver has exhibited at the D'Arcy Galleries, American Institute of Graphic Arts, Society of Illustrators, and Art Directors Clubs in New York, Washington, and other cities. The Society of Illustrators awarded him a Gold Medal in 1964.

Weaver has also been teaching at the School of Visual Arts, in New York for the past seven years.

A. Illustration for *Steelways* magazine, published by the American Iron and Steel Institute.
B. One of Weaver's sketchbook drawings as part of his research for a projected book on juvenile delinquency.
C. Here, for an *Esquire* article, Weaver painted a portrait of the Presidential candidate, Jack Kennedy, symbolizing his emergence from the background of local politics to the rotunda of national statesmanship. "Kennedy's Last Chance to be President," by Richard H. Rovere, April, 1959.

Whittingham

WILLIAM H. WHITTINGHAM (1932-   ) is typical of today's illustrator who approaches his picture-making from a painter's viewpoint and who exploits the latest pictorial trends in either field.

He was born in Detroit and studied at the University of Michigan as well as with Reuben Tam at the Brooklyn Museum. His work won a first prize at the New York City Center and has also been exhibited at the Society of Illustrators.

Whittingham has had his illustrations reproduced in many women's magazines in England as well as in *The Saturday Evening Post, Ski* magazine, *TV Guide, Parents* magazine, and Bantam Books in this country.

This illustration, printed with an overlay of red, was used as a cover design for *The Saturday Evening Post.*

Ben T. Wohlberg

BEN WOHLBERG (1927-   ) had an early interest in architecture, which he studied for a year at Kansas State College. Classes in drawing stimulated him to shift his interest to art, and he transferred to the Chicago Academy of Fine Art and on to the Art Center School in Los Angeles.

Wohlberg's paintings are done in large scale, marked by bold color and strong composition yet with subtle value changes and sensitivity of form. The majority of his work has been for *Redbook*, for which he did his first illustration in 1960, but he has also painted for *Good Housekeeping, Ladies' Home Journal, Woman's Day*, Dell Books, and Crowell-Collier publications.

Ben exhibits with the American Water Color Society and the annual shows of the Society of Illustrators from which he won the Award of Excellence in 1962.

Illustration for *Redbook* magazine story, "Heirloom," by Florence Engel Randall, 1963.

The Future of Illustration
by Robert Weaver

DRAWING BY ROBERT WEAVER

The Future of Illustration

by Robert Weaver

Interviewer: Since your long-awaited paper, "The Future of Illustration" has not been forthcoming, we are compelled to adopt the format of an interview. Have you any excuse?

Mr. Weaver: I have an ear for dialogue. Also I don't believe in amateurism. The essay form should be entrusted only to writers. The question-and-answer method seems to me to be appropriately direct and utilitarian. In a word — journalistic.

Int: Are you leading into something?

Weav: What journalism is to literature, illustration is to fine art.

Int: Is illustration art?

Weav: Why should it be? . . . or even try to be? . . . It is possible that illustration and art might one day merge, at some vanishing point in history, but for the moment their aims and purposes are quite different. It seems to be the function of the artist to produce art. The illustrator may use the ideas of the contemporary painter; but it is communication that is his ultimate goal. I wish I could remember that phrase of Ezra Pound's . . .

Int: "Literature is news that stays news."?

Weav: Exactly.

Int: We have both seen banal and trashy work that clearly tells a story. On a level of pure communication a cigarette ad or an example of Soviet social-realism is highly successful, but is it art?

Weav: The point is, the examples you cite don't *really* communicate.

Int: Contemporary attitudes in art seem to put the stress on form, not on content. What counts is what a picture *does*, not what it *says*.

Weav: That won't work in illustration, and I suspect not in fine art, either. It is certainly not true for literature, to say nothing of journalism. If you will forgive me, form is the fire under the pot, and content is what's in it.

Int: I see. Is this emphasis on the communication aspect of painting the only thing that separates the illustrator from the fine artist?

Weav: No, there's the crucial matter of reproduction. In a mass-production society, the original work, the handmade object becomes increasingly precious. Painting, as someone else has pointed out, is the last of the manuscript arts; almost all other art forms undergo a translation of some sort from manuscript to finished stage. It is the physical being of the painting that the fine artist projects — its reproduction not only doesn't interest him, it threatens him. The illustrator takes just the opposite position: the original is disposable. Have you never seen those patched-up ruins from which the reproduced image somehow miraculously emerges? In some cases an original doesn't even exist as in the case of color separations. Does reproduction diminish the quality that makes a work of art great? Does it reside in the paint itself — a non-photographable essence?

Int: It's the painting's uniqueness that makes it valuable.

Weav: True, but it is essentially a financial valuation you are talking about. The uniqueness comes in the way the artist did it, not in the fact that he only made one of its kind.

Int: Going back to Pound's statement, can you cite examples of illustration which have become art?

Weav: Daumier . . .

Int: No, I mean in the present.

Weav: Hmmm. Well, I'm afraid that until the illustrator enjoys complete independence from outside pressure and direction, complete responsibility for his own work, and complete freedom to do whatever he deems fit — all necessaries in the making of art — then illustration cannot be art but only a branch of advertising. Illustration is less an art than a profession in our time. Mind you, I'm not cavilling at the deadline, the space and color restrictions, the lack of choice in subject matter, and the rest of it — these are the necessary edges against which you choose to work.

Int: Are you suggesting the illustrator is being muzzled?

Weav: Why put a muzzle on a dog that has no teeth? It is hardly likely that the artist of strong opinions would be drawn into a medium of expression that subordinates personal opinion in favor of the larger, corporate editorial image. The kind of artist I'm talking about would find little to encourage him in the illustration of today.

Int: The fault lies with the present concept of the magazine, I gather?

Weav: The large-circulation magazine, as we know it today, cannot permit the kind of uncensored pictorial journalism I'm talking about, because inherent in any creative work is an awareness of the artist's identity — of authorship. A man without an opinion is dull company, but an opinion without a man is duller still. The concept that there can be a "correct" position that resides up in the air somewhere, woven out of many private opinions — the chaos of divergence simplified into The Truth — is possibly dangerous but certainly nonsense.

Int: How would you run a magazine?

Weav: Albert Jay Nock ran a first-rate literary magazine called *The Freeman*, in the 'twenties, with this simple editorial policy: "The writer must have something to say, and he must make it out in 18-carat English."

Int: Don't magazines like *Sports Illustrated*, *Fortune*, and *Holiday* give the illustrator the freedom as well as the space he requires.

Weav: Yes. But I would like to bring the artist's eye to bear upon more dangerous and volatile aspects of our time. The illustrator cannot influence the outcome of a tennis match or the policies of U.S. Rubber.

Int: You see the artist then as an instigator?

Weav: Has he not always been?

Robert Weaver

Bibliography

Bibliography

Abbott, Charles D., *Howard Pyle, A Chronicle*, New York & London: Harper & Brothers, 1925.
Advertising Arts & Crafts, Volumes I & II, New York & Chicago, Lee and Kirby Inc., 1924
American Art Annual, Washington, D. C.: American Federation of Arts, 1898 to 1936.
American Art by American Artists, New York: P. F. Collier & Son, 1914.
The American Historical Scene as depicted by Stanley Arthurs, Philadelphia: University of Pennsylvania Press, 1935.
Annual of Advertising and Editorial Art and Design, New York: The New York Art Directors Club Yearbook, 1921 and annually thereafter.
Arts Yearbook I, *The Turn of the Century*, New York: The Art Digest, Inc., 1957.
Biographical Sketches of American Artists, 5th Edition, Lansing, Michigan: Michigan State Library, 1924.
Bolton, Theodore, *American Book Illustrators*, New York: R. R. Bowker Company, 1938.
Calkins, Earnest Elmo, *Franklin Booth*, New York: Robert Frank, publisher, 1925.
Clark, Eliot, *History of the National Academy of Design 1825-1953*, New York: Columbia University Press, 1954.
Cornwell, Dean, *The City of the Great King*, New York: Cosmopolitan Book Corporation, 1926.
———, *The Man of Galilee*, New York: Cosmopolitan Book Corporation, 1928.
Craven, Thomas, Editor, *Cartoon Cavalcade*, New York: Simon and Schuster, Inc., 1943.
———, *A Treasury of American Prints*, New York: Simon and Schuster, Inc., 1939.
Creative Artists, 1940, New York: Sackett & Wilhelms Lithographing Corporation.
Darton, F. J. Harvey, *Modern Book Illustration in Great Britain and America*, London: The Studio Limited, New York: William Edwin Rudge, 1931.
Downey, Fairfax, *Portrait of an Era as Drawn by C. D. Gibson*, New York and London: Charles Scribner's Sons, 1936.
Drawings by Thulstrup and Others, New York: E. R. Herrick & Co., 1898.
Dunn, Harvey, *An Evening in the Classroom*, Privately printed at the instigation of Mario Cooper, 1934.
Fawcett, Robert, *On the Art of Drawing*, New York: Watson-Guptill Publications, Inc., 1958.
Fielding, Mantle, *Dictionary of American Painters, Sculptors & Engravers*, (from Colonial times through 1926), Flushing, N.Y.: Paul A. Stroock, publisher, 1960.
Flagg, James Montgomery, *Roses and Buckshot*, New York: G. P. Putnam's Sons, 1946.
Frost, A. B., *A Book of Drawings*, New York: P. F. Collier & Son, 1904.
Gallatin, Albert Eugene, *Art and the Great War*, New York: E. P. Dutton & Co., 1919.
The Gibson Book, A Collection of the published works of Charles Dana Gibson in two volumes, New York: Charles Scribner's Sons, R. H. Russell, 1907.
Gill, Bob, and Lewis, John, *Illustration: Aspects and Directions*, New York: Reinhold Publishing Corporation, and London: Studio Vista, Ltd., 1964.
Goldsmith, Oliver, *The Deserted Village*, Illustrated by Edwin Austin Abbey, New York and London: Harper & Brothers, 1902.
Gottschall, Edward M. and Hawkins, Arthur, Editors, *Advertising Directions*, New York: Art Directions Book Co., 1959.
Guitar, Mary Ann, *22 Famous Painters and Illustrators Tell How They Work*, New York: David McKay Company, Inc., 1964.
Guptill, Arthur L., *Drawing with Pen and Ink*, New York: The Pencil Points Press, Inc., 1928.
———, *Norman Rockwell – Illustrator*, New York: Watson-Guptill Publications, Inc., 1946.
Hall, W. S., *Eyes on America*, New York: The Studio Publications, and London: The Studio, Ltd.
Halsey, Ashley Jr., *Illustrating for The Saturday Evening Post*, Boston: Arlington House, 1951.
Harrison Fisher's American Beauties, Indianapolis: The Bobbs-Merrill Company, 1909.
Held, John Jr., *The Works of John Held, Jr.*, New York: Ives Washburn, publisher, 1931.
Holme, Charles, Editor, *Modern Pen Drawings: European and American*, Special Winter Number of "The Studio" 1900-1901, London, Paris, New York, 1901.
Hydeman, Sid, *How to Illustrate for Money*, New York and London: Harper & Brothers, 1936.
Illustrators Annuals published by the Society of Illustrators, New York: Hastings House, 1959 to date.
Johnson, Merle, Compiler, *Howard Pyle's Book of Pirates*, New York and London: Harper & Brothers, 1921.
Kent, Norman, Editor, *The Book of Edward A. Wilson*, New York: The Heritage Press, 1948.
Landgren, Marchal E., *Years of Art*, The Story of the Art Students League of New York, New York: Robert M. McBride & Company, 1940.
Lucas, E. V., *Life and Work of Edwin Austin Abbey, R.A.* in two volumes, New York: Charles Scribner's Sons, London: Methuen and Company, Ltd., 1921.
Lyon, Peter, *Success Story: The Life and Times of S. S. McClure*, New York: Charles Scribner's Sons, 1963.
Mallett, Daniel Trowbridge, *Mallett's Index of Artists*, New York: R. R. Bowker Company, 1935. Supplement published in 1940.
Marshall, Francis, *Magazine Illustration*, New York: The Viking Press, Inc., London: The Studio Ltd., 1959.

Mather, Frank Jewett, Jr., Morey, Charles Rufus, and Henderson, William James, *The American Spirit in Art*, from the "Pageant of America," Vol. XII, New Haven: Yale University Press, 1927.
Morse, Willard S. and Brinckle, Gertrude, Compilers, *Howard Pyle — A Record of his Illustrations and Writings*, Wilmington, Delaware: The Wilmington Society of the Fine Arts, 1921.
Murrell, William, *A History of American Graphic Humor*, New York: The Macmillan Company, 1938.
Official Directory, American Illustrators and Advertising Artists, Washington, D. C.: American Federation of Arts, publisher, 1949.
Pennell, Joseph, *The Adventures of an Illustrator*, Boston: Little, Brown and Company, 1925.
———, *Modern Illustration*, London and New York: George Bell & Sons, 1895.
———, *Pen Drawing and Pen Draughtsmen*, New York: The Macmillan Company, 1889.
Phillips, Coles, *A Young Man's Fancy*, Indianapolis: The Bobbs-Merrill Company, 1912.
Pitz, Henry C., *Illustrating Children's Books*, New York: Watson-Guptill Publications, Inc., 1963.
———, *Ink Drawing Techniques*, New York: Watson-Guptill Publications, Inc., 1957.
———, *The Practice of Illustration*, New York: Watson-Guptill Publications, Inc., 1947.
———, *A Treasury of American Book Illustration*, New York and London: American Studio Books and Watson-Guptill Publications, Inc., 1947.
Rockwell, Norman, as told to Thomas Rockwell, *Norman Rockwell — My Adventures as an Illustrator*, New York: Doubleday & Company, Inc., 1960.
Simon, Howard, *500 Years of Art in Illustration*, New York: World Publishing Co., 1942.
Taft, Robert, *Artists and Illustrators of the Old West 1850-1900*, New York: Charles Scribner's Sons, 1953.
Thirty Favorite Paintings by Leading American Artists, New York: P. F. Collier & Son, 1908.
Watson, Ernest W., *Forty Illustrators and How They Work*, New York: Watson-Guptill Publications, Inc., 1946.
Wenzell, A. B., *The Passing Show*, New York: P. F. Collier & Son, 1903.
Whiting, John D., *Practical Illustration, A Guide for Artists*, New York and London: Harper & Brothers, 1920.
Who's Who in American Art, Washington, D. C.: American Federation of Arts, publisher, 1936 to present.
Who's Who in Graphic Art, Zurich, Switzerland: Amstritz & Herdeg, Graphis Press, 1962.
Wortman, Denys, *Mopey Dick and The Duke*, New York: Fairchild Publications, 1952.
The Year's Art/The Quarterly Illustrator, New York: Harry C. Jones, publisher, 1893, 1894, 1895.

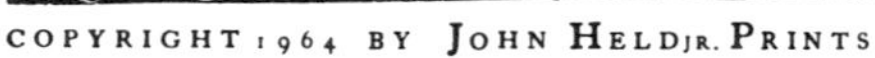